D0883138

The Changing Definition of Masculinity

PERSPECTIVES IN SEXUALITY
Behavior, Research, and Therapy

Series Editor: RICHARD GREEN

State University of New York at Stony Brook

NEW DIRECTIONS IN SEX RESEARCH
Edited by Eli A. Rubinstein, Richard Green, and Edward Brecher

PROGRESS IN SEXOLOGY
Edited by Robert Gemme and Connie Christine Wheeler

HANDBOOK OF SEX THERAPY
Edited by Joseph LoPiccolo and Leslie LoPiccolo

THE PREVENTION OF SEXUAL DISORDERS: Issues and Approaches
Edited by C. Brandon Qualls, John P. Wincze, and David H. Barlow

IMPOTENCE: Physiological, Psychological, Surgical Diagnosis
and Treatment
Gorm Wagner and Richard Green

SEX EDUCATION IN THE EIGHTIES: The Challenge of Healthy
Sexual Evolution
Edited by Lorna Brown

THE CHANGING DEFINITION OF MASCULINITY
Clyde W. Franklin, II

The Changing Definition of Masculinity

Clyde W. Franklin, II

Ohio State University
Columbus, Ohio

Plenum Press • New York and London

WITHDRAWN

LIBRARY
MOUNT ST. MARY'S
COLLEGE
EMMITSBURG, MARYLAND

Library of Congress Cataloging in Publication Data

Franklin, Clyde W.
    The changing definition of masculinity.

    (Perspectives in sexuality)
    Bibliography: p.
    Includes index.
    1. Men—United States. 2. Masculinity (Psychology) 3. Sex role—United States. 4.
Men—United States—Sexual behavior. 5. Social role. I. Title. II. Series.
HQ1090.3.F73   1984   305.3'1   84-1967
ISBN 0-306-41554-2

First Printing—March 1984
Second Printing—March 1986

© 1984 Plenum Press, New York
A Division of Plenum Publishing Corporation
233 Spring Street, New York, N.Y. 10013

All rights reserved

No part of this book may be reproduced, stored in a retrieval system, or transmitted,
in any form or by any means, electronic, mechanical, photocopying, microfilming,
recording, or otherwise, without written permission from the Publisher

Printed in the United States of America

Preface

The Changing Definition of Masculinity is an outgrowth of four years of developing and teaching the course "Social Factors in Male Personality" at Ohio State University, Columbus.

This volume reflects, in addition to my thoughts and feelings about what should be discussed in a sex-roles course taught from a male perspective, the thoughts, feelings, and knowledge of scores of students, colleagues, and friends. These are persons who either have taken the course or discussed with me appropriate material to be included in such a course and/or book.

Chapter 1, for example, is influenced greatly by the work of Elizabeth and Joseph Pleck's *The American Man,* dealing with the periods of masculinity in the United States up to 1965. The chapter also deals with emerging meanings of masculinity after 1965, and female and male responses to these meanings.

The second chapter is devoted to male sex-role socialization and examines the roles of biology and environment in male socialization. It is also concerned with agents of male socialization and with male assumption of such sex-role traits as dominance, competitiveness, the work ethic, and violence. In Chapter 2, I also propose two general masculine roles frequently assumed by American males which may or may not be race-specific—the *White masculine role* and the *Black masculine role.*

"The Male Self" is the topic of Chapter 3, which discusses three perspectives on the male self—*The Life-Cycle Approach, The Cognitive-Developmental Approach,* and *The Social-Learning-Theory Approach.* In addition, a *Symbolic Interaction Approach,* referred to as *The Male Self as a Dynamic Process,* is offered as a viable framework for study of the male self. The latter approach allows us to see how male socialization in the United States frequently places men at odds with their "selves."

Chapter 4, on male social perception, offers the *gestalt* thesis that males' perceptions of their social worlds is some function of their own structuring of those worlds. It is acknowledged that some male perceptual-organization factors are beyond the control of males, but others males bring with them to their social worlds. These factors are explored as well as the specific topics on male nonverbal sensitivity, male impression formation, and male impression management.

The next chapter (Chapter 5, "Male Social Roles") looks at men as husbands, parents, friends, and employees. The chapter also invites the reader to go beyond androgyny in determining male gender—a perspective only recently suggested by the work of Freimuth and Hornstein.

Chapter 6, on male interpersonal attraction, deals with the dynamics of male liking, male friendship, male love, and male respect. Key questions addressed in this chapter are "what do men want?" and "what do others want in men?"

Chapter 7 is entitled "Themes in Male Sexuality" and offers a general discussion of men and sex. In addition, more specific discussions are presented of men's heterosexual involvements, using Donald Mosher's provocative work. Highlights of this chapter include the relationship between women's freedom and men's sex, men's dominance in sexual matters, men's "socialized" penises, violent aspects of men's sex, and extensive coverage of men, homosexuality, ambisexuality, and asexuality.

Chapter 8 is the concluding chapter of this volume; it raises questions and attempts to answer some about the male sex-role in the future. Topics include interracial and intraracial male–female interaction, men's future interaction with other men, men's responses to sex-role changes, and career paths men take toward sex-role equality. The chapter ends with a discussion of men's emerging social forms.

Finally, while this book is entitled *The Changing Definition of Masculinity*, it is my firm belief that it is a book about much more than males. From my perspective, it is a book about past, current, and future sex-roles, and one that can offer an essential perspective to all of us in America as we nurture new generations of females and males.

Clyde W. Franklin, II

Acknowledgments

So many have contributed to this volume and in so many ways. The influence of my children, Coy, Sean, Clyde and Alison, who have kept me honest when I have discussed sex-roles in the United States with them, is apparent throughout. Women relatives, friends, students, and colleagues who have related their experiences as females in this country have also been invaluable sources of information. Men relatives, friends, and students whom I have observed struggling to fit themselves into society's masculinity model have been the primary impetus for *The Changing Definitions of Masculinity*. In fact, a great debt is owed my friend, Larry L. Spencer, who spent numerous hours with me talking about masculinity and mulling over problems facing males in the United States as well as problems caused by males in America.

To Lisa Boyer, my research assistant, Cindy Brown, who provided indispensable typing assistance, Aleta Geib, who prepared the index, and to Kim Hawkins, my production editor, I give a warm thank-you.

The above persons and groups mentioned contributed directly to this book and I thank them. There are others who contributed, however, whom I have not met, but their influence is great. Some of these are the men who were at the Berkeley Men's Center in the early 1970s—Jack Nichols, Herb Goldberg, Warren Farrell, Robert Staples, Robert Brannon, John Scanzoni, Alvin Poussaint, and most of all, Joseph Pleck. These men are forerunners. This volume continues in some way, I hope, the important work they have done.

Contents

CHAPTER 1

Meanings of Masculinity in the United States

A saner society will flower when men liberate themselves from contrived, socially fabricated prohibition, cultural straitjackets, and mental stereotypes that control and inhibit behavior through arbitrary definitions of what it means to be a man. (Jack Nichols, 1978.)

During the early and middle 1970's, authors such as Jack Sawyer (who is credited with starting the male liberation movement in 1970), Joseph Pleck (1973), Marc Fasteau (1974), Warren Farrell (1974), Jack Nichols (1974), and Herb Goldberg (1976; 1979), to mention a few, began to write about the male experience in the United States. By this time there was a growing literature about the female experience and distinctions were being made between concepts such as sex, gender identity, and gender. Komarovsky's popular work on sex roles nearly forty years ago was the forerunner of much of the literature on sex and gender emerging during the 1970s. Yet, until the above authors made their contributions, the full significance of the distinctions being made between being *male* and being *masculine* was not felt by many—not even those who had developed interests in sex-roles, gender and like study areas. Part of the reason for this oversight was the fact that males in the United States were perceived simply to have a power-advantage over females. Most attention was focused on the victimization of women, and little devoted to the disadvantages associated with the male sex role.

Another plausible explanation for the blurred distinction between "male" and "masculine" may have been the lack of clear-cut definitions of key concepts in sex-role analyses prior to the 1970s.

Walum's (1978) distinction between *sex, gender,* and *gender identity* in her popular text, *The Dynamics of Sex and Gender: A Sociological Perspective,*

1

is representative of work that began to explore three basic concepts during the 1970s. Let us examine briefly these three concepts, since they form the foundation of our concern in this volume.

Three Basic Sex-Role Concepts

Sex

Describing *sex* as an ascribed status assigned to persons at birth, Walum states that *sex* refers "to the biological aspects of a person such as the chromosomal, hormonal, anatomical, and physiological structure" (p. 5). For our purposes, this means that a person at birth who has an XY chromosome pattern, male and female hormones, a penis, testicles, seminal vesicles and prostate glands generally is categorixed as *male*. A person is generally assigned to the female sex category at birth if an XX chromosome pattern and female internal and external sex organs are determined. As Walum indicated, in many instances chromosomal, hormonal, anatomical, and physiological structural information used to classify persons can be inconsistent and/or ambiguous, making assignment to one of the dichotomous categories a function of chance, choice, or some factor other than biology. One such factor which has been documented is the case of a normal male infant who at the age of seven months suffered a surgical accident during circumcision. The mishap resulted in the complete destruction of the penis. Money and Ehrhardt (1972) report that the male infant was reassigned to the female category following surgical genital reconstruction as a female and anticipated medical regulation of pubertal growth and feminization.

Gender

The stage is now set to distinguish between sex and gender. Sex is a descriptive biological concept. Male fetuses develop reproductive systems, musculature, and other biological features that distinguish them from females. On the other hand, gender refers to an achieved status (Walum, p. 5) which is a function of socialization and has social, cultural and psychological components. As the result of direct and indirect experiences, formal and informal learning, we develop images, conceptions, perceptions and the like, of masculinity and femininity. Furthermore, generally people behave, hold attitudes and feel the way society says that a male or female should do so. When a male does *so*, he is seen as masculine and when a female does *so*, she is seen as feminine (Walum, p. 5).

While the definition of male has undergone little change since 1630 (the beginning of the Plecks' Agrarian Patriarchal period), the definition of masculinity has undergone numerous changes. Some of these changes are explored in a later section. The major point is that the concept "sex" refers to *biology* while gender refers to the *social*.

Gender Identity

The above comments about sex and gender lead us to a third concept, *gender identity*. There are persons in our society who are perceived as male who identify themselves as masculine, and others who are perceived as male who identify themselves as feminine. It is essential, though, that at least some others confirm a person's self-identification, lest the person be thought psychotic (Berger and Berger, 1979). Gender identity ('I am male', 'I am female'), then, is some function of the interaction between self-identification and others' identification. Transsexuals are examples of people who appropriate the opposite gender identity through interactions with themselves and others. It may even be possible to say that only when a given female who identifies with the male gender convinces some others (e.g., a physician who can perform corrective surgery, friends, relatives) that she is a member of the male gender, is the male gender-identity construction real to her. Gender identity, therefore, refers to *an individual's view or belief that he or she belongs to a particular gender, supported by self-identification and the identification of others.*

In the abovementioned case of the sex-reassigned normal male infant, Money and Ehrhardt report that after six years, the child, though exhibiting some so-called "tomboyish" traits, behaves like a "normal" female child. They report further that the mother consciously reinforces "female" behavior and that this has resulted in a child with numerous feminine characteristics who is considered by others to be a member of the feminine gender and who considers herself such.

Now that we have discussed three basic sex-role concepts (others will be discussed as the need arises), it is possible to explore meanings of the major concept of concern here: *masculinity*. In doing so, definitions of feminity also will emerge. The major thrust of this analysis, however, remains a full explication of *masculinity*.

Traditional Meanings of Masculinity in the United States

It is true that the concept *masculine* existed long before the 1970s. Its full meaning was not developed, however, until the 1970s. In a sense, then, it has been possible to distinguish between being male and being masculine only in relatively recent times. Ironically, this has been due, in part, to the modern-day women's liberation movement and male responses to the movement. Authors like Jack Nichols, Marc Fasteau, Warren Farrell, and Herb Goldberg saw women struggling for social equality and heard them blaming men for their victimization. These men recognized that males, too, were victimized, and offered the point of view that men were imprisoned by dysfunctional social roles. Thus, the beginning of the development of the concept of masculinity in the United States. The titles of their books, which would become widely read, underscore the meanings of masculinity they found as they delved into the subject. Fasteau's *The Male Machine*, Farrell's *The Liberated Man*, Nichol's *Men's Liberation: A New Definition of Masculinity*, Goldberg's *The Hazards of Being Male: Surviving the Myth of Masculine Privilege* all suggested that masculinity meant more than the 1968 checklist by Rosenkrantz *et al.* describing masculine personality traits. Consider the reproduction of the checklist in Table 1, which gives attributes often associated with masculinity, and with femininity.

The major contribution made by authors writing about the male experience in America in the early '70s was to alert us to the fact that the meaning of masculinity goes beyond items on a checklist indicating power, privilege, and machoism. In addition they contended that masculinity in America has meant *being caught in destructive binds, being emotionally crippled, losing one's health,* and so on. Finally, as Goldberg sums it up, being masculine has meant *males spending their time trying to prove what they are not* (not feminine, not passive, not weak, not soft, not sensitive, etc.). I hasten to add, however, that two points must be considered when examining the meaning of masculinity in the United States: (1) there has not been a unitary meaning of masculinity in the United States since its beginning; and (2) a large portion of males in the United States only recently have been considered for inclusion in the masculine gender. I contend that these two points are important. Regarding the first point, to say that the traditional meaning of masculinity in the United States has been dysfunctional for males obscures the fact that masculinity did not always mean what it has meant in the past fifty or sixty years. Pleck and Pleck (1980) have explored the multiple meanings of masculinity in the United States, and some of their ideas are presented below. On the second point, since the 1960s, meanings of masculinity in the United States have been affected by the recognition, albeit reluctant, of a sizeable number of males as "men" (notably, Black males). On the last point, it remains questionable whether Black men are thought of as masculine today, but they are seen as men, and, as a result, impact conceptions of

Table 1
Stereotypic Traits

Male-Valued Traits

Aggressive	Feelings not easily hurt
Independent	Adventurous
Unemotional	Makes decisions easily
Hides emotions	Never cries
Objective	Acts as a leader
Easily influenced	Self-confident
Dominant	Not uncomfortable about being aggressive
Likes math and science	Ambitious
Not excitable in a minor crisis	Able to separate feelings from ideas
Active	Not dependent
Competitive	Not conceited about appearance
Logical	Thinks men are superior to women
Worldly	Talks freely about sex with men
Skilled in business	
Direct	
Knows the way of the world	

Female-Valued Traits

Avoids harsh language	Interested in own appearance
Talkative	Neat in habits
Tactful	Quiet
Gentle	Strong need for security
Aware of feelings of others	Appreciates art and literature
Religious	Expresses tender feelings

masculinity (this point is explored extensively in Chapters 2 and 8). At any rate, these two points make the examination of masculinity a delicate and difficult task. Moreover, they dictate the recognition of *multiple meanings of masculinity*. There *is* one major consideration, however, and that is that, regardless of the shifting meanings of masculinity in the United States down through the years, each meaning appears to have placed the male sex in a power-advantaged position relative to the female sex with respect to many social resources. Just being in this position, though, may have affected males negatively and, in addition, may have placed them in some power-disadvantaged positions.

Joseph and Elizabeth Pleck (1980) identify five general periods of masculinity. They are: (1) the Agrarian Patriarchal period, 1630–1820, (2) the Commercial period, 1820–1860, (3) the Strenuous Life period, 1861–1919, (4) the Companionate Providing period, 1920–1965, and (5) after 1965. An examination of each period of masculinity presented by Pleck and Pleck reveals that, indeed, meanings of masculinity have shifted over time in such areas as sexuality, male–male relationships, father–child relationships, authority within the home, and so forth. Let us examine briefly each period.

The Agrarian Patriarchal Period

To be masculine in the United States in 1630 meant first of all that you were white, since male slaves were felt to be outside the "man" category and only a "man" had the potential to be masculine. Being male undoubtedly was a valued status in America during this period; men were favored in all legal and economic matters (only men could sign contracts, and husbands owned joint property). Moreover, men were the dominant figures in affairs of the home, the political institution, and the religious institution. While this may not seem generally different from men's control today, it *is* different, as we will see.

To be masculine in 1630 probably meant that you were an aggressive and competitive member of the male sex who believed in the familiar "double standard" regarding male and female sexual activities. You also felt that women were temptresses and should be handled basically as one would handle a child. Sons for you were valuable, but they were also people to be controlled, which you could do by holding an inheritance over their heads. Illustratively, you were in control of all societal institutions, you were competitive, you drank, you might even duel and gamble, but you were affectionate toward other males and believed in *manly intimacy*, as long as it did not extend to sex. You were a patriarch, in control, and sensitive to other men, but you did not include women in your circle of intimate friends. Basically, then, you were a ruler over children and women (who were child-like). You stood at the apex of a scale which included all of society's basic institutions.

The Commercial Period

With the growth of cities came changes in the meaning of masculinity. Because so many young men were leaving the land, moving to cities and entering the worlds of business and public affairs, older and wealthier men began to lose their patriarchal status. In addition, there was a decline in apprenticeships which affected older man–younger man instruction, laws were passed abolishing primogeniture, and women began to teach (thus placing young minds under the control of women). This latter part, however, did not affect male comradeship, as a separate male culture grew enormously during this period, with men meeting at taverns, coffeehouses, churches, blacksmith shops and the like.

During this period women were to make modest gains. In fact, an ancestor of the modern-day women's movement emerged in 1848: the organized feminist movement best know for formulating the Seneca Falls Declaration of Principles. Rejecting the tyranny of men over women, the signers (one-third of whom were men) and supporters sought equality for women in matters of law and the home. Given the political, social, and economic climates it is perhaps not surprising that women, on the surface, made modest gains during the Commercial period.

Pleck and Pleck note that two separate vertical scales emerged—one for males, and one for females. The male sphere consisted of business and public affairs, while the worlds of home and church were proclaimed the women's.

The rationale behind the emergent "separate but equal" spheres for men and women during the Commercial period was simple. Men were thought to be innately competitive and practical, while women were perceived as delicate, sensitive, pious, and virtuous. (During this time, men were envisioned as the more passionate sex.) This meant that men were more suited to business life and public affairs, while women's "natural" places were the home and church. A crucial additional statement is important, in that the home was thought to be a refuge for men from the competitive, aggressive, and practical world. Moreover, because men now were viewed as passionate creatures, women became responsible for helping men to control their passion by being good mothers to sons and good wives to husbands. Underneath all of this it is easy to see that the 'Phyllis Schafly' orientation for women began during the Commercial period.

The Strenuous Life Period

During this period, masculinity and physical strength became inextricably interwoven. There were still separate spheres for men and women, but women were beginning to ride bicycles, unfasten their corsets, and take jobs as typists, sales clerks, and librarians. In short, women seemed to be beginning to threaten men's stronghold on traditionally male occupations. This led to the construction of a rationale based on male–female differences in physical strength that was used to justify the exclusion of women from most jobs other than those mentioned above.

Masculinity during this period continued to imply that males had questionable moral standards, control over most affairs in the business world, male subcultures, and an emphasis on being physically active and fit (with the rise of organized male athletics and the founding of the Boy

Scouts of America by Ernest Seton, who blamed females for boys' flabby muscles). Some have felt that men during this period actually increased their camaraderie because of the perceived threat of women. One thing appears certain, and that is that the meaning of being masculine shifted from being the opposite of childish to being the opposite of feminine. It was during this period that some men became labeled as "effeminate," specifically those remaining in occupations that had been invaded by women. It is safe to say, then, that not only is a societal definition of femininity formed during the Strenuous Life period, but also a societal devaluation of femininity begins, the remnants of which remain today.

The Companionate Providing Period

During this period of masculinity, several significant changes occurred. Men began to interact socially with women as romance became a feature of male–female relationships. (Marriages began to take place between males and females more equal in age.) Male friendships diminished as males increased their participation in the competitive business world. Also significant was the fact that the *male as provider* became a dominant characteristic of masculinity. A "real man" paid his bills on time, took care of his family by purchasing numerous goods and providing for them in the best way possible. Obviously, this meant that work, aggressiveness, providing, competitiveness, and, in essence, "getting ahead" became integral features of masculinity. In the sexual arena, sex was perceived as recreational; premarital sex, extramarital sex, and homosexuality all became recognized as quite common occurrences with the publication of Kinsey's *Sexual Behavior in Males*. (The latter sexual activity was still defined by society, however, as a mental illness.) The Kinsey Report, then, added a new dimension to masculinity. The Plecks suggested that this new dimension included the relatively high incidence of homosexuality in the male population reported by Kinsey, his view that while most men did not act upon their homosexual potential all had that potential, and the assertion that male adolescents were "restrained by traditional sexual mores against premarital sex and outmoded views toward masturbation" (p. 31).

After 1965

According to Pleck and Pleck, three major social movements have altered the meaning of masculinity in the United States since the 1960s. They are the women's movement, the gay liberation movement and the men's movement. Let us examine some of the implications of these movements for meanings of masculinity. To these three movements, a fourth movement is added—the "Moral Majority," whose impact has been felt early in the 1980s

The Women's Movement

The early and middle 1960s marked the beginning of a resurgence of the women's movement, with the founding of the National Organization for Women (NOW) and the emergence of groups of young, college-educated women who had participated in civil rights movements, leftist movements, and the Vietnam anti-war movement. The NOW group consisted primarily of professional women demanding equality in pay, promotion, and opportunity for leadership, while the younger group of women focused their attention on an even wider range of issues. These women sought equality between the sexes on such issues as sexuality, socialization, and domestic responsibilities. The two general groups of women, together with numerous others, have been successful in effecting sex-role changes in the social order. Yet the success has been limited, as menifested by the failure of the Equal Rights Amendment to be ratified by the required number of states by June, 1982. Nonetheless, definitions of masculinity have been altered by the women's movement.

The Gay Liberation Movement

Another movement altering definitions of masculinity has been the gay liberation movement. Following the now-famous "Stonewall Rebellion" in 1969, when homosexual men and women resisted the tyranny of New York police in Greenwich Village, the gay liberation movement was born. Prior to the movement other gay organizations had pressed for legal changes, but none had been as vocal, as daring, and as active as organizations like the Gay Liberation Front, Gay Activist Alliances, and The National Gay Task Force, to mention a few. Using a variety of activist strategies, these and numerous other state and local gay organizations have promoted gay rights and prerogatives. The decision to remove homosexuality from the list of mental illnesses by the American Psychiatric Association in 1974 undoubtedly was due in part to the activities of various groups comprising the gay liberation movement. These men and women certainly have affected emerging conceptions of masculinity by their "out-of-the-closet" activities. As Pleck and Pleck state, "gay liberation's critique of the Western taboo against male expression of intimacy and affection raised unresolved issues for all men, regardless of sexual orientation" (p. 37). In addition, with the increasing numbers of males becoming "self-proclaimed gay men," fewer persons are ignorant of the fact that one may feel he is male (gender identity, masculine), behave in a societally-defined masculine manner (gender, masculine) and prefer sex with a male (sexual orientation, male). Introducing this clarification in basic sex-role concepts has been but one of the gay liberation movement's effects on emerging meanings of masculinity. Other effects are discussed throughout the volume.

The Men's Movement

In 1970 a Men's Center was formed in Berkeley, California, and for the next few years a surge of activity related to men's issues occurred. Men's consciousness-raising groups were developed, books about men were published, forums were held, and National Men's Organizations appeared on the scene (Men Allied for Liberation and Equality and Man Awareness Network are examples). Because the women's movement had created problems for men in their own role assumptions, the men's movement first concentrated on male–female relationships, only to extend its concern to issues affecting men as they relate to the male role. Issues like relations between men, father–child relationships, myths surrounding maleness, male intimacy, homophobia, and so on, have become dominant ones in the men's liberation movement. Certainly this last movement has not had the visible impact on society's definitions of masculinity that the other two have had. Nevertheless, I contend that the impact has been felt, albeit subtly. But, this impact presently may be difficult to discern, due in part to another movement—the Moral Majority.

The "Moral Majority"

The Moral Majority, a religious-based movement, has had broad appeal in the 1980s. It has been given some credit for the conservative political and social climate in the United States, because of its stance on critical social issues. These are issues directly related to the above three movements' aims and objectives. On a very general level, the moral majority has been in direct opposition to the women's movement's stands on abortion and equal rights, to the gay movement's stand on equal rights for homosexuals, and as a result, opposed to many aims of the men's liberation movement. While the moral majority's influence certainly has been felt in the United States, its effects on definitions of masculinity are only speculative at this time. However, should definitions of masculinity undergo tremendous change in the opposite direction in the near future, the effect of the moral majority might be more accurately assessed.

Emerging Meanings of Masculinity

Daniel Levinson *et al.* (1978), in *The Seasons of a Man's Life,* suggest that men during the mid-life transition stage (which occurs from the late thirties to the early forties) experience an emergence and integration of the more feminine aspects of the self. In fact they contend that the crucial issue during the mid-life transition period for males is learning to love devalued aspects of the self. How unfortunate it is that many males in the United States repress emotions and remain essentially unexpressive or nonhuman until they reach middle age. Changing meanings of masculinity in the United States will free men to become human much earlier in life. Let us discuss briefly the nature of emerging meanings of masculinity and the implications for males in our society.

A close examination of the preceeding pages of this book should show that meanings of masculinity in the United States from one point in time to another is some function of three factors: (1) *the nature of the relationship between men and women;* (2) *the nature of the relationship between men and other men;* and (3) *the nature of the relationship between men and themselves.* If, for example, the relationship between men and women generally is one where men tend to be domineering, violent, aggressive, chauvinistic, etc. toward women, then some portion of the prevailing definition of masculinity will include these traits. Similarly, if men distrust other men, if they are competitive and aggressive toward each other, if they are homophobic (afraid to be close to other men), then a full definition of masculinity must include these characteristics. Finally, if men generally in the United States accept the blame for a *few* men victimizing children, for a *few* men raping women and for a *few* men being insensitive animals, then *self-hate* is likely to be a part of the gender definition of masculinity. I do none of these things, and few men (if any) reading this book engage in these behaviors or have such feelings. Yet, these are stereotypes and/or meanings of masculinity held by many people which make relatively innocent men feel guilty. As Goldberg (p. 103) has stated, "men may very well be the last remaining subgroup in our society that can be blatantly, negatively and vilely stereotyped with little objection or resistance."

Based on the above comments, then, we see that to be masculine in the United States today, for some, means *to be a male chauvinist pig!* Such a sweeping generalization is unacceptable here, and the reasons are threefold: (1) *relationships between men and women are changing,* (2) *relationships between men and other men are changing,* and, (3) *male self-hatred is dissipating.* First of all, it should be remembered that the modern-day women's movement has had an enormous impact on male–female relationships in the United States. Power analyses of male–female relationships typically have focused on male power advantages in basic societal institutions. To be sure, males have enjoyed (?) "advantages" in societal wealth, power, and prestige. It is questionable, however, whether all of these "advantages" have been enjoyable. For example, to believe that being masculine means the assumption of a protective, condescending, providing, and generally patriarchal role regarding one's female mate and women in general has meant a reduction in psychological power in vital human areas for males.

Joseph Pleck (1976) has described two kinds of power women have in traditional male–female relationships. This is significant because most power analyses of male–female relationships in the United States posit power advantages for males (e.g., Polatnik, 1973–1974). Undoubtedly this is due to the basic premises accepted by many writers about male–female relationships, one being that males are in control of the major sources of power in the United States. Specifically these sources of power include political, economic, social, and physical institutions. What is obscured when such premises are accepted without qualification is the nature of power–dependence relations, long explored by exchange theorists. Joseph Pleck implicitly recognizes the nature of power–dependence relations in his work, which is the reason it is so important to mention.

Most social-exchange theorists would accept the point that social power resides in dependence. This means, for example, that a particular male might wield a good deal of power over a particular female in a given situation. This power, however is contingent upon the female acquiring or accepting the subordinate position. Collectively, this may mean that much male power in the United States is the result of female dependency, even when the power is institutionalized. Colette Dowling presents this thesis as the core of her analysis of male–female relationships in the United States in *The Cinderella Complex* (1981). In her analysis, however, Dowling does not adequately allow for the possibility that the reciprocal nature of sex roles produces social power for females. In other words, as Emerson (1962) pointed out over two decades ago, power in social relationships may not be a zero sum game. Undoubtedly males have power over females in America, but females also have power over males in vital human areas.

More specifically, Joseph Pleck states that women hold two kinds of power over males in our society. These two kinds of power are (1) *expressive power*, and (2) *masculinity-validating power*. In explaining *expressive power* held by women, Pleck refers to the fact that "masculinity" is often interpreted to mean that emotions should not be displayed. As a result, many men who internalize masculine traits and who act out the masculine role are able to express their emotions only vicariously through women. Therefore, many men come to depend on women to make them feel emotionally alive, thereby giving women *expressive power* over them.

A second kind of power men attribute to women is *masculinity-validating power*. Men do this because of their need to have women play certain roles which will make them feel powerful. Because few men accept self-definitions of masculinity from other men, according to Pleck (and this is explored later), most men depend on women to tell them emotionally that they are members of the masculine gender. Pleck feels, by the way, that most women only *pretend* for men, realizing that this is a need that men have. At any rate, women assuming submissive roles for men often do so only to make men feel good. Women also sometimes refuse to accept their submissive roles in an effort to make men feel bad. The mere fact that women often determine whether men feel masculine or non-masculine attests to the power that women have over men.

The emerging definition of masculinity will affect men's dependency on the above two dimensions of female power. As men become emotionally more expressive, they will depend less on women in this area of humanity. This should have far-reaching implications for all kinds of social relationships. One kind of relationship that will be affected is the parent–child relationships. No longer will it be necessary for fathers to wait until their children are adults and until they, themselves, are past middle-age before they relate to them on an emotional level. Men will be free to laugh, cry, share pain and joy with their children during early childhood years and throughout the childrearing process. The emerging definition of masculinity will also allow males to feel more secure in their gender. Men will learn how to define themselves! Rather than depending on women to tell them they are "men," males in the United States will look to themselves as masculinity-validating sources. Interestingly enough, this may be precisely what some female opponents of the Equal Rights Amendment fear.

Emerging meanings of masculinity also are being affected by the recognition by growing numbers of men that it is alright to feel affectionate toward men. Men are growing increasingly weary of the "latent homosexual" label applied to them when they develop caring and warmth toward each other. As men are becoming more secure in their sexual identities and less fearful of their feminine characteristics; they are becoming more relaxed in their relationships with other men. If such a trend continues, undoubtedly it will affect the male's need to *prove himself* in all areas of social life, his need to live up to certain male images constructed by society (and often supported by women), his need to use women in competitive games with other men, and his need to strategize ways of destroying other men.

The above changes are intricately related to still another source of changes occurring in men—change in self-concept. Just as women have been used by men, *men have been used by women.* Men, too, have been used as symbols of success and security by women, often being driven to lead emotionally self-denying lives. As a result, men have been plagued by feelings of doubt, self-hate and guilt. What happens, for example, to the man who internalizes all that society says a man should be and yet is denied the opportunity to become that man? This happens to a large portion of the male population—Black men, poor White men, Chicano men, American Indian men, and so on. Even when men are "successful" in our society, they are often castigated for not participating in the child-rearing process, for not being a companion to a mate, for being too competitive or too aggressive. All of this contributes to male self-hate. Men gradually are coming to realize that much of the masculine role places them in a no-win situation. The result is that men are examining more closely the feelings they have about themselves. Moreover, as men are becoming more expressive, and turning to themselves for masculinity-validation, they are beginning to experience the positive aspects of maleness and to resist the sexist and intimidating labels often stereotypically applied to them, as well as the behaviors which perpetuate stereotypical masculine traits.

Women and Masculinity

That American women generally have always represented an underclass is a conclusion reached by many scholars of the status of women in the United States. Within the last decade or so, many articles and books have suggested and documented the assertion that women in America suffer discrimination that affects their power, prestige, and wealth. The Women's Movement has been a response to the power disadvantages experienced by women. Within the Women's Movement itself, according to Yates (1975, p. 21), three ideologies exist: (1) the feminist ideology, (2) the women's liberationist's ideology, and (3) the androgynous ideology. These ideologies are important to understand because they have diverse implications for the relationship between women and masculinity. The *feminist ideology* seemingly accepts male perogatives, privileges, values, and so on, but embraces the philosophy that women, too, should enjoy equally all of these dubious advantages. Much more radical is the *women's liberationist's* ideology which questions masculine values, standards, and traits. Undoubtedly, these are the women Goldberg says pin unfair, sexist, and chauvinist labels on all men. The androgynous ideology appears to be more conciliatory than the latter without sacrificing *women's* standards, values and in a sense, *femininity*. The ideology calls for compromise and negotiation between men and women with the ideal product being a society where men and women are equal and masculinity and femininity are equally valued.

An interesting feature of the ideologies existing within the Women's Movement is the extent to which women within the Movement (and many who do not identify with the movement) agree on certain aspects of each ideology. For example, the responses of many women to public opinion polls indicate a substantial number *separate* themselves from masculine traits like violence and aggression (women's liberation ideology). Many women also believe in *equality* for men and women in all present societal institutions (the feminist ideology). In addition, a great number of women feel we "must embrace a set of humanistic and socially conscious values that embrace the best of both traditional masculinity and traditional femininity" (Chafetz, 1978, p. 258; an androgynous ideology).

What often is *not* emphasized is the fact that literally thousands of women have responded to traditional masculinity in traditionally feminine ways. Moreover, as Nelson reports in her interviews with Yale undergraduate women, "the younger generation tempers its hope with realism." The result, as explained by one of the interviewers, and reported by Nelson (1982, p. 231) is that a vast number of younger women seem quite apathetic about feminism. The fact that many women in the past have been willing to assume traditional feminine roles and numerous ones *presently are* assuming traditional feminine roles does not obviate the need for women's-movement issues to be addressed by society. Indeed, the earlier assumption of traditional feminine roles by many older women contributes to a crucial problem facing the United States today—the feminization of poverty. Moreover, the striking increase in the number of female-headed households indicates that young women who do not embrace aspects of the Women's Movement may be on the verge of contributing enormously to the problem in the future. In the next section, I discuss household characteristics and comparative income statistics which give credence to the above contention.

Women and Households

Of the eighty-two million, three hundred sixty-eight thousand (82,368,000) households in America as of 1980, forty-nine million two hundred ninety-four thousand (49,294,000) consisted of married couples. Women headed another twenty-one million eight hundred sixty-two thousand (21,862,000) and men headed eleven million two hundred twelve thousand (11,212,000) households. Women, then, headed 27% of the total number of households in America while men headed only 14% when married couple households are excluded. Furthermore, when only single-sex headed households (33,074,000) are examined, according to the Bureau of the Census, women headed 66% and men headed 44%. This supports Chafetz's statement that "no female can assume any longer that she will be supported for the rest of her life" (p. 31). In fact, further examinations of Census Bureau data indicates that a large number of women will not only have to fend for themselves, but also will have to fend for other family members.

Approximately one-third of the single-sex headed households (11,015,000) had other family members present. Eighty-two percent (9,082,000) were female-headed and 18% (1,933,000) were male-headed. Within female headed households, 69% (6,299,000) had related children under eighteen. Only 41% (2,000) of the male-headed households contained related children under 18 years of age. Moreover, of all the households with children under eighteen (7,101,000) excluding married couples, females were heads of households in 89% while males were heads of households in only 11%. If single-sex heads of households with other family members present are restricted to include only "own children under 18 years of age," females head 89% (5,634,000) and males head 11% (666,000). This accounts for nearly 11 million children living in households headed by females (over 1,092,000 children under 18 live in homes headed by males). To be sure, these figures and percentages illuminate the awesome responsibility befalling growing numbers of females in American society. Unfortunately, societal values, standards, and priorities have not facilitated women's preparation to shoulder the responsibility. Ross (1976, p. 137) reported that in 1972, 43% of all poverty-level families were headed by females. By 1980, according to the Census Bureau, 48% (12,972,000) of the 6, 217,000 families below the poverty level were headed by females. Furthermore, 25.7% of the White female-headed households with other relatives present were below the poverty level, as were 49.9% of the Black female-headed households and 51.3% of the female-headed Hispanic households. Pearce (1978) has suggested that approximately 150,000 women per year who head households are recruited into poverty and predicts an increase in this number. Ehrenreich and Stallard (1982, p. 217) have echoed the National Advisory Council on Economic Opportunity's forecast that "all other things being equal, if the proportion of the poor in female-householder families were to continue to increase at the same rate as it did from 1967 to 1978, the poverty population would be composed solely of women and their children before the year 2000." Let us explore some Census Bureau income data as they relate to women in the United States.

Women and Income

Two reasons often advanced for the impoverished status of females in the United States is that (1) women live longer than men and (2) divorce is on the rise in the United States. I submit that these so-called causes simply are *proposed justifications* for female poverty, and that they have a spurious relationship with female poverty. *Divorced females*, for example, in 1980 had the *highest* median annual income ($12,983) for any group of female year-round full-time workers. Widowed females had the second highest median income at $12,279 (see Tables 2 and 3). Widowhood and divorcehood do not *cause* female poverty, but the fact that these two groups of women have median incomes that are only 72% and 70% respectively. of their male counterparts' median incomes, may contain the reason for female poverty.

Given that female divorcees and widows have higher earnings than married women with husbands present or absent; and, that married women earn only 57% of their male counterparts' incomes, it does not seem feasible to use marital status as an explanatory variable for *female* poverty. The real culprit responsible for female poverty, I contend, is institutionalized sexism, which manifests itself partially in lower total money incomes for females and occupational segregation that excludes females from the opportunity to earn higher incomes. Saying that the marital statuses *divorced* and *widowed* cause female poverty is similar to saying that marriage causes women's year round earned income to depart significantly from men's year round earned income. A glance at Census Bureau statistics shows that the median income for single females more closely approximates their male counterparts' than in other marital status groups. In 1980, the year-round earned median income for single females was $11,111, while single males had a year-round earned median income of $12,924—female income was 86% of male income.

Table 2 reveals a great deal of information about the comparative financial statuses of women and men in the United States. Data from the March 1981 population survey show that approximately 74,972,000 males had incomes in 1980, and that 77,487,000 females had incomes for the same period. Two % of the males 18 years of age and older (76,876,000) were without income, while 9% of females 18 years and older (85,237,000) were without income. Seventy-six % of the females without income did, however, have a husband present. The problem for females is not lack of income; it is lack of an *adequate* income. Table 2 gives a more informative picture of women's financial status compared to men when total money income is divided into three broad categories: income below $7,000; income below $15,000; and income above $15,000.

As shown, 60% of those females with incomes in 1980 (46,785,000) had incomes below $7,000 compared to 26% of the males (19,244,000) in the same income category. When the income ceiling is raised to $15,000, 89% of the females (68,712,000) are accounted for, while only 54% of the males (41,150,000) are covered. The result is that only 11% of the females in 1980 had incomes above $15,000, while 46% of the males in 1980 had incomes above $15,000. This discrepancy in income by sex is further reflected in the fact that the median total money income in 1980 for female year-round full-time workers was $11,594, while it was $19,194 for their male counterparts. Females' median total money income in this

Table 2
Total Income by Sex for Persons 18 Years and Over in the United States[a]

	Male		Female	
	Number	%	Number	%
Total	76,876,000	100	85,237,000	100
No Income	1,904,000	2	7,750,000	9
With Income	74,972,000	——	77,487,000	——
Below 7,000	19,244,000	26	46,785,000	60
Below 15,000	41,150,000	54	68,712,000	89
Over 15,000	33,822,000	46	8,774,000	11

Year-Round Full-Time Workers

	Male	Female	Female % of Male Income
Median Income	$19,194	$11,594	60
Mean Income	21,464	12,738	59

[a]Source: *Current Population Reports*, (Table 11, p. 21) 1980.

instance was only 60% of males' total money income. The comparative mean incomes were $12,738 for full-time working females and $21,464 for full-time working males—females' mean income was 59% of males' mean income.

Tables 3 and 4, below, show a similar pattern of income distribution by sex for widowed and divorced persons. However, discrepancies between the sexes decrease. In addition to the specific income-category decreases, widowed female full-time workers have a median income ($12,379) which is 72% of the male median income ($17,245); and, a mean income ($14,204) which is 70% of the male mean income ($20,233). For divorced persons working year-round and full-time, the female median income ($12,893) and mean income ($14,360) are 70% of the male median ($18,359) and mean income ($20,465).

While discrepancies in male and female total income and earned income reveal much about how society responds to women, when the previous discussed household statistics are included the story becomes a rather chilling one. As women continue to experience economic-under-class status, they are increasingly assuming a provider role for other family members as well as for themselves. At the same time, government-subsidized day care has been drastically reduced, as have training programs and many other services benefitting women and their children directly.

Table 3
Total Income by Sex for Widowed Persons in the United States[a]

	Male		Female	
	Number	%	Number	%
Total	1,949,000	100	10,845,000	100
No Income	290,000	1	263,000	2
With Income	1,920,000	——	10,582,000	——
Below $7,000	1,132,000	58	6,984,000	66
Below $15,000	1,521,000	79	9,584,000	91
Over $15,000	397,000	21	996,000	9

Year-Round Full-Time Workers

	Male	Female	Female % of Male Income
Median Income	$17,245	$12,379	72
Mean Income	20,233	14,204	70

[a]Source: *Current Population Reports,* (Table 11, p. 21) 1980.

Table 4
Total Income by Sex for Divorced Persons in the United States[a]

	Male		Female	
	Number	%	Number	%
Total	4,391,000	100	6,438,000	100
No Income	119,000	3	156,000	2
With Income	4,282,000	——	6,282,000	——
Below 7,000.00	938,000	22	2,489,000	40
Below 15,000.00	2,389,000	56	4,883,000	78
Over 15,000.00	1,883,00	44	1,399,000	22

	Year-Round Full-Time Worders		
	Male	Female	Female % of Male Income
Median Income	$18,359.60	$12,893.00	70
Mean Income	20,465.00	14,360	70

[a]Source: *Current Population Reports,* 1980 (Table 11, page 21).

Perhaps one of the most interesting and telling things about all of this is the rationale developed to explain the female's increasing underclass status in America. The fact that women live longer and that the divorce rate is continuing to rise are thought by some to be major factors responsible for female poverty. In a nutshell, this is tantamount to saying that the reason so many women face poverty is that they do not have *protective, condescending, providing and generally patriarchal males* by their sides. Ehrenreich and Stallard (1982) report that Kathleen Teague, director of the New Right American Legislative Exchange Council, feels that the solution for poor and unmarried women is to make more of an effort to attract husbands. In other words, if women would assume the traditional feminine role, they would not be poor. It is this kind of simplistic and illogical thinking that contributes enormously to the underclass economic status of women and the underclass emotional status of men in the United States today.

Teague's thesis seemingly ignores the previously discussed income discrimination against women. Also unimportant, apparently, is the fact that *occupational segregation* remains a part of the American labor scene. While women's participation in the labor force has increased in recent years, women are still underrepresented in many high-paying occupations, and overrepresented in low-paying ones. Ehrenreich and Stallard (1982, p. 220) have stated that "only 20 out of 420 listed occupations account for 80 percent of employed women." According to the July 1982 edition of *Employment and Earnings* published by the U.S. Department of Labor's Bureau of Labor Statistics, women workers are concentrated in the occupational categories *clerical work, service work,* and *professional and technical work* (which includes nurses, grade school teachers, etc.).

As Table 5 indicates, 78% of women workers are found in these three broad categories. Table 5 also shows the median weekly earnings of full-time wage and salary workers by occupation and sex and the percentage females' median earnings are of males' median earnings. In no category is the female median income comparable to the male median income. The occupational category most comparable by sex is the *non-farm laborer* category, where women's earnings are 90% of male earnings. The occupation category where the greatest income discrepancy by sex occurs is in the *manager and administration* category, where female earnings are only 60% of male earnings. This is also the category where males had the highest median weekly earnings. Incidentally, males had the lowest weekly median earnings in the category where females were most comparable to them. These statistics tend to support the idea that, while females may share similar occupational categories with males, differences

Table 5
Occupational Percentage Distribution and Median Weekly Earnings by Sex[a]

Occupation	% of persons employed		Median weekly earnings		Female % of male income
	Males	Females	Male	Females	
Professional and Technical Work	16.3	16.8	$465.00	$330.00	71
Managers and Administrators	14.2	7.3	502.00	301.00	60
Sales Workers	6.2	6.9	362.00	195.00	54
Clerical Workers	6.2	34.8	342.00	232.00	68
Craft and Kindred Workers	20.2	1.9	377.00	278.00	74
Operatives, Except Transport	10.1	9.9	304.00	198.00	65
Transport Equipment Operatives	5.5	0.7	321.00	239.00	74
Nonfarm Laborers	7.7	1.4	249.00	223.00	90
Service Workers	9.4	19.4	245.00	175.00	71
Farmworkers	4.3	1.4	189.00	Less than 100,00 median not shown	——

[a]Source: *Employment and Earnings,* July, 1982 A-22; A-79, p. 25, p. 66.

in rank and function seem to result in income differences between the sexes.

Another factor recently identified as inimical to increases in the financial status of women is the *reorganization of the work structure.* Because of advances in technology, numerous intermediate-level skilled jobs are disappearing and being replaced by low-skilled and semi-skilled jobs. These are jobs for which women are seemingly slotted, and tend to be both meaningless and low-paying.

Based on our discussion, then, the feminization of poverty is some function of (1) *income discrimination,* (2) *occupational segregation,* and (3) *work-structure reorganization.* Given these three factors, marital status seems inappropriate as a casual variable in explaining female poverty.

While women in the United States remain in a subordinate economic status, we would be remiss not to recognize that women's subjugated economic status, albeit important, is *not* the only source of female subordination. Another important source is the fact that women constitute only 4% of Congress, 12% of state legislatures, and 8% of mayors in the United States. These statistics reflect the subordinate status of women in society's political institutions. This is so despite the fact that women have a history of resisting militarism and/or violence—an ideology that is certainly needed in a world occasionally bordering on total destruction. Increased violence toward women in our society also indicates their low status, and the idea that real *men* must dominate and control. Indeed there are numerous signs in the United States of continuing sexism which cannot be given full treatment in this volume. The major question that arises, though, is 'How are women responding to all of this?' In the following section some of the responses women have to traditional masculine ideas and/or behavior will be explored.

Female Responses to Traditional Masculinity

No claim is made here that women hold a unitary view of traditional masculinity. I do believe, however, that certain themes stand out in the multiplicity of views women hold. They seem to be similar to Yates's ideologies characterizing the Women's Movement. In this section, several views of masculinity written or implied by women in their work are explored. The sources are both popular and academic.

Laurel Walum Richardson, in her second edition of *The Dynamics of Sex and Gender: A Sociological Perspective* (1981), undoubtedly echoes the views of a large and growing number of women. Referring to herself as a feminist, she seems to accept the worth of certain traits like competitiveness, aggressivenes intellectualism, logical thinking, and so on—all of which traditionally are associated with the masculine gender. Richardson, in no uncertain terms, expresses the need for a redistribution of power in the United States to include women. Interestingly, while traditional feminine traits like nurturing, passivity, and warmth are discussed positively, they are stressed only minimally as characteristics males should adopt. Perhaps this is why she agrees with Lamm's (1977) contention that men do not need to meet with each other in an effort to develop their awareness and sensitivity, rather, they should read feminist literature and begin to *behave* in a feminist manner. I feel, however, that unless men recognize and appreciate in themselves those traits traditionally associated with femininity, behaving in an equitable manner toward women is unlikely to occur. Men's liberation groups, I contend, are catalytic agents toward change in men's behavior.

Another sociologist, Janet Saltzman Chefetz (1978), pens a slightly different view of traditional masculinity. She believes that some aspects of both traditional masculinity and traditional femininity should be discarded and/or altered. Believing that simply "allowing males to get into the costly 'bag' females have long been in, and vice-versa, is no solution" (p. 258). Chafetz argues for androgynous sex-role assumptions. She believes that this would be both personally and collectively rewarding to men and women. Chafetz's view toward masculinity, then, is that there are both negative and positive aspects of the gender. We should discard the negative aspects and embrace the positive aspects. For Chafetz, then, masculinity should be modified.

Jean Stockard and Miriam M. Johnson (1980) offer still another view of masculinity, similar to Chafetz's and different from Richardson's. They feel that the world would be a much better place if maintenance of hierarchies and dominance over others could be lessened. This obviously means that the traditional masculine traits of aggressiveness and domination should be devalued, from Stockard and Johnson's perspective. In fact they summarize their volume as an analysis that suggests that women should not become more like men; rather, men should become more like women, in the sense of using a more female world-view or paradigm. This means that the meanings of masculinity should be modified much more in the direction of the new meanings of masculinity discussed earlier in this chapter. Drawing upon the work of Geils (1978) and Neil (1979), Stockard and Johnson (p. 277) write:

> ... Cultural symbols would be altered to show an equal evaluation of females and males, and cultural values would express complementarity and interdependence rather than priority and social hierarchy. It would be recognized that nurturance, expressiveness and concern for other people are

more important than the maintenance of hierarchies and dominance over others. Aggression would be viewed as a threat to social integration and to human survival itself. In this world, the form of domination would be seen as undesirable, and stratification by race, class, and sex would lessen.

Chafetz's and Stockard and Johnson's views of masculinity parallel the view of Phyllis Chessler (1978), who contends that it is crucial for men to enter fully the family of women and children as "wise and gentle" nurturers. Chessler feels that male relationships, especially those between men, have been characterized by ambivalence, hostility, homicide, and full-scale warfare—all the result of a "specifically male sense of primal guilt and damnation" (p. xvi). In Chessler's opinion, men could benefit greatly from assuming more androgynous roles in our society. Thus, the masculine image for Chessler is in need of modification.

During the same period in which Chafetz, Stockard and Johnson, and Chessler wrote their views on traditional masculinity, two other women advanced ideas on the subject. These women's ideas are significant because they dared to broach a topic that up until that time largely was neglected—Black males and masculinity. Jeanne Noble's book, *Beautiful Also Are the Souls of My Black Sisters* (1978), made a distinct statement about Black males following the modern day Black movement. She wrote that Black males had destructive, sexist attitudes toward Black women, and she basically blamed Black men for the negative interaction between Black men and Black women.

Michele Wallace, another Black female author, published the popular *Black Macho and the Myth of the Superwoman* in 1979, which told the story of how Black women were disillusioned with Black men. Black men, according to Wallace, raised the expectations of Black women during the Black movement of the late 1960s and early 1970s. Wallace states "When she stood by silently as he [the Black male] became a man, she assumed that he would finally glorify and dignify Black womenhood, just as the white man had done for white women" (p. 122). The problem for Wallace seems not to be a general dislike of traditional masculinity as much as a dislike of the fact that few Black men seem willing to take on the shackles of traditional masculinity for Black women.

Noble's and Wallace's theses raise the same kind of dilemmas for Black women as expressed in "Diary of a Native American Feminist" (1982) by Rayna Green. She alludes to historical tribal differences in sex roles and to life-and-death issues that affect Native Americans—both of which threaten "sisterhood" among Native American females. As Green says (p. 172), "The double bind of sex and race is too real. . . . Whose version of tradition and whose version of equality should we fight for?" These particular points make it extremely difficult for Native American women to reach a consensus on masculinity, but it does not negate the concerns they express about the plight of Native American women. These women, who have been subjected to sterilization abuse, whose infant death-rate is 1.2 times higher than the general population's, who themselves die during childbirth at alarmingly high rates (1.2 times as high as the general population), whose suicides and alcoholism rates are on the increase head half of all Native American households (p. 213). To be sure, the issue of traditional masculinity in the United States *is* related directly to these issues affecting Native American women. Judging from Green's interpretation of numerous meetings with Native American women across the United States, their cry is "Bring on the new ways, bring on the new ways"—a tacit disapproval of traditional masculinity, and an implied preference for equality among the sexes and the races. It is not clear, however, whether, from Green's perspective, the masculine model needs alteration.

The forgoing views on masculinity in the United States lead us to the views of another author whom many would claim raised the consciousness of many women in 1981. Just as many, however, would probably say that Colette Dowling raised the ire of women in *The Cinderella Complex*. Though her perspective on sex roles in America is in contrast to Richardson's, their conclusive views about masculinity are strikingly similar, in that both ultimately are interested in making women equal to men in a man's world. Dowling wants women to become less dependent, "pull themselves up by their bootstraps," and at least rid themselves of irrational fears and the deep wish to be taken care of by others. Scant attention is given to the power that men traditionally have held over women, which would not facilitate such a miraculous rise in status. Of course, much of Richardson's volume is devoted to pressing this point. Nevertheless, with few minor differences, both offer few alterations in the traditional masculine model—their basic ideas seem to be, *make women equal to men.*

Still another response to traditional masculinity has been an exhortation by some to women that they should separate themselves from men—at least psychologically, if not physically. One of the early statements implying this philosophy is contained in Robin Morgan's (1970) introduction to *Sisterhood is Powerful.*

> I can no more countenance the co-optive lip-service of the male-dominated Left which still stinks of male supremacy than I can countenance the class bias and racism of that male "movement." I haven't the faintest notion what possible revolutionary role white heterosexual men could fulfil, since they are the very embodiment of reactionary-vested-interest-power. But then I have great difficulty examining what men in general could possibly do about all this. In addition to doing the shitwork that women have been doing for generations, possibly not exist? (p. xi)

LIBRARY
OF
MOUNT ST. MARY'S
COLLEGE
EMMITSBURG, MARYLAND

The above statement is a powerful one, but it is safe to say that most women have not chosen to totally separate themselves from men as the solution to inequality between the sexes. There are, however, variations on the theme. For example, Freeman (1979) discusses the fact that numbers of women are engaged in building alternative institutions that incorporate feminist values, such as self-help medical clinics and self-help training centers for legal services. This has come about, she says, because many women feel that "the institutions of society are corrupted by their weddedness to masculine values . . . " (p. 603).

Regardless of whether the appropriate response to traditional masculinity is seen as assimilation or as pluralism or as separatism, they all have in common the goal of raising the status of women in our society. This in itself implies change in the definition of masculinity. As we have seen, some views have more direct implications for change than others. Nevertheless, I feel safe in saying that increasingly more women are demanding modification on some level of society's traditional masculinist model.

Men and New Definitions of Masculinity

The voices of women opposed to their subordination in America are not as loud as they were during the 1970s. Yet there is a determined effort underway by women of all races, ethnic groups and socioeconomic backgrounds to eradicate sexism in the United States. The approaches used by these women are as varied as the women themselves, and range from expressions of indignation at overheard sexist comments to directing women's self-help organizations like the ones mentioned above. The question raised and discussed in this section focuses on the meaning of these changes in sex roles for men. In other words, what is the realtionship between men and new definitions of masculinity?

The above question is difficult to answer because many men subscribe verbally to equality for women; yet the status of women has not changed appreciably in recent years (Richardson, 1981, p. 266-7). Why? Are men only paying lip service to equal rights for women? Are men resisting changes in their behavior toward women? The answers are "yes" and "no" to the latter two questions.

Some changes have occurred in men's behavior within the past decade. Men's groups have been formed to combat sexism in the United States. Men have written with great compassion in support of women's equality and issues affecting women. Men also are assuming certain roles traditionally associated with women, such as doing domestic work, sharing childrearing duties with their mates, engaging in nurturing behavior, and so on. In fact, some studies of male and female elementary school teachers are showing that males are often more nurturant than female teachers to both boys and girls. Beverly Fagot (1981) found in her study that male teachers gave more positive comments to children and were more likely to give children physical affection than female teachers.

Despite the fact that some men do support women's equality in most societal areas both verbally and behaviorally, male resistance to women's rights does exist. Nowhere is this resistance more apparent than in *The Myth of the Monstrous Male* (1982). In this scathing attack on feminists, Gordon challenges generalizations about relationships between men and such things as pornography, rape, historical discrimination against women, and, in general, male dominance. Claiming to agree with the "standard" feminist platform calling for greater freedom for women, Gordon feels that the women's movement has come to be represented by "the sour, the mean and the dumb" (p. xiv). Furthermore, he contends that the reason for the degeneration of the women's movement is discrepant expectations between men and women about sex.

What Gordon does not address in his book reveals more about his resistance to women's rights than what he does address. I think he is correct to criticize the tendency of some feminists to overgeneralize about men, he is correct to criticize those women who still use traditional feminine ploys in their dealings with men, and I think he is correct to question the wisdom of those female chauvinists who would exclude men from participating in the Women's Movement. I question, however, Gordon's failure to adequately address economic, political, and other social issues affecting women. I question also his contention that unless women retain the idea of sexual freedom in their movement, there cannot be an equal sharing of rights and responsibilities between men and women. I doubt seriously Gordon's thesis that all of this boils down to an upheaval in the bedroom.

Gordon, however, is not the last bastion of discrimination against women. Men in their everyday lives resist changes in their behaviors toward women. When we do not encourage women to be independent, when we lapse into traditional ways of thinking about women, when we behave toward female acquaintances, friends, lovers, wives, and even strangers in condescending and sexist ways, we resist changing our behavior. But we do not need to resist the Women's Movement. In fact, our energies should be devoted to participating in the Men's Movement. This would alert many of us to the idea that traditional masculinity is hazardous to our health. Joseph Pleck (1981) has stated:

1. Aggressiveness and competitiveness cause men to put themselves in dangerous situations;
2. Emotional inexpressiveness causes psychosomatic and other
   health problems;
3. Men take greater risks;
4. Men's jobs expose them to physical danger;
5. Men's jobs expose them to psychological stress;
6. The male role socializes men to have personality characteristics
   associated with high mortality;
7. Responsibilities as family breadwinners expose men to psychological stress;
8. The male role encourages certain specific behaviors that endan-
   ger health, specifically tobacco smoking and alcohol consumption, and;
9. The male role psychologically discourages men from taking adequate medical care of themselves.

In the chapters to follow, not only will we see that our sex role is
hazardous to our health, we will see that we, too, are in the process of
becoming free. Hopefully, we will recognize the need for our facilitation
of the process.

CHAPTER 2

Socialization and the Male Role

Invariably, couples who express the desire to have children will respond that they want 'a *boy* first . . . and then, a *girl*'. Persons interested in the status effects of sex and gender often interpret such a response to support the notion that boys are more valued than girls in our culture. One problem with this interpretation of the "boy-first" response is that it tells only part of the story. The story unfolds further when couples are asked "why do you want a boy?" Responses given usually will include "to carry on the family name," "to follow in his father's footsteps," " . . . so that a boy will be the oldest of the children," and the list goes on—most, if not all, indicating male assumption of responsibility. Thus, *if* boys *are* more valued than girls, then the question must be asked, *valued for what?* To assume responsibility? To be placed in a cultural straightjacket? To become prematurely dysfunctional persons both physically and psychologically? These are questions which must be answered by society, given the hazards faced by many males as a result of learning the male role and attempting to behave according to its prescriptions (Goldberg, 1976). Long before many of them are born, and certainly during infancy, specific and general expectations are established regarding the roles most males are to perform. Obviously, this means that little attention is ordinarily given to the individuality of a particular male child. As Zane Grey is supposed to have said, "Every boy likes baseball, and if he doesn't, he isn't a boy" (Pleck and Pleck, 1980).

Some changes have occurred in role expectations for boys since the time of Zane Grey's. It is questionable, however, whether changed role expectations are any less rigid for boys as most little league games reflect.

All boys do not have to play baseball, but if they don't they should play softball, soccer, football, or *something* that will teach them the competitive spirit . . . teach them to be *men*.

One familiar example of the rigidity of modern day role expectations for a male infant can be seen in the case of a newborn outside of the United States which was popularized in the mass media in June, 1982. What is revealing about this foreign birth is the excitement and/or furor it created in the United States—a country thought to be undergoing modification in traditional sex-roles. On June 21, 1982, Princess Diana gave birth to a boy and Britain seemed elated as were literally millions of Americans. Princess Di had a boy—the future king? The child was hardly wrapped in clothing before a plethora of expectations had been established in England and in America regarding the role he is to perform in the coming years. To ensure that he will meet these expectations, a long and arduous socialization process awaits the "future king" that only the masochistic would enjoy, and, perhaps, only the sadistic would administer.

In America we do not have "future kings." Nevertheless, we cannot afford to be smug because practically every male born here has similar (though lesser in degree) shackles placed upon him at birth. This is due to the male *socialization process*—the process of acquiring the physical, mental, and social skills that a male needs to survive and to become both a man and a member of society (see Light and Keller, 1979, p. 109). A myriad of agents and artifacts are responsible for this process including the child's primary group (which includes parents, relatives, friends, other children) the mass media, the schools, toys, the sports institution, clothes, and so on. It is a complex process, made even more so by the existence of racial and ethnic substructures. While our discussion of male socialization will be general, later in the chapter specific attention is devoted to two relatively large groups of males in the United States— White males and Black males. First, however, let us consider the socialization of males generally and some of the agents responsible for the process.

"At the beginning of a child's life, we signal to ourselves and others that here is, not simply a new life, but a new male or female" (McKee, 1981, p. 265). This in itself is the beginning of sex-role socialization for the child. Parents as well as others are expected to, and do, act differently toward the child if it is male than if it is female, and vice-versa. The child may not be aware of it, but its sex-role socialization has already begun, moments after its birth. If the child is male, though, he will learn soon that there are certain kinds of behavior he is expected to engage in and certain kinds which he should not engage in. Maccoby and Jacklin (1974) have pointed out that from early childhood greater pressure is exerted on males than on females to conform to appropriate sex-role behavior. And to what does society generally want males to conform?

Since the reasons usually given by parents and prospective parents for preferring boys imply responsibility to be assumed, the following statement seems appropriate: *Boys are expected to conform to the norm of responsibility for learning how to maintain and perpetuate the society.* Furthermore, the idea can be proferred that these expectations are lodged in a general belief that biological factors are responsible for differences between the sexes. Thus, for many persons, boys should be given the responsibility for societal survival because they are innately more capable of assuming this responsibility than females. This line of thought leads us to a discussion of the roles of biology and environment in sex-role socialization generally, and in male socialization specifically.

Biology and Male Socialization

An extremely informative article by Lewis and Weinraub (1979) examines research related to the direct role of biological factors in influencing sensory, attentional, and temperamental sex differences in infants and young children. They point out first of all that research on cerebral dominance suggests sex differences in maturational rates. These differences, they feel, may result in earlier verbal development in girls but slower development of spatial skills. However, Lewis and Weinraub conclude, "It is clear that sex differences in cerebral dominance are probably *not* responsible for the appearance of sex differences before the fourth year of life" (p. 138).

With respect to sensory functions, Lewis and Weinraub report that findings indicate slight sex differences are rather inconsistent. Some studies have shown that newborn girls are more sensitive to touch than newborn boys, but other studies have not confirmed the findings. Few conclusions can be reached about sex differences in the areas of taste and smell, because of the paucity of studies. There is evidence, however, that female infants show more interest in and pay more attention to complex auditory events than males; Lewis and Weinraub cite Birn (1976) and Maccoby and Jacklin. They also report that there is evidence that there may be sex differences in infant temperament. Citing work by a number of investigators, Lewis and Weinraub state that boys under three months, when compared with girls of the same age, demonstrate higher levels of irritability and lesser amounts of sleep. Infant boys also seem more affected by stress and are more distressed when separated from their mothers than girls.

Despite the above findings, Lewis and Weinraub feel that the existence of early sex differences probably does not necessarily mean that the differences are biological in origin. Differential parent–infant interactions by sex of child have been observed which show that girls receive more verbal stimuli from their mothers than boys. Referring to work done in the area by Lewis and Freedle (1973), Lewis and Weinraub conclude that sex differences in infants, indeed in young children, may be a function not so much of biological sex differences, but of differential expectations and/or adult behavior exhibited toward infants and children. Even if the clearly observed physiological differences between the sexes exist, we must be aware of the influence of adult expectations and the experiences they provide for children in preparation for future adult roles to be assumed. The future King of England in all likelihood will perform "kingly" when the time comes. However, it is quite unlikely that this will be due entirely to his "royal blood" or the fact that he is male. Expectations and experiences will play vital roles.

Environment and Male Socialization

It was emphasized at the outset of this chapter that boys seem to be preferred more frequently than girls. Hoffman (1977) offers evidence for this assertion and also states that when girls are wanted, the reasons are different. Girls are wanted to play with, for companionship, and to be cute and sweet. In addition, Lewis and Weinraub state that newborn females are described differently than newborn males by their parents. Boys are seen as strong, more alert, fussier, and better coordinated while girls are thought to be softer, have finer features, and to be more attentive. Boy infants seem to be handled more roughly than girl infants, and while they are touched more than girls for the first three months, they are touched less afterwards. As a result, by the age of six months, girls are touched more. On the environmental side, then, we already see that boys, during the early months following birth, receive less *verbal* stimulation *and* declining *physical* stimulation from their parents. To be sure, others, too, respond differently to boys than to girls. The environmental influence is certainly apparent in gender development, as the above comments indicate, and cultural artifacts such as the child's name, toys, clothes, room, and experiences enter the picture. Little boys *are different* from little girls. As to what extent these differences (aside from biologically obvious ones) are due to biology and to what extent they are due to environment, we are much less certain. It is perhaps safest to say, at this juncture, that sex-role socialization is some function of biology and environment. Much of the biological, however, seems to be guided by social interactions with others. The following section is devoted to some of those vital "others" who assist new male members of society in becoming social beings.

Agents of Male Socialization

The Family

For most infants, the family is the primary agent of socialization during the first year following birth. Regardless of race, ethnicity, or social class, the male infant usually derives the first information about himself, others, and, in general, the world from the family. The information he derives and how it relates to the acquisition of the male sex role is the subject of our concern.

First of all, *gender* appears to be important for parents and other family members during a child's infancy period. The importance of gender to family members is reflected in their comments about the infant shortly following its birth. It is quite common to hear family members exclaiming "What a strong boy!" "My, how muscular he is!" "What a darling girl!" "My, she is dainty!" Such comments, connoting social meanings attached to the sex of the infant, begin a labeling process that is used by the child as it gets older to form some notion of self. Many social scientists (Varma, 1980) feel that this labeling process, together with *cultural artifacts* (e.g., clothes, toys, and room decor) and direct tutelage facilitate the internalization of sex-role definitions by the child.

Two general perspectives on sex-role socialization have been popular in sex-role literature in recent years. These perspectives are the *social learning* or *purposive reinforcement perspective* and the *cognitive perspective.* The social learning or purposive reinforcement perspective is reflected in Constantinople's comments that "positive and negative reinforcement serves to focus the child's attention on relevant stimuli and to endow sex-role-related behavior with positive or negative support" (p. 128). According to this perspective, children are differentially reinforced for sex-typed behavior. This means, for example, that one reason boys are more aggressive, autonomous, and competitive than girls is that caretakers within the family reinforced these behaviors in boys but not in girls.

Schau *et al.* (1980) found that parental expectations for sons were related to actual toy preference and toy play in boys. While parents expected sons to play with masculine toys and girls to play with feminine toys, only boys played consistently with sex-typed toys. Similar results were obtained by Fu and Leach (1980) in a study of toy preferences in a rural, traditional setting. These latter findings are consistent with earlier findings by Minushin *et al.* (1969) that family orientation is associated with sex-typed play activities. When children from "traditional" family orientations were compared with those from "modern" family orientations, boys from traditional families were found to be more aggressive and girls had stronger family orientations and dependence. However, girls from "modern" families were significantly less sex-typed in their play activities than girls from "traditional" families or boys from modern or traditional families.

In addition to these studies which suggest caretaker manipulation and differential reinforcement of stereotyped children's play, other studies present a more complex picture of the role of caretaker reinforcement in sex-role socialization. Bearison (1979) has stated that *opposite-sex parents* may tend to reinforce stereotypic sex-roles in children. He found that parents tended to be more person-oriented in regulating the behavior of same-sex children ("Is that a nice thing to do to a person?") and more position-oriented in regulating opposite-sex children ("Little boys don't treat little girls that way"). Along similar lines McBroom (1981) found that university women who accepted traditional expectations for females viewed their relationships with their fathers as "good." Those who perceived their relationships with their fathers as negative tended to reject traditional expectations for females. Moreover, rejection of traditional expectations for females was related to the women's perceptions of negative relationships with their fathers irrespective of socioeconomic class. When the father–daughter relationships were perceived positively, social class made a difference. Class-specific role models of *fathers* were thought to explain the difference.

Other studies, too, have found a relationship between sex-typed behavior in children and caretakers' differential reinforcement of behavior in boys and girls. However, the data are not consistent (Maccoby and Jacklin, 1974; Block, 1977; Lewis and Weinraub, 1979). Lewis and Weinraub state that there is not a consensus that boys and girls are differentially reinforced "for aggressive behavior, for autonomous behavior, for dependent behavior, or for competitive behavior" (p. 142), although there is some evidence of more widespread punishment for sex-inappropriate behavior. Moreover, Lewis and Weinraub report, some studies have not found a correlation between parental attitudes toward sex-typing and parental behavior that encourages children to conform to sex-typed behavior (p. 142).

The cognitive perspective assumes that sex-role socialization is less a function of direct tuition than it is of "a shift in the child's knowledge of the world and the dimensions along which experience can be ordered" (Constantinople, p. 127). Drawing upon the work of Kohlberg (1966), scholars espousing this point of view feel that the child, at a very early age, actively structures his/her own experiences, categorizes himself/herself, and then begins to categorize the rest of the world (Walum, 1979, p. 38). Once the child has generated sex-role categories and the self has been assigned to a category (both of which involve such cognitive processes as perception, memory, attention, pattern recognition) categorizing and ordering of the rest of the world occur. Seen in this light, then, a young boy acts aggressive, competitive, violent, or whatever because he is acting consistent with other "objects" (males) in his category.

Three rather convincing propositions advanced and explained by Lewis and Weinraub will serve as the basis for our brief discussion on the influence of cognition in male socialization. They are as follows:

1. The infant acquires knowledge about itself and at the same time the infant acquires knowledge about others.
2. Gender and sex-role knowledge is acquired early.
3. The infant acts in a manner consistent with "like objects" (p. 145).

Based on Lewis and Weinraub's work, as well as numerous other studies published by Lewis and several other co-authors, some cognitive ability develops rather early in children. In fact, these authors found that by the time an infant has reached 18 months, he or she has developed some knowledge of self and others. Given the existence of support for the first two propositions, Lewis and Weinraub address the third proposition. The proposition implies, for example, that a male infant who has knowledge that he is male and, who can differentiate other males and females, will tend to behave like the other males rather than like females. They explore a variety of literature showing that infants prefer to *attend to* pictures of other infants of the same sex, they prefer to *play with* others of the same sex, they *look up* at parents of the same sex during free play, and they tend to *imitate* the behavior of same-sex parents. Lewis and Weinraub conclude that infants are active, complex, and competent organisms who actively interpret their environments and who *choose* to be like those who have similar characteristics and labels to themselves. They state:

> the earliest forms of knowledge may be based on the smallest differences, for example, hair length, the color and nature of clothes. These provide the

first information necessary for differentiation of self and others. On the basis
of this differentiation and on the principle of attraction, the infant moves
toward conformity with sex-role stereotypes (p. 147).

As Lewis and Weinraub pointed out in a discussion of Kohlberg's
cognitive–developmental idea and Mischel's social learning approach,
both positions acknowledge the critical role social cognition plays in sex-
role acquisition. This means that the child is aware that behavior in one
of the gender categories is more likely to be rewarded than behavior in
the other category (p. 143). The infant's "choice" to move toward conformity obviously is related to *likelihood of reward*. I submit that the motivational aspects of sex-role behavior involve more than "if I am an 'A'
and I can differentiate other 'A' and 'not A,' I will under most conditions
act like the other 'A'" (Lewis and Weinraub, p. 146). In other words, a
more complete approach to sex-role acquisition should give equal weight
to both perspectives. *Why* I will act like the other "A" is just as important
as the fact that I *do* act like the other "A."

Despite the competing perspectives discussed above and the contradictory findings on differential reinforcement by parents, one thing is
clear. Many children *do* exhibit sex-typed behaviors, and young males,
in particular, develop such traits as aggressiveness, competitiveness,
independence and the like quite early.

For example, Moely *et al.* (1979) found that there were sex differences in competitive and cooperative behavior of very young boys and
girls. Using preschool- and elementary-school-age-level children, Moely
and colleagues found that boys showed a developmental change toward
traditional masculine competitiveness. In fact, the older boys in the study
(7–11 years) tended to compete with other children regardless of sex,
while girls were much less competitive toward other girls and tended to
compete only with boys. Succinctly, boys exhibited competitiveness to a
greater degree than girls and the behavior tended to increase with age.
Does the *family* play a role in male children's behavior? I think so, and
the precise role it plays is discussed below.

The family facilitates the young male's socialization in two major
ways: (1) It provides *a setting whereby he can observe and learn how males are
supposed to behave,* and (2) it *provides direct and indirect tuition about the male
role to the child.* In the first instance, the child observes male and female
models in the family. From these observations, he gains a clear understanding of his role and the roles of others (e.g., his father's role, his
mother's, his siblings' roles). In everyday family social interaction, which
includes both task-oriented activities and socioemotional activities (e.g.,
play activity, sports activity, and the like), differences between the sexes,
even if subtle, are emphasized. The male child, as a cognitive being, can

be expected to come to understand that when he engages in certain kinds of behavior, certain kinds of rewards are likely to be received. It should not be surprising to find that in America the behavior most likely to bring a young male rewards remains *sex-typed behavior*. Relatively few parents and other relatives have become comfortable with a three or four year-old boy playing nurse or playing with a "Barbie" doll, and many more still prefer him to play with trucks, cowboy guns, toy soldiers, football games, and such. As noted earlier, Schau *et al.* (1980) found that parents *expect* boys to play with masculine toys and girls to play with feminine toys, and boys tend to be more consistent in regard to these parental expectations.

Besides providing a setting for sex-role socialization of the male child and indirect tuition for him, the family also directly teaches the boy the role he is expected to assume. Parents, siblings, and other relatives inform the male child that he *is a boy*. Inherent in this information are expectations about boy's roles that are usually caricatures of father's, male siblings', and other male models' roles. Moreover, much of the informing is not necessarily subtle. Even in "progressive" families where, for example, sex education is taught to the male child at a very early age, he learns not only differences between the sexes but also the sex category to which he belongs. Perhaps it is axiomatic, then, that the male child in these "progressive" families also is taught directly to differentially value *his* sex category. Thus, in the process of teaching the child a "good" self-concept, "progressive" families may also teach the male child to differentially *value* males and females and the behaviors often associated with them—traditional masculinity and traditional femininity. The young male may not be *taught* that the female role is subordinate to his role but a relatively great emphasis on his role, to a relative neglect of the female role, produces the same result.

Actually, it would be difficult to explain the role of the family in sex-role acquisition without referring to the reinforcement perspective *and* the cognitive-developmental perspective. With respect to male youth, both perspectives are important in explaining conformity to sex-role stereotypes and are implicit in our examination of other agents of male socialization. Let us turn to the role of the peer group in male socialization.

Peer Groups

When the role of the peer group in socialization is discussed references are usually made to the influence of adolescent peer groups. One possible reason for this is that peer group importance is thought to increase as children grow older, and peak during adolescence (Light and Keller, p. 128). It is possible to argue, however, that peer group influence at an even earlier age may be responsible for most sex-role internalization, especially for males. Connor and Serbin (1978) found that fourth, sixth and eighth grade boys' responses to stories with male and female characters indicated a decidedly positive bias toward stories about males and male activities and a negative bias toward stories about girls and girl activities. The idea that learning to avoid a nonstereotyped activity when it is associated with girls in a particular story may be a subtle form of learning not experienced until elementary school implies early peer-group influence. Fagot's (1981) research indicating that boys receive negative feedback from peers when they exhibit feminine behaviors also supports the idea of early peer-group influence on boys.

Boys, I believe, are especially susceptible to early peer-group influence because of societal emphasis *on traditional masculine traits* and *societal devaluation of feminine traits*. Both societal emphases lead to the encouragement of male bonding at an earlier age, generally, than the encouragement of female bonding. Young male children are frequently encouraged by their caretakers to bond with other male children for reasons of masculine identification. This early encouragement is especially likely to occur in female-headed families because of the popular belief that boys need to be with boys and/or other males so that they do not identify too closely with females and therefore experience gender-identity problems. Also, in 'couple families' where a father is present, young male bonding has been encouraged by parents for the same reason, because fathers traditionally have devoted only a modicum of time to the childrearing process (often this has been unavoidable because of the family-provider role traditionally assumed by fathers) and were not available to be a role model.

The idea that intrasex bonding occurs at an earlier age for males than for females has implications for the peer group as an agent of male socialization, as will be shown. First, however, let us examine the rationale behind the assertion of earlier male bonding. Research has shown that caretakers tend to be less protective of male children than of female children (Minton et al., 1971). Young male children are more likely than female children to be encouraged in independence, adventure, risk-taking, and so on. Frequently, young male children are allowed to spend more time away from the family (with, for instance, friends or older male role models) than female children, and at a much earlier age. Furthermore, male children are encouraged to participate in activities that reinforce and/or teach the young male stereotyped sex-roles (Fling and Manosevitz, 1972). Tyron's findings (1980) that boys in her study generally seemed to believe that boys were more competent than girls in boys' activities and vice-versa are important here. Also, Connor and Serbin's (1978) study revealed that elementary school boys tended to respond somewhat negatively to stories when the main character was female, and they also indicated a negativism toward the activities the "girl" main character might be engaged in (p. 643). The responses to stories involving "boy" main characters and their activities were much more positive. It is not possible to conclude from these studies that peer-group influence is *responsible* for sex differences in beliefs and preferences. Nevertheless, we can speculate that at the very least, young male peer groups support such beliefs and preferences.

Within young male peer groups, boys also learn first-hand such traits as competitiveness, aggressiveness, and violent behavior. In other words, not only do young males learn to devalue femininity, but they also learn that to be masculine means to become independent and relatively unreliant on, and to some extent unsusceptible to peer-group influence. Experiences many males have when they participate early in peer groups inhibit substantial peer-group influence over them in later years. If a boy learns early to be independent, competitive, aggressive, and so on, in all likelihood, peer-group influence during his later childhood, adolescence, and adulthood will be minimal. Those adolescent and young adult males who *are* susceptible to peer-group influence most likely have not experienced early peer-group influence of the kind discussed above. As a high school senior recently replied "Around tenth grade, guys begin to go for themselves . . . they go solo . . . girls begin to run in cliques."

It should be remembered that most females around the age of 15 are given more independence and freedom to interact with other females outside of the home. It would seem to follow then that as females approach later adolescence and early adulthood, female bonding increases. Increases in female bonding result in increases in the amount of influence female peer groups exert over female socialization. As implied earlier, the reverse seems to occur for males. As males approach later adolescence and early adulthood, male bonding decreases. Decreases in male bonding result in *decreases* in the amount of influence male peer groups exert over male socialization.

Adolescent male peer groups, however, do remain important for most males. They constitute a kind of reference group, but most males around 16 or 17 actively filter, alter and/or modify peer-group information, standards, and values to fit their own perspectives (derived, in part, from early bonding). These perspectives, more often than not, stress male individuality. Unfortunately, the perspectives also have included in the past some of the dysfunctional aspects of traditional masculinity. Changes in contemporary definitions of masculinity promise to correct these deficiencies.

The Mass Media

Television, radio, newspapers, magazines, popular lyrics and the like all contribute to sex-role socialization. Inauspiciously, research shows that many mass media messages contain stereotypes of male and female sex-roles. As agents of socialization, the media relate specifically to the cognitive development of the child in the area of sex-role socialization. It can be proferred, then, that some unknown portion of male socialization is attributable directly to the mass media. Supportive evidence for this contention is provided by McGhee and Frueh (1980) in their study of children's perceptions of sex-roles and television viewing. McGhee and Frueh reveal that children (in grades 1, 2, 5, and 7) who viewed television 25 hours or more per week had more stereotyped perceptions of males than those who were labeled light viewers (10 or less hours per week). Additionally, these perceptions among heavy viewers persisted with increasing age while they declined for light viewers.

Such findings as the above are not surprising in view of another study conducted by Mamay and Simpson (1981). In the study of female roles in television commercials, men generally were shown engaged in active work outside the home, being experts about mechanical and chemical products, being pampered at home by their wives, and generally *not* participating in household activities. Women in the commercials could be fitted into three roles—all connoting the woman's "place" in society: the maternal, housekeeping, and aesthetic roles (p. 1224).

In addition to numerous other studies of the influence of television on behavior, Carter and Strickland's (1975) experiments are important, in that they demonstrated that television programs focusing on sharing and cooperation encourage positive social interaction. The implications are that television can be used to alter sex-role socialization in an equitable manner for both sexes. Drabman *et al.* (1979) state more specifically that "television programming which *directly* informs the child that nearly all life roles are available to both sexes might prove more fruitful in attempts to alter traditional gender stereotypes" (p. 388).

Direct gender socialization is thought to be especially important by Drabman *et al.* since school-age children tend to alter their perceptions or memories of counterstereotyped videotaped presentations. In their study, when first-graders were shown videotaped presentations of males and females in counterstereotyped occupations, such as male nurse and female doctor, there was a tendency to reverse sex-role information in the stereotyped direction. They concluded that the strength of sex-typing by six years of age dictated a more direct gender socialization approach if sex-role changes were to occur.

The newspaper is another medium which contributes to gender socialization. While newspaper-reading probably is not as prevalent among young children as television-viewing, it does exist. In fact, most children are encouraged to read newspaper stories while they are still in elementary school. Foreit et al.'s (1980) conclusions, reached in their content analysis of news stories, imply that we may be encouraging children to read material which at the very least supports stereotyped sex roles indirectly. They allude to the existence of a sex bias in newspaper treatments of male-centered and female-centered news stories. According to their analysis of news stories, women were described in terms of personal traits to a greater extent than men. Personal attributes such as appearance, age, marital status, spouse, and parenthood seem to be more important to reporters in reporting on women than when reporting on men.

Many interpretations of this sex bias in news stories are possible. One inescapable interpretation that deserves mention is the fact that personal variables give "newsworthy" persons warmth, humanity, affectivity, and the like. The absence of these variables in newspaper reports on males leaves "newsworthy" males cold, objective, and "traditionally masculine." No effort is made here to discuss the newspaper as a medium which generally perpetuates explicit stereotyped sex roles (this may vary from one newspaper to another by region, city, or community). It is important to realize, however, that seemingly harmless techniques of reporting, foci of attention, descriptions of news characters, and other accoutrements of newspapers may contain messages implicitly conveying stereotyped sex roles.

Along the same lines, Brabant (1976) content-analyzed four family-oriented Sunday comics and found that traditional sex-role stereotyping existed. Directly relevant to male socialization was the finding that males' "places" tended to be outside of the home. Even when males were in the home, they were seen as maintaining "distance" from household duties and/or as being bumbling idiots within the home. Family politics as portrayed tended to pit the wife and children *against* the father. The messages in the comics analyzed seemed very clear with respect to the male role: The man is a provider, while women and children are consumers. If the man does not provide adequately, he is belittled both by his wife and children—not to be respected—in fact, to be dismissed. Brabant says of The Born Loser:

> Gladys constantly belittles poor Brutus in size as well as action. She throws a pie at him, depreciates his income-producing ability, watches while his son lights dynamite behind him. . . . " (p. 334).

While Brabant concentrates on the fact that female characters over-whelmingly are shown in domestic situations, this analysis of her find-ings has been directed toward the stereotypical manner in which *men* are shown.

A final medium to be discussed here which often furnishes tradi-tional stereotyped sex-roles for youth is the *popular song*. Of notable inter-est is the fact that men are more consistently stereotyped in popular song than are women. Freudiger and Almquist (1978) reported in an analysis of sex-roles in the lyrics of popular songs that men are presented less positively than women, and that there is less lyrical variability in mas-culine traits across "Country," "Soul," and "Easy-Listening" music than there is in feminine traits across the music categories. Males in all music categories were found to be aggressive, demanding, consistent, active, and confident. On the other hand, women were praised for being depen-dent and submissive in the Country music category and were portrayed as strong and independent in Soul music. In the Easy Listening category, male and female roles were less stereotyped.

While we know little about the extent to which lyrics in popular songs influence sex-role socialization, one thing that seems certain is that the male image suffers. As one aspect of the mass media, obviously some modification in popular song lyrics is necessary in order to support changing definitions of sex-roles.

Other Societal Institutions and Male Socialization

The early educational institution, more than any other, provides a setting whereby masses of children learn "appropriate" and "inappropriate" sex-role behavior. Unlike the family setting, in school, children's peer groups flourish, interact, and influence the sex-role socialization process, especially during "free play" activities. In addition to conforming to parental expectations regarding play behavior, then, children (especially males) also are expected to conform to peer-group expectations of play behavior. These expectations are especially pronounced in school envi-ronments. Serbin *et al.* (1979) suggest that peer groups may function as discriminative stimuli, setting the occasion for sex-appropriate play activities. This means that when peer-group members are present, chil-dren, because of the attention and praise they receive from others, engage in sex-appropriate play activity. Obviously, this means, too, that the presence of peer-group members inhibits opposite-sex play activities.

Fagot's (1981) findings that boys in school who engaged in opposite sex-appropriate play activities receive negative feedback from peers, and those who engage in sex-appropriate play activities received positive peer-group feedback is instructive here. In addition, teachers, too, were found to differentially reinforce boys and girls for high activity levels (Fagot, 1979; 1981).

Phillips (1982) in a study of sex-role socialization on a school playground, noted that boys and girls had their own areas of play. The girls' play space, however, was limited (although girls tended to dominate use of the playground apparatus). Also, girls' play spaces were "easily invaded by boys, but the boys' play space was 'inviolable.'" She noted, too, that boys had a large play area where they engaged in competitive games excluding girl participation. However, when boys chose, they used the playground apparatus and girls submissively left the equipment to their use, which was much more aggressive than the girls' use. Finally, girls' play was seen by Phillips as cooperative and either dyadic or triadic, while boys played in relatively large competitive groups. She concluded that boys' play was preparing them for future work roles that would consist of the networks of competitively based groups necessary for success and achievement in the workplace. In addition to research findings showing family, peer-group and mass media influences on sex-role socialization, the school environment also may be seen as an agent of sex-role socialization. Implications from studies of the role of the school environment in sex-role socialization indicate that certain aspects of the school environment tend to support stereotyped sex roles.

As an agent of sex-role socialization, the *religious institution* in the United States has always played a vital role. The role generally has been supportive of traditional definitions of masculinity and femininity. It is from this institution that the family has received support for its sex-typed instruction of boys and girls on sex roles. Within the past two decades, the religious institution has undergone numerous changes, and these changes have had implications for sex-role socialization. Prior to the 1960s, religious institutions were seldom involved in secular concerns like civil rights movements, anti-war demonstrations, women's rights. The 1960s and 1970s saw increased participation of the religious institution in such concerns.

By the end of the 1970s, rank-and-file church members began to call for an end to religion's active participation in secular concerns and church officials returned to serving their congregations. Moreover, religious cults began to rise as well as evangelical fundamentalism with its emphasis on *salvation* and the *divine spirit.* Americans became disillusioned with the "new" definitions of sexual morality, economic crises, and societal policies in general. Steiber (1980) has suggested that the recent rise of fundamentalism in the United States may very well affect the trend toward religious tolerance and liberalized social attitudes which have characterized the religious institution. Given this fact, and that parents tremendously influence religious identity and in turn are influenced by their religious affiliation, future progress in the area of sex-role equality might be impeded. In other words, the rise of evangelical fundamentalism in the United States has important negative implications for changing sex roles. It is important to remember that sex-role distinctions are important aspects of this movement. Great emphases are placed on the "traditional" family which can be translated to mean that the woman's place is *in the home with the children;* and the man's place is outside of the home *assuming the protector-provider role.* This developing trend is important because, as Roof (1978) has pointed out, it cuts across socioeconomic, racial, and ethnic groups. Thus, while new definitions of masculinity and femininity seem to be emerging in some of society's basic institutions, in one, the religious institution (which serves both individual and group needs), recent trends toward conservatisim and/or fundamentalist ideas appear inimical to sex-role equality. To the extent that the religious institution in the United States has an impact on sex-role socialization, some portion of sex-role socialization of boys and girls will be sex-typed in nature.

Males and the Assumption of Masculine Roles

We have discussed several agents of male socialization and in this section we will explore the results of male socialization in the United States. In other words, if young males are exposed to a particular kind of learning process, what does this learning process produce? Succinctly stated, male socialization prepares the male child to assume the "masculine" role. The *nature* of the masculine role is what will concern us here. First of all, let us explore the concept "role."

Vander Zanden (1977) offers a conception of role that is broad, encompassing, and suitable for our analysis. He suggests that roles "are shorthand conceptions embracing expectations and obligations." Vander Zanden states further that we are locked into the social order through reciprocal social roles, and that interpersonal relationships are some function of linkages between social role relationships—the obligations of one end being the expectations of the other (p. 173). Males in the United States learn *via* the agents of socialization to embrace certain general expectations and obligations held by members of society regarding their behavior.

Due to the multiplicity of roles men assume in our society, it is impossible to give adequate attention to all male roles. Chapter 5, however, is devoted to some specific social roles males assume, such as the role of friend, spouse, or father. Our concern here is with two *general masculine roles* assumed by males in America. The masculine roles are ideal types and men assuming one or the other can be expected to deviate from the roles to some degree.

The two general roles assumed by American males are the *White masculine role* and the *Black masculine role.* I maintain that while subcultural, ethnic, racial, and socioeconomic factors may modify the specific masculine role assumed by a specific male, the role that he makes and plays is derived either from the White masculine model or the Black masculine model. These models, I contend, have developed through a long historical process involving social, demographic, and socioeconomic factors. What this means is that masculine role assumptions *may* or *may not* be race-specific, although a race-specific pattern of masculine role assumptions is usually the case. Possible exceptions include those *few* Black males and White males who are exposed early to opposite-race socialization influences and live most, if not all, of their lives in opposite-race social and physical environments.

Undoubtedly as many of you think about some of the above statements, questions about Native American men, Chicano men, Chinese-American men, Japanese-American men, Cuban-American men and others arise. What about these men, and what roles do they assume? My response to your probable question is that these men have not made the impact on American society that Black males have made, nor has society constructed specific strategies for meting out resources to these men. Men in the above ethnic groups usually find themselves assuming either the White masculine role or the Black masculine role. For these men, socioeconomic variables usually determine which masculine role model is assumed. Let us now turn to the nature of these two general masculine roles. Because of the complexity and diversity of the two, they are examined separately. The White masculine role model will be examined first because so few men from other ethnic and racial groups use the model (often reference will be made to the "White male").

The White Masculine Role and Males

On the White masculine role in America, Jack Nichols has stated:

> It is not that they (many young men today) want to stay home and clean house or to be womanly but that their families and neighbors expect them

to follow a certain course to 'fulfill their responsibilities as a man.' These responsibilities are too narrowly defined, and the interpretation of such words as 'independent,' 'self regulating,' and the like does not allow for deviation from a norm that makes these words little more than suspenders for the Calvinist work ethnic (p. 65).

With these comments about the White masculine role, Nichols implies that characteristically the role is restricted and disallows role options for males who subscribe to the model (essentially, White males).

White males in the United States, as we saw in Chapter 1, have a long and complex legacy with respect to meanings of masculinity. What has evolved over time is a White masculine model which, to reiterate, defines relationships between men and women, men and other men, and men and themselves. It is how those relationships are defined in terms of four related traits internalized by males that makes the White masculine role a distinctive one. If a White male is to be considered masculine in our society, he must embrace certain obligations and expectations associated with domination, competition, the Calvinist work ethic, and violence. The nature of these obligations and expectations is discussed below.

Male Dominance

In "The Social Origins of Dominance" Johnson and Stockard's (1979) point of departure is that male dominance is learned and supported by basic institutions in the society. This view is consistent with the position advanced here. That is, that males reared under the White masculine role paradigm (and a vast majority are reared under this paradigm) develop quite early in their lives strategies aimed at securing positions of dominance in all three types of relationships mentioned above. Male dominance in relationships with females begins during mixed-sex play in children's early years. Caretakers, peer groups, school teachers, the school environment, and other societal institutions and artifacts support and, in some instances, encourage sex differences in dominance between boys and girls. When boys are supported and encouraged to be active, aggressive, competitive ("be a boy") and the like, while girls are supported and encouraged to be passive, coooperative, and submissive ("to be ladylike"), male dominance is promoted.

Encouragement and at least tacit approval for the development of male dominance by adult caretakers and society's basic institutions frequently occur within the context of children's play activities. Phillip's findings, related earlier, show that boys in her study easily invaded girls' play spaces, but their play spaces were not invaded by girls. Moreover, while boys generally did not use playground equipment, when they wanted to, they took over the equipment and the girls simply left it to their use.

These early traits of male dominance in male–female relationships are developed even further during the later childhood period and adolescent years. During these periods, male youth begin to turn their attention to sex and thus, the beginning of male perceptions of females as subordinate sexual objects. Male youth during these periods spend a good deal of time becoming proficient in the use of sexual language which reflects the superordination of men and the subordination of women. Stockard and Johnson (1980) allude to this point when they examine "male dominance" characteristics of concepts used often by males to describe sexual intercourse. They state:

> Many slang words used to describe sexual intercourse also connote dominance and aggression. To get 'fucked', 'screwed', 'reamed', or 'had' implies that one has been victimized. While this is not the typical male view of intercourse, there is within the masculine paradigm a symbolic association between sexual initiation and aggressive dominance (p. 244).

Learning a language often means more than simply uttering empty words or phrases. It often means realizing that certain behaviors are possible, and, in addition, acquiring attitudes congruent with possible behaviors. It should be obvious, then, that when young males learn language that devalues femininity and/or places women in submissive statuses, young males also acquire attitudes and behaviors congruent with the language—all of which devalue femininity and place women in submissive and/or inferior positions.

Females are not the only objects of domination in the white masculine paradigm. Young males also are instructed quite early in the art of dominating other males. Male youth sports frequently emphasize not only winning a competitive game but also total domination of the opposing team members. For totally dominating another team, a male youth team will be showered with affection and accolades for coaches, parents, and other youth (both male and female). The pattern begins in early male youth sports and continues through periods of adulthood.

The sports institution for male youth is not the only one responsible for the perpetuation of male dominance over other males. When parents, education, and social environments directly and indirectly support "labels" for certain male youth such as "sissy," "woman," "wimp," and so on, young boys are encouraged to exhibit dominating behavior toward other boys. (The labels also imply a devaluation of femininty and the perception that females are to be dominated by males.) While dominating behavior is known to be displayed by some young males toward others who exhibit cross-sex behavior, a recent study has shown that some boys who do not exhibit cross-sex behavior may also be the objects of ridicule, name-calling and, possibly, domination. Hemmer and Kleiber (1981) found that male youth creativity was the highest correlate of the "sissy" label in their study.

As with male domination over females, males continue to develop strategies for dominating other males well into adulthood. From occupational domination (when men strive to *control* large numbers of other men in the work arena) to sexual domination (as occurs in homosexual rape, especially in prison settings) many males develop and sustain strategies of male–male interaction which reflect male domination of other males. Basic societal institutions, subtly and not so subtly encourage and support these forms of interaction which serve as interaction models for male youth.

The idea of male dominance does not end with attempts to control women and other men, it also involves a rather complicated effort to control self. Male youth are taught a kind of dualistic approach to "self." Extreme demands are made upon boys to develop self-control, logical thought, and intellect. Simultaneously, males traditionally have been taught to eschew emotion, intuition, equivocation, and the like—all associated with femininity. This type of socialization, I suggest, leads to a perception that males can dominate themselves and then control any situation in which they find themselves. This means that males ultimately are responsible for all situations — those between males and females, males and other males, and those between males and selves.

Male Competition

Closely related to those aspects of socialization emphasizing male dominance is another trait associated with the White masculine role paradigm—competition. Male youth begin early to compete with others, and this competitive tendency is not only directed toward other males but also toward females (Moley et al.). Males probably remain competitive indefinitely with those few females who continue to exhibit assertive and active behavior beyond late childhood. For the most part, however, competition between males and females abates during adolescence. The reason for decreased competition between males and females during adolescence is that a vast majority of females begin to engage in "sex-appropriate behavior." This generally means that they relinquish and/or reject competitive positions that might have been maintained through childhood and adopt more submissive and/or subordinate roles relative to males during adolescence.

For males, competition during adolescence is intensified and extended beyond competitive sports games, although athletic achievement still seems to be a major area of competition for males during adolescence (Moreland, 1980). Bringing with them all of the competitive strategies learned during childhood and *personal modification* of these strategies, young males engage in intense one-upmanship games (in a variety of arenas) with other males as they prepare to enter adulthood. The prizes to be won in these often seemingly goal-less games are peer females. Ironically, it is frequently during this period that peer females begin to assume masculinity-validating power over these competitive males. *While females are pawns in these competitive games they also are sources of masculinity-validation.*

Competition between males continues well into adulthood because of the enormous demands made upon them to be successful in American society. It is true, as Moreland (1980) suggests, that during early adulthood, many men begin to develop a combination of intellectual and interpersonal skills which allow them to participate in the adult world. It is questionable, however, whether such skills alone result in men becoming "tender" and "intimate" in heterosexual relationships or developing relationships with men that are characterized by emotional sensitivity, cooperation, and playfulness (Moreland, p. 808). For the vast majority of men, while the arena of competition changes from one requiring physical strength to one requring intellectual and interpersonal skills, competitive strategies learned during early male socialization still characterize male social interaction with others, especially other males. Moreover, because men increasingly are required to accept women as equals (Pleck, 1976, p. 159), hetereosexual competition can be expected to increase.

In sum, Moreland presents a cogent argument when he says that a man cognitively and affectively reorganizes his conception of masculinity in order to more adequately meet the demands of new age-related roles he accepts as he progresses through adulthood. These demands, however, rarely until after midlife, require that men change the *basis* for reorganizing their conception of masculinity. While relatively few adult men continue to engage in competitive sports after entering the adult world, most engage in competitive intellectual and interpersonal games well into adulthood. In fact, male success and achievement in the workplace often depend upon how well the male competes. Success in the workplace, in turn, determines how well a male has *competed* generally in life. Certainly this is one reason why the work ethic is such an important part of conceptions of masculinity.

The Work Ethic

Pleck's (1976) early distinction between traditional and modern male roles contains those aspects of "masculinity" related to the work ethic. Tolson (1977, p. 12) states that "in Western, industrialized capitalist societies, definitions of masculinity are bound up with definitions of work." He states further:

> Whether it is in terms of physical strength or mechanic expertise, the qualities needed by the successful workers are closely related to those of the successful men.... The roots of man's gender identity are interfused with expectations of achievement.

In American society, achievement rarely occurs at the expense of no one else. Someone usually wins and someone usually loses. This is expected in the work place and thus, in America, *espousal of the work ethic implicitly means espousal of a competitive ethic.* Men, I contend, always tend to be far ahead of the game. Early male socialization nurtures the quality necessary for success in America—competition.

We must remember that men are cognitive beings. Therefore, men should not be expected to continue emphasizing physical strength when it is no longer necessary for success or when they are no longer capable of delivering (after young adulthood). Most men, as stated earlier, opt out of the physical game and into intellectual and interpersonal games bringing with them competitive strategies. What Moreland has called "emotional warmth," "expressiveness," "cooperation," and so on all relate to interpersonal skills which might be more appropriately labelled *symbiotic strategies*—all used to "win" the work game as well as other social games.

Male Violence

The rudiments of male violence can be found in early male socialization. Nichols (1978) feels that violence is some function of encouraging competition. He contends that "the American male has been nursed by a violence-prone ethic" (p. 109). In a sense, Nichols is correct. Boys generally are not taught directly to be violent, but neither are they taught to avoid or condemn violence. As David and Brannon (1976, p. 29) indicate, "the message is more often 'this world is full of dangerous bullies, son, and that's too bad, but you'd better know how to handle them or you're going to have a rough time . . .' or 'never *start* fights, boys, but always *finish* them.'" David and Brannon also feel that the line of distinction between self-defense and violence is often blurred (in practice) during child inter-action and adolescent interaction away from adults.

Aside from caretakers' subtle encouragement, other agents of social-ization also play a role in teaching young males violence. Little league football, for example, encourages young males to be violent toward other young males. Adult coaches, parents, and adult spectators all participate directly in this kind of violence-oriented male socialization. Little league football is not alone in this, however, since adults often exhort young males to annihilate the "enemy" in every type of little league sports game.

Another agent of socialization, the mass media, participate heavily in the instruction of male violence. From comic books to television to pac-man, young males are taught the violent dimension of masculinity. In Chapter 7, we will explain more thoroughly violence as a form of social interaction occurring between males and males, males and females, and males and themselves. For now, it is appropriate to say that male violence is *not* an innate propensity in males, but rather a function of society teaching young males *what it means to be a man.*

Comments About the White Masculine Role

Much has been written in the last decade about the White masculine role in the United States. Some authors (e.g., Farrell, 1974; Fasteau, 1974; Goldberg, 1976; 1979; Nichols, 1978) have stated that males are charac-terized by conceptions of masculinity which are inimical to themselves, other men, and women. Others (e.g., Pleck, 1976; Moreland, 1980) have made distinctions between the masculine roles to which men subscribe. Pleck distinguishes between the *traditional male role* (characterized by an emphasis on physical strength, angry and impulsive behavior, the expec-tation of submissiveness in women, functional relationships between men and women, and strong male bonding) and *the modern male role* (characterized by Pleck as emphasizing intellectual and interpersonal skills, heterosexual tenderness and emotional intimacy, the prohibition of anger and impulsive behavior, the expectation that women will serve as refuges and weak male bonding). His distinction between male roles served as one point of departure for another analysis of the male sex-role by John Moreland (1980).

Moreland's analysis is important to consider in this book for two major reasons. First of all, Moreland's analysis of the masculine role *is progressive in its discussion of male sex-role socialization beyond adolescence.*

This view is consistent with some current views of the socialization process as extending throughout the life cycle (e.g., Levinson et al.). The second reason why Moreland's analysis is important lies in the fact that it implicitly obscures the need for changes in the masculine role. Moreland concentrates on conflict between existing conceptions of masculinity at a particular stage of the life cycle and expectations associated with age-related roles accepted by the male. He suggests that resolution of the conflict occurs *via* changes in the male's conception of masculinity as a result of reassessment of the internalized masculine sex-role standards and incorporation of new values used to evaluate self.

Moreland's analysis is provocative. He acknowledges that men during the midlife transition stage of the life cycle are still interested in being competent, successful, respected, sexually attractive, and the like, with a realization of their strengths and weaknesses. However, to imply that many men eventually become androgynous during middle-age does not address the dysfunctional aspects of masculine sex-role assumptions during a male's earlier years. In fact, it is because male sex-roles are dysfunctional for many men that they do not *live* to reach middle-age or else do not progress through the life cycle in a positive, growth-oriented manner. Quite simply, the question to be asked is *'Why do men have to wait until middle age before they become human?* I contend that men do not, and aspects of this volume are devoted to elaborating individual and societal strategies that promise more positive and human relationships between males and females, males and other males, and males and themselves.

The Black Masculine Role and Males

Few things in America are more hazardous to a male than *assuming the Black masculine role.* This is ironic, since only relatively recently have Black males been able to assume a masculine role in the United States. Alvin Poussaint (1982) outlines this situation when he says:

> A fundamental change in the Afro-American male psyche occurred with the advent of the Black Power Movement in the late 1960s. A fresh, virile, sexually potent image appeared, bolstered by an assertive, more confident Black man. The Negro male became the Black male—a transformation that henceforth would never be completely safe for White society (p. 39).

Poussaint implies in the above quote that adult Black males have been recognized as *men* by most of society only since the late 1960s. Given this view of the status of Black males in America, the following quote from Poussaint is even more significant. He states:

No one can deny that being a Black man in America is a high-risk adventure. The social and health status of the Black male is alarming. The life expectancy at birth is about 65 years for Black men, 70 years for White men, 73 years for Black women, and over 77 years for White women. Black males have higher age-adjusted death rates for cancer, heart disease, cirrhosis of the liver, strokes, accidents, and lung disease than White males, White females and Black females.... the leading cause of death among young Black men has become Black-on-Black homicide. And significantly, about 45 percent of police killings in recent years have been of Black men, who are, in general, frequent victims of police brutality. The suicide rate of young Black males has more than doubled since the 1960s and is more than four times the suicide rate of a comparable group of Black females (pp. 39–40).

Poussaint's statement describes the Black masculine experience as one that is "life-threatening" and "psychologically brutalizing." The nature of the Black masculine role that results in this experience should become apparant as we explore how most Black male youth come to assume the Black masculine role. Just as with our discussion of White masculine role assumption, Black masculine role assumption is examined within the context of Black males' internalization of certain traits society associates with masculinity—domination, competition, the work ethic and violence.

Black Male Dominance and Competition. The dominance trait of the Black masculine role typically is expressed in Black male–Black female relationships and Black male-Black male relationships. Only rarely do Black men express dominance with "self" or with others outside of the Black subculture. Black male youth learn early that society does not permit Black males to express dominance in the larger society. As a result, much of the dominance learned during Black male socialization is directed toward others within the Black subculture.

While there are some similarities between Black male socialization and White male socialization, in the sense that there are numerous agents of socialization, there also are some striking differences. A large proportion of Black males are *reared in families headed by women, and an overwhelming number of Black male youth engage in apprenticeship sex-role socialization.* Black females headed 47% of all Black family households with one or more children under 18 years of age as of March, 1981, according to the U.S. Census Bureau. While this does *not* mean that Black male youth are deprived of Black male role models, it does mean that large numbers of Black male youth develop and establish unique relationships with female caretakers. Such relationships, I feel, are qualitatively different from relationships established when male and female caretakers participate in the socialization of male youth. This point is elaborated further below.

Due in part, but not totally, to the high incidence of female-headed households, the socioeconomic status of Blacks in the United States, and the primary group-like living patterns in Black communities, Black male youth often learn directly the Black masculine role. In addition to (and many times instead of) engaging in organized male youth sports, which teach male youth domination, competition and the like, as do their White counterparts, Black male youth get first-hand instruction in these traits. They do so because Black male youth quite early in their lives are exposed to the often harsh realities of life.

Learning dominance and a competitive spirit often are felt to be essential for Black male survival. Caretakers frequently teach the young Black male that in order to survive he must be able to take care of himself. Moreover, many Black male youth are burdened with the responsibility of being prepared to defend the entire family, which in many cases includes female caretakers as well as siblings. Who are Black male youth learning to defend themselves and their families from? The answer to this question has implications for understanding Black male-on-Black male violence. The object of Black male youth defense, more often than not, is other Black males! How and why this kind of socialization comes about is discussed in a later section.

As stated earlier Black male youth do learn the masculine traits of dominance and competition. However, they learn simultaneously that these traits are to be exhibited only within the Black subculture. Grier and Cobbs's (1968) observation over a decade ago is still applicable today. They noted that Black parents, especially Black mothers, tended to curb dominance and competitiveness in their male offspring. Black caretakers take this posture because they believe that it is too hazardous for Black males to exhibit traits of dominance and competitiveness in American society. In Grier and Cobbs's words "Black men continue to exhibit the inhibitions and psychopathologies that have their genesis in the slave experience" (p. 60). Not only do Black parents and/or caretakers impart these inhibitions, but they also are taught to Black male youth by another influential socializing agent—the *peer reference group.*

Because Black male youth, much earlier than their white counterparts, are exposed to agents of socialization external to the family, the peer-reference group assumes a powerful role in Black male youth socialization. Unique to Black male youth socialization is the tremendous influence that older, Black, unrelated males have on young Black males in the absence of adult supervision. Young Black males, for a variety of reasons, spend a good deal of time in the company of older Black males. These older Black males teach younger ones the nuances of Black male masculinity. One example of this socialization process can be seen in urban Black barbershops, where continuous instruction in Black masculinity is given, usually six days a week. Reminiscent of adult male meeting places in early America, the urban Black male barbershop differs in one important respect. Not only do adult Black males share ideas about worldwide issues, most of which deal with the Black male's role or its absence in world affairs, but Black male youth also passively, and sometimes actively, participate in the social interactions.

At the heart of peer-reference group instruction in the Black male sex role is the learning by Black male youth of what Alvin Poussaint calls "that commonality of social and psychological experiences affecting their adaptation" to an often-hostile society. This learning is what enables the highest-status Black male to be able to identify with and feel those things that the lowest status Black Male feels. It is what is responsible for the concepts "brother" and "blood" in Black male parlance, and cuts across age, social class, and geographical regions of origin. This quality of Black male youth socialization is what causes a Black man like Roger Wilkins to bare his soul in *Ebony* magazine to the Black population, forsaking his "successful" prodigal-son status in White society and expressing a desire to return to the Black fold.

What is the nature of these qualities that teach Black males dominance and competitiveness within the Black subculture and simultaneously feelings of intimacy with other males, as well as passivity with those outside of the Black subculture? Black male youth receive several kinds of messages in early socialization. One message received is that to be a Black man means that one internalizes those traits of dominance and competitiveness. One should be able to handle himself physically and, to a certain extent, mentally. However, Black male youth also learn that passivity and noncompetitive behavior are expected of them outside of the Black subculture. Many Black male youth also learn that a *lacuna* exists between those traits of dominance and competitiveness internalized and their exhibition in the larger society. They are very much aware of the high rate of Black male unemployment, Black male underrepresentation in high-paying, high-prestige occupations, and the generally inferior status of Black males in American society. Black male youth also know on some level that Black males are overrepresented in crime and delinquency rates—all adding to their knowledge of what it means to be a Black man in America.

Just as contributory to Black male sex-role socialization is the influence of Black female caretakers. Black females teach Black males the importance of being able to compete successfully, work hard, and so on, but they also frequently assume a protective posture toward young Black males that ill prepares them to participate in the larger society. Black males do, however, learn first-hand the strength of so-called feminine qualities like intuition, warmth, and empathy. In fact, it may be precisely because of this that Black males frequently score more androgynous on masculine–feminine scales than white males (Pettigrew, 1964). While some have referred to this kind of socialization as responsible for emasculating Black males (e.g., Moynihan, 1964) and causing them to have sex-role identity problems, few have pointed to the positive results of Black female influence on Black male socialization.

While Black male socialization, as we have seen, produces many positive results for the Black masculine sex-role, it also leads to some less-than-positive consequences for the adult Black male. American society is based on a White masculine sex-role paradigm. This means that success, achievement, security, and in general, *the good life* all are some function of subscribing to and acting in accordance with the White masculine sex-role paradigm. At this period in American history, Black males are still largely excluded from the paradigm because of obvious racial and not-so-obvious experiential reasons. Because American society, in spite of sex-role changes in recent years, continues to function in terms of power, prestige and wealth on the basis of a white masculine model, the Black masculine sex-role remains a subjugated and hazardous one for Black males. This can be seen further in an examination of the relationships between the Black masculine role and two other "masculine" traits— *work and violence.*

Black Males, Work, and Violence

Nathan Hare wrote in 1964 of the "frustrated masculinity" of the "Negro" male. His analysis lamented the inability of Black males to assume the provider-protector role in Black families. Hare suggested that American society was responsible for this because it presented Black males with numerous structural barriers to equal occupational opportunities and participation. He concluded his article with a quote from John O. Killens's novel *And Then We Heard the Thunder:* "The only thing they [white society] will not stand for is for a Black man to be a man. And everything else is worthless if a man can't be a man."

Hare's early analysis of the Black male sex-role is important for us in two ways: (1) Black males remain inhibited in their efforts to assume the provider-protector role by structural barriers, and (2) society (the Black subculture included) still considers internalization of the work ethic as a necessary trait of masculinity.

First, only the naive are unconvinced that structural barriers to Black males' occupational and general socioeconomic upward mobility remain the major impediments to Black males' progress in American society. To be sure, in recent years individual Black males have been *permitted* to experience upward occupational mobility, often *via* affirmative-action pressures. However, as a group Black males experience the following: residential concentration in central-city areas (while business and industry are moving to outlying areas); technological changes that are altering the composition of the occupational structure in such a way that opportunities are disproportionately available to Whites; governmental refusal, in large part, to eliminate employment difficulties facing young Black males; denial of membership in White-dominated unions; and generally, exclusionary practices by organized labor for the higher-paying, more-highly-skilled jobs (Neubeck, 1979). Such barriers have functioned to keep the Black male as a group "in place" despite the advancement of indivudual Black males.

A second point to be made about Hare's analysis which remains important today is that he considered the breadwinning role to be inextricably interwoven with the concept of masculinity. The thesis is salient today only in the sense that society still tends to measure a male's masculinity in terms of the degree to which he fulfils the work role (this includes also the amount of money he earns). It is appropriate to point out that because of national economic difficulties in the early 1980s, some alteration in society's measurement of masculinity according to occupational status has occurred. Still, the overall conservative political trend in the United States in the early 1980s has served to emphasize the importance of the work ethic in definitions of masculinity. Female entrance into the labor force in large numbers in recent years also has served to alter the work dimension of masculinity, although as one undergraduate female student remarked recently in a class on the male sex-role, "The men I know don't mind if I work, as long as I am not working in their job area . . . (or earning as much as they are earning?)"

In the Black subculture, I contend, work and masculinity have never been as closely associated as the two have been in the larger society. While Black men and women often have decried the fact that large numbers of Black men have not assumed the provider role, it has been recognized by many that societal restraints were responsible. Generally nonassumption of the provider role has not had a halo effect on perceptions of Black male masculinity within the Black subculture. This has resulted in an extremely complex socialization of Black male youth on the work dimension of masculinity. Let us explore this aspect of Black male socialization.

Black male youth receive two messages about the work ethic during early socialization. These messages come from the Black subculture directly and indirectly; and the larger society (mostly *via* formal educational institutions and the mass media). One message the Black male receives, both from the Black subculture and the larger society, is that he must enter training and develop skills that will enable him to assume a masculine role in society in order "to become a man." Contrary to some opinions this ideology is imparted to Black male youth throughout the Black socioeconomic structure. Black parents, Black spokespersons, Black ministers and even formal school authorities *do* make efforts to teach Black male youth the work ethic.

Another message received by Black male youth from the same sources, however, often mitigates against Black male youth internalizing and/or acting upon the former message. The essence of the second message is that *Black male youth are going to be constrained by white society from fulfilling the work role.* Young Black males learn the value of certain occupations, as do their white counterparts. They also see and hear who occupies the high-status positions and who occupies the low-status positions (or *no* occupational positions) in American society. This information comes not only from the Black subculture but also from the larger society through the news media, television, movies, and the like.

The result of these conflicting messages is that Black male youth frequently do not internalize conceptions of masculinity closely associated with the work ethic or dimension. This means also that Black male youth, in all likelihood, develop measures of masculinity based on other traits such as physical strength, aggressiveness, dominance, sexual conquest, conspicuous consumption, exterior emotionlessness ("coolness"), and so on.

In a society where masculinity (which is the Black male's major gender identification) is determined, in part, by internalization and acting upon the work ethic, failure to do both or at least the latter has implications for the Black adult male psyche. Moreover, because little distinction is made by others between *failing to internalize the work ethic* and an *inability to act upon the work ethic due to societal impediments*, Black males frequently receive information from others that is psychologically devastating. A major point here is that Black males themselves usually realize the distinction between their conceptions of masculinity and actual assumption of the work role. However, society's insistence upon linking the two, and society's failure to allow Black males to assume this important dimension of masculinity result in much Black male dysfunctioning. In fact, Black-on-Black violence may be one result, as we see below.

In his discussion of *Black male violence,* Curtis (1976) takes as his point of departure Cloward and Ohlin's (1960) "blocked opportunities model" and suggests that:

> racial-economic constraints have causal primacy in determining Black (male) behavior . . . with only a limited number of avenues open . . . a more distinguishable cluster highlighted by physical toughness and sexual exploitation emerges among some poor Black males than among middle-class Black or White males. The process heightens when the quality of youth is added to blackness, maleness and poverty (pp. 121–22).

Curtis' statement is consistent with our contention advanced earlier that since some Black males frequently do not use the work ethic (or expressions of it) as a measure of masculinity, many emphasize other traits associated with masculinity. Others, too, have spoken of the tendency in some Black males to exhibit hypermasculinity or other masculine traits (e.g. Liebow, 1967, and Hare, 1964). Unfortunately one of the "other" culturally condoned masculine traits exhibited by increasing numbers of Black males is male violence.

It must be remembered that Black male youth, like their White counterparts, learn to value masculine traits as well as their expressions. They, too, learn to devalue certain traits associated with femininity, in particular those such as passivity and submissiveness. These traits, unlike the "feminine traits" intuition, warmth and empathy, are not valued by Black males. While passivity and submissiveness may be exhibited by Black males outside of the Black subculture (and this is becoming more infrequent), there is a rationale available to them for exhibiting these traits. Within the Black subculture, however, no such rationale exists for exhibiting passive and submissive behaviors. This is precisely where America's cultural masculinist model (including male violence) influences Black males in a most dysfunctional manner. Moreover, Black male acceptance of certain aspects of the White masculine sex-role model is reflected in high Black-on-Black homicide rates, high rates of Black-on-Black rape, and in general, high incidences of Black-on-Black violence.

Further elaboration of these ideas is given throughout the book; however, one final point should be made about Black male socialization into violence. Black male youth, as we have discovered, are taught the value of empathy, warmth, and intuition. They also learn and come to value the masculine traits of dominance and competition. It is entirely possible that learning such an androgynous sex-role with no appropriate outlet for the latter two traits may interact to produce a male who is especially likely, in certain situations, to engage in *violence of passion.* Indeed this may be one reason why Black male violence seems less calculated than White male violence. Still, much of the responsibility for Black male violence, as is true for White male violence, lies with American culture's acceptance and encouragement of violence in males generally.

Comments About the Black Masculine Role

Aside from being hazardous, the Black male sex-role is extremely complex. Its complexity arises from Black males being socialized to adopt an androgynous sex-role and simultaneously being expected to perform according to the White masculine sex-role paradigm in certain instances. An additional factor which makes the Black male sex-role difficult for Black males to fulfill in a functional manner (as far as the larger society is concerned) is that Black males are only permitted to exhibit certain "masculine" traits of their androgynous sex-role within the Black subculture.

An androgynous sex-role, in itself, is not difficult for most persons to fulfil. Many social scientists concede that, generally, persons exhibit both "masculine" and "feminine" traits in social interaction. However, when a society encourages its males to consistently *express* their masculine traits, those males who consistently *express* an androgynous sex-role are at a distinct disadvantage. Such is the case for Black males in America. Black males are expected (both by society and the Black subculture) to exhibit dominance, competitiveness, aggressiveness, and so on. They also are expected to display submissiveness, passivity, cooperativeness, and the like. The larger society expects Black males to exhibit their "feminine" traits in social interaction outside of the Black subculture but expects (and to some extent encourages) the exhibition of their masculine traits within the Black subculture. The Black subculture (especially peer Black women) expects Black males to exhibit androgynous traits within the Black subculture and masculine traits outside of the Black subculture. Yet, the Black subculture's socializing institutions teach Black men to *inhibit* their "masculine" traits outside of the Black subculture and to *exhibit* them within the Black subculture. If you are confused by this, imagine how Black male youth must feel.

Many Black male youth, confronted with these contradictory socialization messages, seem to develop a gender identity which is at best only marginally functional for them in American society some of the time, and oftentimes dysfunctional. Given Black male youth socialization, which also has been affected by the remnants of the Black male-led movement of the late 1960s (a point to be discussed later) Black males tend to internalize a masculine role which can be characterized as follows: *An emphasis on physical strength, an expectation of both submissiveness*

*and strength in women, angry and impulsive behavior, functional relationships
between men and women, and strong male bonding.* The Black masculine role,
then, lies somewhere between or is some combination of Pleck's *traditional male role* and *modern male role.*

Male Socialization in Retrospect

One underlying assumption in this chapter has been that much of what
is called "male behavior" is acquired through direct and indirect socialization processes. Recognizing, of course, that sex-role behavior is influenced by biological factors, the position taken here is that the precise
nature of the *direct* role of biology in sex differences is open to question.
Physiological sex differences have been observed at early ages; however,
research findings on whether biology influences sensory, attentional,
and temperamental sex differences have been inconsistent (Lewis and
Weinraub, 1979, p. 139). Furthermore, it is not known how early physiological sex differences directly influence later behavior in males and
females. It is possible, however, to speculate on the indirect influence of
such early sex differences on later male and female behavior.

Using males as an example, many social scientists would agree with
the point that people hold certain expectations and behave in certain
ways toward male infants. These expectations and behaviors encourage
and support the development of certain types of traits and behaviors in
males. More specifically, as a result of differential societal *expectations of*
and *behaviors toward* young males, biology indirectly influences the
development of male sex-roles.

The influence of environment in sex-role differences is thought to
be profound by most social scientists. Again, however, the exact nature
of the influence remains open to empirical investigation. Certainly this
is due in part to the fact that the influence of biology is not known. In
addition, the specific role of parental reinforcement of appropriate sex-
role behavior in sex-typed behavior of children is controversial according to research findings. However, given the wide variety of environmental influences that support "sex-appropriate" behavior in children
and adults, few would be unwilling to admit that the role of environment in sex-role behavior appears at this time to be quite influential.

A strictly cognitive-influence approach to sex-role socialization
seems somewhat limited, as we have seen. However, our approach has
been to recognize the fact that children are active participants in their
sex-role socialization. Together, then, with environment and biology,
cognitive influences are thought to influence the process whereby male

and female infants become adult men and women. It is the kind of adult man that the socialization process produces in America that has been a focal concern in this chapter. Throughout the rest of the book, we will explore the possibility that with alterations and/or modifications in sex-role socialization, better social psychological and psychological functioning for men *and* women will result.

CHAPTER 3

The Male Self

> Whatever decision we make, whatever action we take, is inevitably predicated on some implicit assumption of what we were like. Without the ability to view ourselves as objects, to assess our dispositions or other characteristics, and to consider these in relation to the particular situation, we are virtually immobilized (Rosenberg and Kaplan, 1982, p. xiii).

"Why, I am a *man*" . . . usually is the first statement made by an American man when he is asked the question "who are you?" Following this statement, American men generally will go on to describe themselves in terms of their behaviors and attitudes about themselves learned from others. In doing so, they reveal, in addition to their gender identity— Richardson (1981) feels that few people are confused on this point— information about whether they think their behaviors and attitudes are consistent with society's norms for them (Richardson's contention here is that many more people worry about this). In other words, self-concept responses are frequently given in males' further elaborations on the "self." But, what *is* the *male self*? How does it come about? What is the "male self's" relationship to "male self-concept," "male self-esteem," "male behavior," and so on? Answers to these questions, as well as others, constitute the focus of this chapter.

First, it is important to distinguish between two related terms— *socialization* and *self-development*. *Socialization,* as we have seen, deals with the process whereby culture and the rules which guide social interaction are transmitted to persons. It occurs when statuses are assumed and social roles are learned (Hess et al., 1982). Socialization involves, but is distinct from, the "development of the self." Development of the self refers to the fact that persons develop role-taking abilities to the point whereby they are able to abstract generalized sets of definitions and expectations, thus enabling them to view themselves as objects and behave toward themselves as objects (Franklin, 1982). In addition, persons construct self-knowledge, self-feelings and numerous conceptions of self—all functions of interaction between themselves and others.

Given the above meanings of socialization and self-development, and the distinction between them, it is now possible to define the "male self." The "male self" refers to *the process whereby males, by taking the roles of others, view themselves and behave toward themselves as social objects.* Out of this process comes self-knowledge, self-conceptions, self-esteem and the like. Thus, a central concern for us will be the *results* of our hypothetical construct, "male self." Before examining these results, however, let us consider briefly the existing explanatory models often used to explain self-development. Our treatment, however is from a male perspective.

Explanations of the Male Self

The Freudian Male Self

Relatively few contemporary social scientists dealing with the male self explore it from a Freudian view point. Nevertheless, Freud's ideas on the subject have played an influential role in shaping popular and academic thought on the subject. This seems true because there is no dearth of attitudes reflecting that male youth become men and female youth become women because they are biologically male and female respectively—a conclusion reached by many about Freud's feelings on this topic. Admittedly, *Mourning and Melancholia* (1917) and *The Ego and the Id* (1905) seem to support such a conclusion.

The idea that, ultimately Freud's conceptions of a person's sexual self are biologically rooted seems unfortunate given his point of departure on (primarily) male self-development. On the surface, Freud's views start out as decidedly androgynous ones. He contended that human beings were characterized by *both masculine and feminine components.* In males, the masculine components usually were stronger and in females, the feminine components usually were stronger. In addition, when Freud stated that "it seems probable that the sexual instinct is in the first instance independent of its object; nor is its origins likely to be due to its object's attraction" (Freud, 1905, p. 148), much of the male self was placed clearly *outside* of the biological. Thus, Freud's idea on the male self seems both androgynous and socialization-based.

Within the context of a more general concern with self-development, Freud's division of the mind into three well-known parts also gives us important information about the development of the male self. He divided the mind into the *id*, the *ego* and the *superego*. The *id* consisted of instinctive desire while the *superego* referred to *conscience* or those values and standards derived from agents of socialization and internalized by the male. The *ego* was seen as the mediator—that entity of the mind which links the mind with reality. The male self, then, from this perspective can be viewed as the dynamic interplay between the id and the superego—one result being male behavior. It is within Freud's *superego* concept that his explanation of the male self lies—or is supposed to lie. Alas, it does not.

Society and the self are functions of the repression of instinctual needs. For our present purpose this means that the male self results from males' repressing their desires for their mothers (the Oedipus Complex). Successful resolution of this complex in boys should produce men. Brown's analysis (1965) of Freud's account of what happens suggests an inherent biological bias. Brown states:

> Both boys and girls take their mothers as their first sensuous love objects for the reason that love develops out of dependence on a caretaker. A boy's love for his mother becomes increasingly passionate and so his father becomes an increasingly exasperating and threatening rival. At length a threat of castration is made to the boy or imagined to have been made. Chiefly because of this thrust but also perhaps because of his anatomical inadequacy, the boy gives up his mother as a love object, represses his desire for her and his hatred of his father, and accepts his father as an ego ideal or model (p. 377–378).

The male self develops out of a *boy's identification with his father!* What determines identification? Ego identification with the last love is said to be the determinant of identification; but as Brown surmises, for Freud it comes out wrong, since the boy *should* identify with the mother. But, as Brown notes further, Freud makes it right by relying on the assumption that "which identification is stronger will depend on the relative strength of the masculine and feminine components in the child's nature." Since boys have stronger masculine components, their identification usually will be with their fathers. The tautology is complete—boys become male selves because they are boys and biological males.

The Life-Cycle Approach to the Male Self

Daniel J. Levinson and colleagues Charlotte H. Darrow, Edward B. Klein, Maria H. Levinson and Braxton McKee have written what many consider to be *the* definitive statement on the male adult life cycle. Entitled *The Seasons of A Man's Life* (1978), the book takes an approach to male adult development which grew out of an intellectual tradition formed by such scholars as Sigmund Freud, Carl Jung, and Erik Erikson (Levinson et al., p. 5). Among other things, the meanings of two concepts are significant in their approach—*life cycle* and *self*.

Life cycle implies that the life course has *a specific character and follows a basic sequence;* that it is a process with both a beginning and an end. Moreover, using the idea of *seasons*, Levinson and co-authors assume that the process is complex and involves periods or stages within the life cycle. While the notion of "season" implies *stability*, it is these authors' contention that this does *not* mean that a particular season is *static*. On the contrary, they believe that change is a crucial part of each season, and that there is transition from one season to another. The life cycle in a sense, then, can be viewed as a *gestalt* with each season contributing to the "whole," linking past and future and containing both within itself (see p. 7).

Male Self, according to the Levinson schema (p. 42), includes "a complex patterning of wishes, conflicts, anxieties and ways of resolving or controlling them." Their view of self is somewhat mentalistic, encompassing the male's fantasies, valor, talents, and ways of feeling and acting. Believing that "self" contains both conscious and unconscious aspects, the authors contend that initial aspects of the self (an intrinsic element of the ego structure) formed in pre-adulthood influence a male's life throughout the life cycle. Let us turn to what many consider to be the major contribution of the volume—a discussion of stages of the male life cycle.

Suggesting that male childhood and male adolescence are parts of a formative phase characterized by pleasures, conflicts, and preparation for male adulthood, Levinson and colleagues turn their attention to male adult development. The first period defined is *Early Adult Transition* (roughly, ages 17–22). Linking male adolescence and male early adulthood, this period begins with the male leaving pre-adulthood, reappraising and modifying self, and creating a life within the adult world. The self during the period is initially characterized by exploration and role-taking regarding male adult participation in the world— all in an effort to forge a male adult identity. The Early Adult Transition period ends at approximately 22, giving way to *Entering the Adult World* (22–28). This period is defined as one where the young man is faced with the avoidance of strong commitments, maximization of alternatives and the necessity to construct a stable life structure—incompatible demands which often produce confusion and anxiety. *The Age Thirty Transition* (28–33) often involves alteration in the life course for men. It is characterized by much self-reflection and/or self-communication. Men, during this stage, are likely to experience stress *and* make changes in the direction of their lives. The end of this period marks the end of the first of the life structures of males.

The second adult life structure begins with what is called the *Settling Down* phase (33–40). During this period, men seem to be characterized by "striving" behavior. Much emphasis is placed on activities which affirm that they are full-fledged adults. Such activities include emphases on social rank, income, power, and indeed all of the characteristics generally associated with masculinity. It is said that a man's self-esteem during this period is a function of his own and other's evaluations of the progress he is making toward "climbing the ladder to success." The midlife transition period (40–45) marks the link between early and middle adulthood and causes men to engage in self-reflection. This self-reflection often causes men to establish priorities, to question their lives, and to begin to seek expression of those aspects of self previously neglected. By age 45, the second life structure takes form for many men—one that is sometimes poorly connected to the self but operable in the world. Other men during this period, however, having reasonably altered "self," experience a full and creative season. Levinson *et al.* state:

> They are less tyrannized by the ambitions, passions and illusions of youth. They can be more deeply attached to others and yet more separate, more centered in the self. For them, the season passes in its best and most satisfying rhythm (p. 62).

The *Entering Middle Adulthood* period (45–50) involves an extension of attempts to create a life structure which is satisfactory for self and the outside world. Thus, the sequence of stable and transitional periods together with familial relationships change, as do occupational relationships. This period leads into the *Age 50 Transition Period* (50–55). During this period, further modification of the life structure may occur, including a reintegration of those feminine aspects of self (if this has not occured during the mid-forties transition period). For those men who did not modify their life structures earlier, it may also be a time of great crisis. From 55–60, men experience *Culmination of Middle Adulthood*. Being somwhat similar to the *Settling-Down* period; men build a second middle-adult structure. The period is thought to be one where men can expect great fulfilment. The ages 60–65 terminate middle adulthood and begin *Late Adulthood*. Levinson *et al.* feel that this is a period of "significant development and represents a major turning point in the life cycle" (p. 62) as the man prepares himself for the time to come.

A **Comment on the Life-Cycle Approach to the Male Self.** Criticisms of life-cycle approaches to self-development include the idea that human development often is irregular and unpredictable (Fishe, 1980). Therefore it may be inappropriate to think of adults as going through a fixed set of stages, or to refer to changes people undergo as "growth." Others feel that life-cycle approaches are too confining and arbitrary (Hess et al., p. 127). Levinson and colleagues attempt to avoid this latter criticism in their presentation of the male-life-cycle approach to self-development. They do so by stating at the outset that their view of the adult male life-cycle is a result of inductive theorizing rather than armchair speculation. Basing their conclusions on interviews with forty men between the ages of 35 and 45, as well as with most of the wives of the married men, Levinson *et al.* present the male life cycle as overlapping categories and/or eras with dynamics within and between eras. They feel also that the heterogeneity of the sample used (in terms of social-class origins, racial-ethnic categories, marital status, and education) contributes to the generalizability of their results.

Another point deserving mention regarding the Levinson work relates to its pragmatic value. Reactions and responses to their work generally have been favorable. However, relatively little attention seems to have been devoted to one of the most important sections (from a sex-role perspective) of the volume—"Fostering Adult Development." In this section, the authors embrace an explicit call for modification in sex-role responsibilities for males in the United States. Such modifications are thought to be necessary for a lessening of conflicts, anxieties, and crises experienced by men as they go through the seasons of life. Furthermore, the authors imply that equality between the sexes would greatly enhance better psychological and social-psychological functioning for men. Implicit in their conclusion, then, is a *call for modification in the traditional definitions of masculinity.* Unless such modification occurs (and continues to occur), indeed, the new epoch in human evolution spoken of by Levinson and his associates *will* have to await hundreds of generations.

The Cognitive-Developmental Approach to the Male Self

Lawrence Kohlberg laid the basic groundwork for the cognitive-developmental approach to the male self in 1966. In an article entitled "A Cognitive Developmental Analysis of Children's Sex-Role Concepts and Attitudes," he set forth a general theoretical framework which assumed "that basic sexual attitudes are not patterned directly by either biological instincts or arbitrary cultural norms, but by the child's cognitive organization of his [sic] social world along sex-role dimension (p. 84)." Recognizing and accepting the viewpoint that both biology and cultural factors are significant forces in sexual development, Kohlberg sought the "basic source of patterning in sexual attitudes, not the quantative contribution of the factors that may influence or deflect this pattern in individual cases (p. 84)." This "basic source," according to Kohlberg, was the child's cognitions—his or her active structuring of his or her own experience. This means, for example, that the male child uses what he knows about his body and his social environment to construct basic sex-role concepts and values. Information gained from the environment, however, can result in alteration and/or modification of these concepts and values at any given point. Let us consider the process for a "typical" male in America.

Between the ages of 3 and 5, a boy generally develops universal conceptions of his role. First, he becomes aware that he is a boy (correct self-labeling). Secondly, he learns to label others according to cultural symbols. Thirdly, near the end of the 5th year and entering into the 6th year, he learns the *constancy* of gender (that if a little boy wears a dress, he is still a little boy). This latter aspect of cognitive development is seen by Kohlberg as *one* part of a general stabilization of constancies of physical objects. Following the development of constant-gender categories, the boy becomes aware of genital differences between males and females. Moreover, he begins to and continues to develop an awareness of different masculine–feminine stereotypes based largely on meanings/symbols of nongenital body imagery (physical size, age, strength, family-role differences, social power differences, etc.). Kohlberg states:

> It appears likely, then, that children's stereotypes of masculine dominance or social power develop largely out of this body-stereotyping of size-age competence. Children agree earliest and most completely that fathers are bigger and stronger than mother, next that they are smarter than mothers, and next they have more social power and are the boss of the family (p. 102).

Once the boy has developed all of the above concepts, sex-typed preferences and values emerge. Kohlberg contends that there is a *natural* tendency for one to ascribe worth to oneself. From his perspective, persons *spontaneously* seek worth, compare their worth with others and evaluate others' worth. Eschewing the idea that children internalize external cultural values, Kohlberg posits the idea that when children learn sex-role concepts, they acquire values and attitudes consistent with those sex-role concepts. Our "boy" then has a natural tendency toward egocentric evaluation and this leads him to think that male is better than female. It also leads the boy to identify with male models, to desire to imitate masculine models, and to accept a moral code consistent with the boy-male model identification (being a good boy means conforming to the male model's expectations, being like the male model, etc.).

A Comment on the Cognitive-Developmental Approach to the Male Self. The cognitive-developmental approach to male self-development "stresses the active nature of the child's thoughts as he organizes his role perceptions and role learnings around his basic conception of his body and his world (Kohlberg, p. 83)." The starting point of this approach is observational learning, which is seen as cognitive because it is selective and internally organized. Basic cognitive organization of the physical world is not static however; it undergoes change with age. As a result, the child's conceptions of his physical world also are thought to undergo transformation. Changes in a child's basic cognitive organization of his physical world are seen as some function of universal age changes in modes of cognition—universal shifts in conceptualization of physical objects.

The sources of such changes and/or shifts in a child's cognitive organization and conceptualization are thought to lie in the child's motivated adaptation to physical–social reality and his *need* to preserve a stable and positive self-image. From the cognitive-developmental approach, we learn that socializing agents like parents, siblings, peer groups, educational institutions, and so on, simply encourage or retard sex-role development. Direct tuition by these agents using reinforcements is *not* thought to be the procedure by which males learn to be dominant, competitive, agressive, violent and the like.

Given the importance of concepts such as "natural tendencies" toward "competence," "effectiveness" and the like, and "spontaneity" in the cognitive developmental approach, it is possible to state that a status quo bias appears to characterize the formulation. In addition, if boys positively value self and thus like self, how do we explain homophobia which becomes apparent in many males as they approach adulthood? In all likelihood we return to "universal shifts in conceptualization of physical objects." I think not! The cognitive development approach to male self-development surely is important. Whether it can be used to explain *all* of the development of the male self is highly debatable. This does not mean that the approach should be discarded; it does mean that we must explain further the phenomenon of male self-development. Let us turn to another explanatory model—the social learning approach to the male self.

The Social Learning Approach to the Male Self

Based on current conceptions of social learning theory (e.g., Bandura, 1977), a male child learns and maintains the male sex-role in two ways: by *response consequences* and by *modeling.*

The male child, as he interacts within the family and outside of the family, experiences many attempts to influence him to adopt "culturally appropriate" sex-role behaviors. Many of these attempts by socialization agents include the use of reinforcements and punishments to modify and maintain selected behaviors. Because he is a cognitive being, the male child becomes *aware* of the fact that some of his behaviors produce positive consequences and others do not. Thus, when the male child's sex-role-related behaviors are differentially reinforced, he is informed of the outcome effects of these behaviors for himself and develops hypotheses about the "appropriateness" of his behaviors. If his hypotheses are correct, future outcomes are positive; if the hypotheses are incorrect, the male child experiences negative outcomes. Through this process, cognitions directly related to behaviors are selectively reinforced and maintained in the male child. In addition, because the young male can reflect on past experiences and can also anticipate future consequences of his behavior, he can *expect* that certain behaviors will produce certain benefits. As a result, some portion of the male child's sex-role behavior falls under the control of anticipatory consequences (Bandura, p. 18).

In social learning, theory, the male child's *learning by responses consequences* is only part of the story. The other part is the male child's *learning by modeling.* In fact, it is Bandura's belief that most social learning occurs *via* this mode. This means that the male child observes other males and then forms ideas about performing these behaviors. These ideas serve as guidelines for the child as he constructs his behavior on future occasions. Several processes are thought to be involved. They include *attentional processes, retention processes, motor reproduction processes,* and *motivational processes.* The male child, in order to learn by observation, has to have the opportunity to observe male models, and must be able to perceive significant features of the models' behaviors. The male child must also be able to experience images of the models' behaviors. The verbal system is thought to be important here, in that the male child can verbally code male models' behaviors. This helps to facilitate the acquisition, retention, and later reproduction of information that serves to guide the male child's behavior. Reproduction of the models' behavior by the young male is thought to be some function of the child's physiological developmental level and cognitive level. Finally, for the male child, when his behaviors which approximate male models' behaviors are rewarded, this increases the likelihood that he will produce the behavior as well as results in self-satisfaction.

A Comment on the Social Learning Approach to the Male Self. Some boys develop into dominating, agressive, competitive, and violent human beings because of the influence of cultural socializing agents. In other words, the male self recognized in many males today is a reflection of American culture. This is the obvious implication of the social learning approach to the male self discussed above. That society can alter institutions responsible for developing and maintaining the male self is a subtle (and I might add, progressive) implication of the social learning approach. As an approach to the male self, social learning "theory" avoids an overemphasis on direct tuition and reinforcement. Moreover, adequate allowance is made both for vicarious learning *and* the influence of cognitive development. It would appear, then, that some combination of the social learning approach to male self development *and* the cognitive developmental approach to male self development *must* be used to give an adequate account of the process whereby boys become men in American society. Elements of both approaches are reflected in the discussion of the male self which follows.

The Male Self as a Dynamic Process: A Perspective and Consequences

If, as stated earlier in this chapter, the male self refers to the process whereby males, by taking the roles of others, view themselves and behave toward themselves as social objects, then it is imperative in a volume of this kind for us to understand something about this process. What is the nature of the male self as process? In addition, what are the results of the male self as process? By this I mean, what are the implications of the male self as process for male self-concept, male self-esteem, and so on?

In order to describe the male self as process, Charles Horton Cooley's classic formulation of the "looking glass self" is used. From Cooley's perspective, the male self may be conceptualized as follows:

1. Males form conceptions of how they appear to others (both females and other males);
2. Males form conceptions about others' judgments of their appearances; and
3. In response to the above, males develop feelings of pride, shame, self-esteem, self-hatred and other attributes of self.

From a sex-role point of view, male conceptions of self appearance to others generally revolve around whether they live up to some ideal masculine image. In more specific terms, this means that males form beliefs about whether they appear to others to be masculine. A particular male, for example, forms conceptions of his appearance to others on such masculine traits as aggressiveness, competitiveness, dominance, control, etc. With these conceptions of self, males also form conceptions of others' judgments of their appearances on the masculine traits mentioned above. During this phase in the process, males arrive at some conclusion about whether they are perceived by others as competitive *enough*, dominant *enough*, controlled *enough*, sexually aggresive *enough* and so on. Those males who perceive that others judge them positively on "masculine" traits develop feelings of pride, high self-esteem, positive self-concepts, etc. Other males who perceive that they are judged negatively on masculine traits by others, develop feelings of shame, self-hatred and poor self-esteem.

Two additional factors are important when considering the male self as process. These factors are (1) *differential cultural valuation of masculinity and femininity in the United States* and (2) *differential cultural negative sanctioning for cross-sex behavior by males and females*. Some studies (e.g., Best et al., 1980) have shown that in some respects the male role is seen as less socially desirable than the female role. In one sense this is not surprising, since dysfunctions associated with traditional masculinity have been popularized in recent years (e.g., Nichols, 1978; Goldberg, 1979). Nevertheless, those characteristics associated with a person's successful adaptation to American society remain, more often than not, traits associated with masculinity. Assertiveness (often substituted for the term *aggressiveness*), competitiveness, logical thought, internalization of the Calvinist work ethic, among other traits, are all thought to be essential for male success—indeed, any person's success in American society. That a masculinist model characterizes American society is also given support by Pleck's (1981) recent exploration into the male sex-role identity (MSRI) paradigm.

Pleck makes the following statement about the MSRI paradigm: "A set of ideas about sex roles, especially the male role, that has dominated the academic social sciences since the 1930s and, more generally, has shaped our culture's view of the male role" (p. 1). Because American society generally accepts the idea that femininity is the opposite of masculinity; and, due to the society maintaining responsibilities inherent in societal conceptions of masculinity, I submit that masculinity is much more valued than femininity in the United States. Verification of this contention can be seen through casual observations of upwardly-mobile women's dress and the expectations held for them.

Women who are "on the move" in American society are expected to defeminize themselves—the classic pump, tailored clothes, functional hairstyles, and little make-up. They are expected to *look* "businesslike" (no "frills"), *act* "businesslike" (show few emotions traditionally associated with femininity), and *think* "businesslike" (rely on logical thought rather than intuitive thought). In essence, women who expect to become full participants in American society (partake of power, prestige, and privilege) are expected to become less "feminine" and more "masculine" in their behavior, feelings, cognitions, and appearances. The only conclusion that can be reached, it seems, is that our culture values masculinity more than it does femininity.

There is evidence suggesting that men experience more negative sanctions when they exhibit behaviors traditionally associated with women than when the reverse occurs (e.g., Seyfried and Hendrick, 1973; Feinman, 1974). Objectively, men exhibiting "feminine" behaviors are doing the same thing as women who exhibit "masculine" behavior—displaying cross-sex behavior. If men experience greater sanctions for cross-sex behavior than women, then one plausible explanation has to be that femininity is less culturally valued. In addition to its meaning for cultural valuation of sex-roles, differential negative sanctioning of cross-sex behavior has implications for male formulation of self conception. Given that masculinity is more valued than femininity in our culture, it follows that self-conceptions constructed by males will be affected. Male self-conceptions are affected by the culture's differential valuation of sex-roles, in that much of a male's conception of himself centers around whether he has constructed an image of others' conceptions of himself as having sufficient distance from femininity. In other words, "is my behavior, in the eyes of others, sufficiently distinct from general conceptions of feminine behavior?" If a male pondering this question arrives at the conclusion that others do, in fact, find his behavior to be "feminine," in all likelihood he will also perceive that he is judged negatively by others for exhibiting these behaviors. As a result, our hypothetical male can be expected to have feelings of low self-esteem, negative self-concept, shame, and so on. Current literature suggests that the restrictive nature of the male role results in many men considering themselves judged negatively by others. This is reflected in studies showing that many males exhibit concern over their masculinity and are affected psychologically (Komarovsky, 1973; Deutsch and Gilbert, 1976).

We see, then, that it is precisely at the point of a male's perception of others' judgments of him that much of the traditional male sex-role becomes dysfunctional. In addition to the dysfunction previously mentioned, many males also exhibit another anomaly—hypermasculinity. This tendency in Black males who are blocked in their efforts to assume the provider-protector role within the family was discussed in the previous chapter. Additional evidence that others' judgments are significant in male self-concepts and behavior comes from rape literature. One line of thought (Russell, 1973; Kanin, 1970) which has been used to explain rape behavior and overly aggressive sexual behavior in some males is that such behaviors are overconforming "male" behaviors. This means that these extreme sexual behaviors are simply extensions of the "masculine mystique." Moreover, the behaviors have been found to be associated with social pressures from associates and thus, conceptions of others' judgments.

Just as overly sexually-aggressive behavior in males can be explained from a hypermasculinity perspective, so, too, can more culturally "acceptable" extreme male behavior. One such type of behavior found in many males is "workaholism." The man who drives himself, has little time for play or for others, and is constantly "producing" for the firm, is a man who is attempting to garner positive evaluations of self from others. Positive evaluations sought may include those on masculine traits like competence, competitiveness, dominance, hard work, and other attributes our society associates with masculinity. Workaholic behaviors in males, like overly sexually aggressive behavior in males, is seen as overconformity to expectations of masculinity.

The male self is seen here as a continuous process of negation of these feminine aspects of self, establishing sufficient distance from femininity. Inherent in this process are continuous efforts to construct conceptions of self that reflect "societally appropriate" definitions of masculinity. Certainly, a male's sexual self is not all there is to the "self," but his sexual self-concept is a core feature of his overall self-concept and influences all major areas of his life.

Males Against Themselves

At the beginning of this chapter, I noted that American males typically state their sexual identity first when asked to describe themselves. This is important because it contributes immensely to our thesis that men in the United States tend to be "against themselves." In order to elaborate this thesis, it is necessary to introduce four additional concepts used by Sheldon Stryker (1980) in his extension of the concept "self." These concepts are "identity," "identity salience," "commitment," and "self-

OF
MOUNT ST. MARY'S
COLLEGE
EMMITSBURG, MARYLAND

esteem." *Identity* is thought to be an aspect of the self and to exist insofar as the person participates in structural social interaction. *Identity salience* is defined as the probability of invoking an identity. *Commitment* refers to the extent "that one's relationship to specified sets of other persons depend on being a particular kind of person" (p. 61). Finally, *self-esteem*, in Stryker's scheme, is an intervening variable between identity structure and role performance. Through role-taking and socialization, persons develop identities based on societal definitions. These identities lead them to seek identity validation. Because persons like to think well of themselves (self-esteem) they tend to behave in accordance with societally suggested and salient identities. Thus, when persons' identities reflect societal norms and values, conforming behavior simultaneously produces self-esteem.

It is within this framework that we can see how many males in America are actually against themselves. Males in the United States are taught to develop those traditionally masculine aspects of self and to repress those aspects of self traditionally associated with femininity. Indeed, many of society's socializing agents implore males, as they participate in social interaction, to invoke their "masculine" identities. Since such encouragement is ubiquitous in our society, males gradually come to have a high probability of invoking their masculine identities in a wide variety of social situations. In other words, a masculine identity becomes highly salient for males. Moreover, males learn quickly that their relationships to numerous others (significant and nonsignificant) depend upon the exhibition of their masculine traits and the repression of their feminine traits. Therefore, for many males, their masculine identity becomes one of high commitment. In seeking validation of their identities and in efforts to think well of themselves, males behave in a sex-"appropriate" way, which in turn produces both *high self-esteem* and *low self-esteem*.

While it is probably apparent that males experience high self-esteem when they engage in sex-typed behavior, it is not so apparent why low self-esteem would also occur. I contend that males, too, are humans, and that because of the fact that much of traditional masculinity negates humanity, males experience low self-esteem. Humanness often is thought to involve traits associated with femininity (Chafetz, 1978). In addition, males *do* develop "human" identities. Male commitment to these identities, however, must often be low, because society juxtaposes them to the highly valued masculine identity. As a result, high commitment to masculinity by males means, in a sense, that males negate other important identities they have. A statement by Fernando Bartolome (1972) is instructive here, and although made over a decade ago, still is applicable, given the conservative trend regarding male sex-role modifications in the early 1980s.

> Man should be free from stereotypes, self-imposed or otherwise, and rigid role definitions that limit his experience. . . . He is limited by a role definition obliging him to be super-masculine, super-tough, super self-sufficient, and super-strong. It allows him very little freedom to be that mixture of strength and weakness, independence and dependence, toughness and tenderness which a human being is (p. 62).

This statement implies, as does our analysis of the male sex role, that many males are "against themselves." In the next chapter we will explain how the process of "males against themselves" has implications for male social perceptions.

CHAPTER 4

Male Social Perception

In developing the psychological portrait of the *Lady Killer*, psychiatrists like Seidenberg and homicide investigators like Detective Michael Chitwood of the Philadelphia Police Department agree that the attacker can't hope to relate to his victim on their level—or on any level other than a pornographic one. "You walk up and down the street in this or any city," Chitwood says, "and you see it in their eyes. They *look* for these women. They wait for them. They only go after the ones they think have it made. . . . that woman who's carrying a briefcase may be in more trouble than she could ever imagine" (Mallowe, 1982, p. 39).

The above is one type of perceptual–behavioral response a few men make to increased participation of women in a world that has been the exclusive domain of men. Many more males make less-physically-threatening responses to women, but ones which are psychologically lethal to women. Many of you reading this will probably ask, "What does this have to do with perception?" The answer is that it has a great deal to do with male perception, because the *Lady Killer* can be seen as a logical, albeit extreme extension or result of many males' perceptions of sex-roles in the United States. It is precisely because of the rigid manner in which the "Lady Killer" views the woman's role in our society as one excluding her from holding power, competing with men, advancing in society and the like, that he makes the criminal political statement of killing "successful" women. I do not mean to justify these heinous crimes; rather, the intent is to show that the ways men conceptualize and form perceptual hypotheses about sex-roles and sex-role-related behaviors are dysfunctional for themselves, others, and society. I hope this chapter will aid in understanding the social-perception process experienced by males in the United States.

To begin with, our concern is with those processes men use to understand and think about their social worlds, including other men, women, and social situations. What is the nature of these processes by which men come to understand themselves and some other men as "masculine?" How do men *know* that women are persons who should be "kept in place?" Why is there a tendency in many men to form conceptions of most social situations as ones requiring the exhibition of so-called "masculine" traits? In sum, what is the nature of male social perception in the United States?

Questions such as the ones above are difficult to answer because numerous (and often individually based) interacting factors must be considered in exploring the nature of male social perception. Perlman and Cozby (1982) feel that social perception involves another person's *actions*, another person's *reactions*, and *interaction*. In order to perceive another person, in this perspective, a man must "understand another's active, independent life (action); in addition, because a man's own actions produce reactions from others, a man must understand that his behavior affects how others behave (reaction) and finally, a man perceiving another is affected by his own actions indirectly as they return from the person receiving them (interaction). Another factor often thought to increase the difficulty of understanding the nature of male perception is the heterogeneity of the male population in the United States. Men in the United States come from diverse socioeconomic backgrounds; they are of many different races and ethnic affiliations; and, they have many different social experiences. Yet, it may be that the difficulty of exploring the nature of male social perception in America is lessened because of a cultural ethos related to masculinity that exists in our society. There are general ideas, expectations, and values most men learn to associate with masculinity, and this contributes to the development of a general perceptual process for most males in America.

These general ideas, expectations, and values that most men associate with masculinity influence male perception. The degree to which male perception is influenced by these factors is related to three concepts discussed in the previous chapter: *Commitment to masculinity, male identity salience* and *male self-esteem. Male commitment to masculinity,* we will recall, refers to the degree that a male's relationship to specified sets of others depends on being a "societal" male. *Male identity salience* is defined as the likelihood that the "masculine identity" will be invoked in social situations; and, *Male self-esteem* connotes male feelings of self-worth. If a given man is highly committed to "masculinity," then this masculine identity is likely to be highly salient for him which in turn contributes to high self-esteem. These three factors, together with general conceptions associated with masculinity, influence how males perceive their social worlds. Let us explore precisely how this works.

Male Perceptual Organization of Social Worlds

Most males' perceptions of their social worlds are some function of how they organize their social worlds. Men, as do women, organize their social worlds around such factors as proximity, similarity, and continuity. These factors, however, are thought to often be beyond the control of the individual male. Nevertheless, there are other factors that are not beyond the individual male's control; in fact, these other factors are seen as originating in the individual male, and are thought to be ones which he *imposes* on his social world. Such factors are referred to here as *central factors affecting male perceptual organization*. They are (1) knowledge of role options, (2) mental states, (3) role-making and/or role-playing strategies, and (4) personal communication techniques (Franklin, 1982, p. 5). These factors, in turn, are related intricately to such aspects of perception as understanding "another's actions," "another's reactions," and "interaction."

Male Knowledge of Role Options

In addition to what already has been mentioned about social perception, the process involves past experiences, contemporary experiences, and perhaps even anticipated experiences. Because males generally learn early to perceive themselves and others in terms of varying degrees of masculinity and femininity, gender must be recognized as playing a vital role in the way males "come to know" their social worlds. A masculine identity is vital for most males, and affects their perceptions of social-role options available to them. For example, if I have learned and believe that "real men don't cook *quiche*," then regardless of my need for employment in hard economic times, a job requiring one to cook *quiche* may not be seen by me as viable employment, for myself or any other man. In this instance, the *"quiche*-cook" role is closed to me because I am likely to see the role as nonmasculine and/or feminine. A man's view of occupants of social roles is affected by whether he tends to view social roles along strict gender lines—that is, in terms of strict definitions of masculinity and femininity. In turn, this tendency to view a specific social role along strict gender lines is related to a man's knowledge (both past and present) of whether both males and females occupy the social role.

Male Mental States

Males in the United States are encouraged to develop systematic and logical ways of thinking. Simultaneously, males are expected to develop a disdain for or to dislike explanations for human behavior based on "the ability to understand one's own feelings and psychological association and, by analogy, those of others" (Nichols, 1978, p. 42). Even Pleck's analysis (1976) of the "modern" male role acknowledges elements of systematic, rational, and logical thought when he says that "interpersonal skills are expected insofar as they promote smooth collaboration with others toward *achievement, as in management.*" When Pleck equates aspects of the modern male role with *management* our idea regarding the endorsement by men of rational and systematic thought is given added support. This is especially the case if men in management fit Bartolome's (1972) description. He feels that men in management "are people with high achievement needs, and one of their characteristics is the desire *to measure accurately* and unambiguously the extent of their achievements" (p. 74). If, in fact, men carry with them into social situations and social interaction the patterns of thought and behavior mentioned above, then what are the implications for men's perceptions of their social worlds? Men's social worlds in the United States are dynamic, changeable and, in essence, unpredictable. Thus, systematic and logical ways of thinking may be inappropriate in numerous instances of men's social interaction where accurate social perception is necessary. Instead, intuitive–passive thought (often equated with femininity) may be required for accurate social perception. Men may, in effect, often reify social situations and social interactions—that is, impose structures where none exist.

Male Role Making/Playing Strategies

It is unlikely that men walk around with specific plans-of-action to direct to others in social interaction. Nevertheless, many men seem to act in a consistently masculine manner when they are involved in social interaction with others. This prompts those who feel that there is a need for changes in men's sex-roles to suggest alteration in men's dominance patterns, competitive patterns, aggressive patterns, and so on. In actuality what is being proposed is that men alter the ways in which they *construct* their behavior during social interaction, which *results* in dominance, competitiveness and aggressiveness. One implication of proposed changes in men's behaviors when viewed from this *processual* perspective is that the persistence and/or maintenance of male dominance, male competitiveness, male aggression, and the like is some function of properties within social interaction.

These properties within social interaction which support traditional male behaviors aid men in constructing masculine behaviors. In addition, emphasis on "masculine traits" during male socialization and past male role-making/playing experiences are sources from which males draw as they construct their behaviors during a particular instance of social interaction. Men whose role making/playing strategies are influenced in traditionally masculine ways by situational and socializing factors organize their worlds along strict gender lines. This affects their perception of other men, women, themselves, and social situations. Richardson and Alpert (1981) provide some evidence that this is what occurs for males in the United States. They found that, in general, men perceive more competition in adult roles than women. While they did not find significant sex differences in competition perceptions of the work role (which they attribute to the competitive orientation of work experienced by both sexes), when the "parent" role is combined with the "work" role, men perceive the combined role as highly competitive while women viewed the combination as "a noncompetitive arena." Richardson and Alpert state:

> In particular, implications of the results that women view segments of their future with more engagement (which is defined separately as high involvement and innovation in role activities [sic]) than men while men perceive most of the roles considered in more competitive terms than women are intriguing. It may imply that women have a greater readiness to invest themselves in life's activities, while men anticipate the future under the stress of a competitive orientation (p. 792).

Male Personal Communication Mechanisms

A fourth factor which influences how males organize their social worlds is the mechanism of personal communication. In general, persons interact with each other in various ways, using a variety of personal communication skills and techniques. These skills and techniques enable information to be transmitted and received and are brought to the social situation by individual participants. Personal communication skills and techniques do more, however, than aid information transmission and reception; they also *influence social perception by filtering information.* When information is filtered, some aspects will be more salient for the perceiver while other aspects will be less salient. The way in which the perceiver organizes his or her world, then, will be related to this filtering process. If, for example, a particular man generally uses controlling communication techniques in his interaction with others, then he will tend to *organize* others in terms of their possession of traits and/or characteristics that allow him to exhibit his controlling behaviors. In addition, these traits or characteristics in others which allow our hypothetical man to exhibit his controlling behaviors are more likely to be perceived by him than those which would disallow the exhibition of his controlling behaviors. Let us review briefly other aspects of personal communication mechanisms in social interaction directly related to males.

A persistent theme in the literature on sex roles is that males are less empathic and less emotional in social interaction than females. Males are also seen as more task-oriented, more aggressive verbally, and generally more controlling than females in social situations (Sampson and Kardush, 1965; Wood, 1966). Pleck (1976), however, contends that modern definitions of masculinity emphasize the development of interpersonal skills. This would seem to indicate that many modern males develop and use communication skills and techniques that insure smooth interpersonal communication. Perhaps this would occur, were it not for the persistence of another characteristic of modern masculinity—*emotional coolness*. While *emotional coolness* mitigates impulsivity and the display of emotionalism in males, it also has implications for males' abilities to form emotionally intimate relationships with others, as will be discussed later. For the time being, however, let us review some findings related to men's perceptions of themselves in interpersonal communication.

Cicone and Ruble (1978) in reviewing research findings on beliefs about males, concluded that men tend *not* to view themselves quite as "traditionally masculine" as the "typical" male. At the same time, according to Cicone and Ruble, men do not perceive themselves to be successful at combining the best parts of traditional masculinity and modern masculinity as the "ideal" male. More specific self-perception findings on males and differences between male self-perception and female self-perception can be seen in a study related directly to self-perception of communication behavior by Fitzpatrick and Bochner (1981). Fitzpatrick and Bochner concluded that there were significant differences in the perceptions of males and females concerning their own communication behavior and the communication behavior of their best friends (p. 531). Males were found to perceive themselves as more controlling in social interaction than did females. Males also viewed themselves as independent and nonaffiliative in social interaction, while females saw themselves as more dependent and affiliative (interestingly, females were not viewed as highly affiliative by those close to them—male or female).

Findings from the Fitzpatrick and Bochner study also have implications for same-sex and cross-sex emotionally intimate relationships. While this topic is discussed in greater detail in Chapter 9, Fitzpatrick and Bochner's findings are significant now because of their impact on perceptual organization. Both males and females perceive themselves as *more* affiliative and less controlling in *opposite-sex relationships* than in same-sex relationships. Males, however, saw females as less controlling but not very affiliative in communication. Males felt that interpersonal communication with their female significant others was generally characterized by their (males') offering support, sympathy, guidance, and the like. Females, on the other hand, perceptually acknowledged affiliative behavior in their male significant others but also saw them as *controlling*.

Undoubtedly when males perceive females in the above manner, just as when females perceive males as stated above, male perception of females is affected, as is female perception of males. Males, like females, attempt to order their worlds. If, in fact, males "expect" females to exhibit less control and less affiliation in communication, then such expectations in all likelihood affect male perceptions of females who meet the expectations and those who do not meet the expectations. This places females in a no-win situation. If they respond in interpersonal communication according to the above male expectations, then they are perceived to be just acting "female." If they respond in an unexpected manner (for example, exhibit more control in interpersonal communication), then they are perceived as "stepping out of their place."

As we have seen in our discussion thus far, the ways that men conceptualize and form perceptual hypotheses about their worlds are affected by four central factors: male knowledge of role options, male mental states, male role making/playing strategies, and male personal communication techniques. In explaining these factors for males, one inescapable conclusion emerges. Many males in our society often bring with them into social interaction ways of organizing their perceptions that may be appropriate for perceiving inanimate objects but inappropriate for perceiving humans. If males, for example, tend to impose on their social worlds communication techniques, knowledge, mental states, and role playing/making strategies that seem devoid of humanness, then perception of themselves, others and social situations is inhibited and, in many instances, inaccurate. Tendencies on the part of males to organize their worlds in the ways discussed may make it impossible for them to perceive their worlds in any way other than along strict gender lines. Moreover, factors affecting male organization of perception have direct implications for impression formation, impression management, and face-to-face interaction with other males, females and in general, social situations.

Males and Nonverbal Sensitivity

Are men incapable of accurately "reading" nonverbal messages of emotion expressed by others? A review of the literature on sex differences in nonverbal sensitivity would not allow one to answer this question affirmatively. However, many probably *would* come to the conclusion, as did Judith Hall (1978) that males appear to be *less* sensitive than females to nonverbal visual and auditory cues in social interaction. The explanations offered for lesser male sensitivity to nonverbal cues in all likelihood would vary. Explanations would probably include biological rationales (where female superiority in nonverbal sensitivity is said to be related to the genetic make-up of females), social-learning-theory rationales (which relate sex differences in nonverbal sensitivity to sex-role related aspects of personality), and social power differential rationales (which suggest that because women enjoy less social power than men, they have to be especially alert to the emotions of "more powerful others" (Henley, 1977; Hall, 1978, p. 274–5). I believe, though, that the explanations for female superiority, and therefore male inferiority, in nonverbal sensitivity given by most of those acquainted with the sex-role literature would overwhelmingly fall within the last two explanatory schemes mentioned.

Hall's ingenious research (e.g., 1976; 1978a; 1978b; 1981) in the area of nonverbal sensitivity has been extremely significant, and is the basis for our discussion in this section. Her study in 1981 with colleague Amy Halberstadt has been quite provocative, because the findings challenged ideas about the relationship between masculinity and nonverbal sensitivity. More specifically, they contend that the assumption of associations between nonverbal sensitivity, prosociality, and empathy (the latter two thought to be correlates of femininity) may be unwarranted. This position is in direct contrast to those which imply that traits in masculinity operate against males being nonverbally sensitive to others.

Hall and Halberstadt provide evidence for their contention by reporting the results of a "meta-analysis" of eleven unreported independent investigations of "decoding ability and/or encoding ability in which measures of masculinity and femininity are employed" (pp. 274–5). They found that while females exhibited overall superiority in decoding and encoding nonverbal cues, "femininity" *did not* seem to account for women's superiority in nonverbal sensitivity. Indeed, they found "a weak tendency for more *masculine types* of people (both males and females) to excel in nonverbal decoding ability" (p. 284). In addition, while women who held more liberated views on women scored higher on decoding nonverbal cues than did "traditional" women, the relationship was obtained only for decoding a woman stimulus-person. When the stimulus-person was male, traditional women tended to understand the nonverbal cues more than liberated women. Hall and Halberstadt conclude that neither social learning explanations nor social power explanations seem sufficient to explain why females are better decoders than males. They offer alternative explanations, including the mediating role of *attention to nonverbal cues,* and feel that the attention might be motivated by *politeness* or by a need on the part of women to seek indication of approval and disapproval (p. 285).

In light of Hall and Halberstadt's findings which question the idea that greater nonverbal sensitivity in women is a function of sex-roles or males' social power (which means that women pay close attention to men in order to observe these powerful others' cues), an alternative explanation is offered which *may be* linked with sex-roles. The bases for the explanation to follow are Hall and Halberstadt's findings and the seemingly uncanny nonverbal sensitivity male "pimps" are said to have in interaction with their "ladies." Hall and Halberstadt, in interpreting their findings that more "masculine people" seem nonverbally sensitive to others, state the following: " . . . the goals of the more 'masculine' person may involve interpersonal effectiveness—accomplishing joint tasks, being a good leader, winning in competition—and this kind of effectiveness may require a more developed ability to judge others' feelings and moods" (p. 284). Along similar lines, the male pimp, while dependent on the earnings of his "ladies," often exhibits hypermasculine behaviors toward them. Male violence, male aggressiveness, male dominance, and so on surely characterize many relationships between pimps and their "ladies." Yet, the male pimp's "success" with his "ladies" often is related directly to his ability to accurately assess their nonverbal emotions.

Given the above observations, it seems possible to distinguish two forms of nonverbal sensitivity: *altruistic nonverbal sensitivity* and *egocentric nonverbal sensitivity.* Before explaining these forms it is significant to point out that testing, itself, is inimical to *altruistic nonverbal sensitivity* and while it enhances egocentric nonverbal sensitivity, a typical test situation (at least the ones reported) constructs an individual goal to be attained in a situation which essentially is devoid of others. This alone *minimizes* the necessity for altruistic nonverbal sensitivity and *maximizes* the necessity for egocentric nonverbal sensitivity. If more masculine persons than feminine persons exhibit high decoding abilities in *test situations,* this is not an unexpected finding, given a distinction between types of nonverbal sensitivity. Additionally, altruistic nonverbal sensitivity may be linked with female sex-role socialization while ego-centric nonverbal sensitivity may be linked with male sex-role socialization. Altruistic nonverbal sensitivity *involves the idea of "reading" other people for the benefit of other people, while egocentric nonverbal sensitivity refers to "reading" other people for the benefit of oneself.* This line of thought recognizes nonverbal sensitivity in males as well as in females; in masculine persons as well as in feminine persons. Such an acknowledgment is consistent with findings reported earlier as well as others. What is significant and deserves mention, however, is that different types of nonverbal sensitivity often found in males and females affect their overall perceptions of and behaviors toward people. In America, males generally develop egocentric nonverbal-sensitivity abilities while females, expecially today, generally develop altruistic nonverbal-sensitivity abilities *and* egocentric nonverbal-sensitivity abilities. The latter point would explain Hall and Halberstadt's suggestion that women's better decoding ability is related to whichever sex is most salient to them—"men in the case of more traditional women, other women in the case of less traditional women."

Egocentric nonverbal sensitivity in males develops out of male socialization stressing competitiveness, individual achievement, and so on, and which often is manifested in male youth-play activities. Likewise, female socialization processes and play activities stress cooperative and sharing behavior which lead to the development of altruistic nonverbal sensitivity. Modern-day modifications in sex-role socialization for female youth and adult females in some social roles (especially occupational roles) have encouraged some females to develop egocentric nonverbal sensitivity. It is very likely that those females who develop both types of decoding abilities use them according to the demands of the social situation. Because males generally develop only one type of decoding ability (the egocentric type) they tend to use this type in *all situations.* In fact, this may be precisely why men are thought by some to be nonverbally insensitive. When men are in situations where personal benefit is perceived to be minimal or unrelated, they probably do *not attend* to cues necessary for nonverbal sensitivity. On the other hand, when men find themselves in social situations where personal benefit is important (e.g., business executives' meeting) because of their acquired abilities to egocentrically decode others' nonverbal messages of emotion, they are quite likely to judge accurately others' feelings, moods, and emotions.

But, what are the implications for male perception if males tend to develop only one type (egocentric) of nonverbal sensitivity while females, especially today, develop both types (egocentric and altruistic)? When males develop only egocentric nonverbal sensitivity, they are rendered incapable of perceiving accurately "whole" persons as well as "whole" situations. Few people or situations can be perceived accurately only in terms of nonverbal instrumental traits or characteristics. For men to egocentrically decode all nonverbal messages means being selectively attentive, which results in selective perceptions for men. When men selectively perceive in this manner, in all likelihood they perceive only those aspects of others and of situations that are congruent with existing preconceptions—those aspects that fit into their highly personalized schemes of things. This idea is consistent with O'Leary and Donoghue's (1978) conclusion in an article entitled, "Latitudes of Masculinity." They state: "If there is a tragedy associated with the adult male role as traditionally defined, it is perhaps the belief that deviation from that role will result in negative consequences" (p. 25). It is hardly necessary to say that when males perceive and believe in the ways described above they *limit* the latitudes of masculinity.

Consequences of Male Perception

Impression formation, impression management, and *face-to-face interaction* are social-psychological phenomena closely associated with social perception. Impression formation refers *to the process by which we arrive at conclusions about the traits, moods, emotions, and other attributes of other(s).* Impression management *involves the regulation of self-disclosure information.* Both impression formation and impression management are related to face-to-face interaction during which two or more persons transmit and receive information.

In our discussion of impression formation as it relates to males perceiving females and other males, several effects of the phenomenon are emphasized. These effects are primary-recency effects, physical-attraction effects, halo effects and stereotyping effects. Impression management for males in our discussion will involve two aspects: how males present themselves in social interaction with both males and females (presentation of self); and, the need for males to avoid the "stigma" of being labeled "feminine." In line with our earlier statement, male impression formation and management influence males in face-to-face social interaction. How males accommodate others' expectations and how others' expectations often result in self-fulfilling prophecies will also be discussed. Let us consider impression formation, impression management, and face-to-face interaction as correlates of male social perception, and how these correlates relate to males perceiving females, and males perceiving males.

Males Perceiving Females: Impression Formation

Berscheid and Walster's (1974) and Miller's (1970) combined findings regarding the effects of physical attractiveness on person perception point to a tendency for males in our society to perceive physically attractive females in a particular way: as sexually warm, personable, kind, and so on. In addition, sexual attraction is also related to physical attractive-ness. Moreover, such effects seem greater for males than for females. When these findings are seen in light of primary and recency effects on person perception, one explanation for the ubiquitous tendency for males to perceive females as sexual objects emerges.

In America, sex category is a core feature of initial information about a stimulus person. According to sex-role literature, sex appears to be a central factor around which males especially organize their perceptions about a stimulus person. Given that numerous "traditional" ideas about feminine traits, feminine moods, and feminine emotions persist in the minds of many males, male perceptions of female stimulus persons are affected. Male perception is affected by the initial recognition that the person is female, which in turn affects any subsequent information pro-vided by and/or about the female person.

Current thinking in social-perception literature is that cognitions affect the way we organize our perceptions; and, that subsequent infor-mation becomes a part of our first impression. If males in our society are predisposed to initially perceiving persons in terms of sex categories and all of their accoutrements, then subsequent information about persons, however objective, will be altered. This means that, instead of some women being excellent surgeons, mechanics and airline pilots, they become excellent *female* surgeons, *female* mechanics, and *female* airline pilots. The implication, of course, is that sex category has both a "primary effect" and a "halo effect" for many males when they perceive persons. This means that sex category systematically biases the formations of males' overall impressions of females, and affects the expectations held by males about how females will behave. For example, Braito, Dean, Powers and Bruton (1981) report that males tend to *overestimate* females' "playing inferior" on dates, while females *underestimate* males' never playing inferior. According to their findings, few differences exist between male- and female-reported "playing inferior" behaviors; yet large differences exist between how men and women perceive others' sex behaviors. However, in their study, women's perceptions were more closely in line with the reported behavior of men than vice-versa. Aside from the tendency to perceive females in terms of stereotypes, impres-sion formation of the kind discussed often leads men, as participants, to construct social interaction strategies with females in ways designed to "keep females in place."

Perhaps one factor affecting male perception of females not consid-ered thus far, which intervenes and causes males to perceive females dif-ferently, deserves mention. This factor, though, does not necessarily operate for the benefit of many women. The factor being referred to is *physical attractiveness.* Bersheid and Walster (1974) have pointed out that physical attractiveness is related to a variety of positive attributes, including personality and romantic and sexual attractiveness. Additionally, males' perceptions seem more affected by the physical attractiveness variable than females' perceptions (Miller, 1970). This was found to be so in a recent study (Janda et al., 1981) even when the "attractive" woman stimulus person also was perceived to be sexually permissive. Males in this study tended to rate the sexually permissive "attractive" stimulus woman higher in terms of warmth, friendliness, and likeability than did females.

I believe, though, that the greater effects of the physical attractiveness variable on males operate against women. What it does is to place some women in an even more precarious position in perceptual terms. Not only are physically attractive women perceived by males selectively because they belong to the female sex category, but physically attractive females are stereotyped and perceived even more selectively by males because they also belong to a subcategory which has its own peculiar ideas about the relationships between "female," external appearances, moods, traits, emotions, and so on. Also important is the fact that perceptions of physical attractiveness are subjective and varied among men. In fact, it is likely that most women are perceived as physically attractive by some men. If the effects of "physical attractiveness" on males generally are consistent with research findings, then the ubiquitousness of sexual harassment experienced by women in our society is explained and sex-role socialization certainly plays a significant role.

Male Impression Management: Manipulating the Perceptions of Females

How males present themselves in social interaction with others obviously affects others' perceptions of them. If males go to great lengths to control and/or manipulate information about themselves—revealing some and withholding other—then others' perception of males and the feedback they give males will be based on partial information. This seems to be precisely what happens when males present themselves to others. Much of the literature supports the idea that males reveal significantly less information about aspects of self to others than do females (e.g., Jourard, 1971; Rubin, 1975). One interpretation of the findings indicating sex differences in self-disclosure is that self-disclosure patterns among males and females reflect sex-role socialization differences. Accordingly, females learn cooperation, sharing, expressive and nurturant behaviors, while males learn assertiveness, independence, and the suppression of emotions. The two different kinds of learning supposedly lead to different rates of self-disclosure for males and females.

Into what does all of this translate when males present themselves to females? If we will recall, Pleck's (1976) analysis of the modern male role includes the notion that males exhibit hetereosexual tendencies and emotional intimacy in social interaction with females. Still, there is little available evidence that males have lessened their avoidance of the "stigma" associated with being labeled feminine. "Tenderness," emotional intimacy, self-disclosure, and the like are all associated with femininity. Therefore, it seems unlikely that many males genuinely present themselves to females even in the 1980s.

A study by Davidson (1981) sheds some light on male presentation of self to females and the reverse. While Davidson found that males tended to show heterosexual tenderness and/or affection, it was exaggerated (females in the Davidson study tended to feign minimal affection toward men). Therefore modern-day heterosexual tenderness exhibited by men appears to be instrumental and/or functional. Basically, this means that much behavior constructed by males in social interaction with females is designed to "manage" a particular impression. As Davidson implies, it seems that modern-day men feel pressure to "express more freely genuine love and affection, yet they also tend to pretend more love and affection than they actually feel" (p. 346). Also, while men in Davidson's study indicated that they tended to be passive with women, they also said that they experienced strong pressures to be active. Why? Davidson suggests we are confronted with a paradox wherein men perceive women as demanding an active man and women perceive men as demanding a passive woman. "The unfortunate irony is that men and women force each other into pressures and pretense, thus perpetuating stereotypical roles and the 'myths' of gender differences" (p. 346).

Let us return to the issue of male self-disclosure, since it is a crucial aspect of impression management with females as well as males. Recent literature in the area indicates mixed findings with respect to levels of self-disclosure for males. In fact, Lombardo and Levine (1981) contend that sex-role may be a better indicator of self-disclosure than sex. On the other hand, significant sex differences on self-disclosure were found too by Gerdes, Behling, and Rapp (1981). In the Lombroso and Levine study, four groups of subjects identified by the (Bem Sex-Role Inventory) BSRI as androgynous males, stereotyped males, androgynous females, and stereotyped females were used to determine sex and sex-role differences in patterns of targets-disclosed-to and amounts-of-information-disclosed. Targets-disclosed-to were male and female best friends and mothers and fathers. Findings of particular relevance for us include those about androgynous males and sex-typed males. Androgynous males were found to self-disclose as much as androgynous females. While they displayed the "peer-first" profile on intimate disclosures, unlike sex-typed males, androgynous males were just as likely to self-disclose to their female best friends as to a male best friend. They also were higher than sex-typed males in their self-disclosures to parents, especially fathers. In addition, androgynous males reported just as much self-disclosure on *intimate topics* as androgynous females to father, best male friend, and best female friend. When both intimate and non-intimate self-disclosures to friends were considered, androgynous males, unlike androgynous females and sex-typed males and females, reported equal disclosures to male and female friends. Also, self-disclosure to mothers and fathers by androgynous males were equal; this was different from any other group. Lombardo and Levine concluded that "self-disclosure is strongly related to the personality construct of masculinity, femininity, and androgyny" (p. 410).

If it were not for another set of recent findings regarding male self-disclosure, we might conclude tentatively that sex-role socialization is indeed related to many males' reluctance to disclose aspects of self. Indeed, this still may be the case. However, Gerdes, *et al.*'s (1981) findings deserve mention here because they feel that some doubt is cast on a sex-role-socialization explanation of sex differences in self-disclosure (Bem, 1974). In a study by Gerdes *et al.* (1981), overall self-disclosure differences were not found between androgynous males and sex-typed males, but significant sex differences and a strong "reciprocity effect" were found. The concept "reciprocity effect" is used to describe the process whereby a person tends to match the level of self-disclosure made by another person with whom he or she is interacting. For example, if you are interacting with a person who reveals a great deal of information about himself or herself, then you are likely to reveal a good deal of information about yourself. The opposite is likely if you are interacting with a person who self-discloses at a low level.

There are additional findings and interpretations from the Gerdes study which are important as we explore male impression management. For example, they found (just as many others have) that females disclosed more intimately than did males; however, they *did not* find that androgynous males self-disclosed more than sex-typed males (p. 995). Gerdes and colleagues interpreted these findings to mean that a social norm existed against *male* self-disclosure to strangers. They believe that their "social norm" explanation differs from a sex-role explanation in the following manner. Regardless of whether a male internalizes a sex-role that makes him likely to self-disclose, his level of self-disclosure is regulated by social expectations of appropriate self-disclosure behavior for males in given social settings. Thus, while I may be androgynous and thus given to intimate expressiveness, I may not disclose intimately in certain settings. Why? Because I am also aware that such behavior is inappropriate in certain settings and this awareness will inhibit my expressiveness.

Gerdes and colleagues *did* find that androgynous males self-disclosed more intimately than sex-typed males when the person with whom they were interacting self-disclosed at a high level—but so did androgynous females in comparison with sex-typed females. They concluded that self-disclosure patterns for *both* males and females may be thought of as reflecting more flexible approaches to social interaction for androgynous males and females in comparison with sex-typed males and females.

While the latter study has not dealt specifically with male self-disclosure to females (and thus, male impression management in male-female social interaction) it does provide support for the idea that many males continue to present themselves in such a way that potential perceivers (including friends) only receive partial information—that is, information that males want them to see. Given the persistence of much "traditionally masculine" behavior, we can only conclude that many males in social interaction with females continue to present themselves in disguised and pretentious ways often designed to control social situations.

Males Perceiving Males: Impression Formation

How do males perceive each other? As stated earlier, sex category is a central factor in male perception. Just as males have ideas, beliefs, and attitudes about females, they also have ideas, beliefs, attitudes and so on about males. Males' perceptions of other males are affected by the cognitions, emotions and behaviors males bring with them into intrasex social interaction. Precisely how male perception is affected becomes apparent when it is recognized that men, too, have been limited by their sex.

It is estimated that over 50,000 men all over the United States have taken part in consciousness-raising groups to discuss and examine men's experiences (Brannon, 1982). While women have been damaged by sexroles, men have also been limited by their sex-roles. It is a different kind of limitation that men have experienced but one that is also faced by women. Brannon explains the limitation in the following way:

> This limitation is based on sex-roles—an invisible network of social pressures, coming from a million sources during all of our lives, that tell each of us what kind of personality we should try to have, what we should do, what things we should be interested in, what we should avoid (p. 42).

This type of limitation is psychological and is as apparent in American definitions of masculinity as in American definitions of femininity. In fact, because the latitudes of femininity do not appear to be as limiting psychologically as the latitudes of masculinity, the effects of "masculinity" on males may be just as damaging, psychologically, as the effects of "femininity" on females. Moreover, early studies have found that men who dare to broaden the limits of masculinity are devalued (e.g., Costrich, Feinstein, Kidder, Maracek, and Pascale, 1975; Spence, Heimreich and Stapp, 1975).

From early socialization on, males are encouraged to relate to other males as though they are instrumental inanimate objects. To be sure, males seem to be given greater latitudes in the male roles as they age; however, strict adherence to male-role expectations is required in most males' early childhood, adolescence, and early adulthood. It must be remembered that these are formative years, and ones when males develop and nurture their knowledge of role options, their mental states, their role making/playing strategies and their personal-communication mechanisms. We must also remember that the latter are factors males use to organize their perceptions in social interaction with others—males as well as females. If strict adherence to and internalization of the male role means inhibiting emotional intimacy with other males, certainly this will affect how males perceive other males. In the United States this seems to be the case (Fasteau, 1974; Goldberg, 1976). Moreover, we cannot expect that relaxing these restrictions at a later age for men will result in most men realizing that the boundaries of their relationships with other men have been extended. Instead, I believe, most men in our culture go throughout their lives forming impressions of other men on the basis of partial information limited by their own and society's definitions of what it means to be masculine.

Literature on social perception suggests that impression formation, as we have seen, is affected by physical attractiveness, primary-recency effects, stereotypes, halo effects, and so on. We know little about the influence of physical attractiveness on males' perceptions of other males. Is it the case, for example, that physically attractive males are perceived by other males as nicer, kinder, more intelligent, and more sexually responsive, than less-physically-attractive males? In other words, if, as many suggest, first impressions of others are affected by the degree to which others are perceived to be physically attractive, then males' first impressions of other males should also be affected by the "physical attractiveness" variable—or should they? One set of findings from a study by Jacobson (1981), which related the effects of victim's and defendant's attractiveness on subject's judgments in a rape case, implies that men *do* tend to be more lenient in their judgments toward male defendants when male defendants are physically attractive. Jacobson, however, was cautious in her interpretation of these findings. She suggested that sex differences in sympathy toward the defendant (women generally were harsher in their judgments) might reflect a "get-tough" attitude on the part of women, who perceive rape differently from men. Males, on the other hand, might have been more lenient because they did not perceive that rape affected them personally. At any rate, Jacobson was inclined to conclude that guilty verdicts for rapes might be more difficult to obtain when the defendant is physically attractive. Of course when discussing males' perceptions of other males as physically attractive, another line of thought is plausible. Societal encouragement and support of "homosexism" defined as "sexism between individuals of the same sex" (Lehne, 1976) may inhibit the influence of physical attractiveness in male–male social perception. Distinguishing between homophobia (which, to use Lehne's definition refers to "the irrational fears or intolerance of homosexuality") and homosexism, I am referring to the tendencies in many males to inhibit certain feelings and behaviors toward other males. However, such inhibiting tendencies often do have their sources in male homophobia. For example, many heterosexual men seem to avoid looking at each other in face-to-face interaction. This tendency in heterosexual men (especially White men, since many Black men do not exhibit this tendency, as we imply in later chapters) is manifested by the limited eye-contact they give each other in social interaction. Heterosexual males frequently, in face-to-face interaction with other males, focus their eyes upward, to the side, downward and anywhere except on the other male stimulus person(s). Fear of being labeled "homosexual" probably contributes to male avoidance and/or nonrecognition of the physical attributes of other males. However, it is also likely that many males have another "fear" which encourages male avoidance of other males' physical attributes and which stems from homosexism. It is the fear many males may have that *they will recognize in other males physical attributes superior to their own.*

To pursue this line of thought further, it is plausible that homosexism alone intervenes in males' perceptions of other males and lessens the effect of the "physical attractiveness" variable. If most males for a lengthy time are required to adhere to strict regulations regarding the masculine role, then this includes adhering to such role expectations as competitiveness, individualism, aggressiveness, and winning. These role expectations can be thought of as sources of homosexism in American males and would certainly operate against males perceiving other males as physically attractive. This is especially so in a society where physical beauty often results in innumerable social rewards. In a sense, for a male to recognize physical beauty in other males means to give his competitors an edge in a world where physical beauty counts heavily in many endeavors. If males tend to diminish the importance of physical beauty in other males, then how do males go about forming impressions of other males?

Most males are likely to categorize male stimulus persons immediately in terms of whether or not external cues of masculinity meet their own general expectations of how males look and behave. If a particular male expects male persons to be tough, aggressive, competitive, and so on, then in social interactions with a male stimulus person, males immediately look for cues which will validate or invalidate their expectations. This indicates that males perceive other males basically in terms of partial information—in terms of stereotypes. Interestingly, regardless of whether a particular male perceives another male as meeting his expectations of a man or as failing to meet his expectations, initial impression formation tends to be based only on these sparse cues. Additionally, those cues stemming from sex categorization have a halo effect which affects the formation of overall impressions of the stimulus male. For example, take the case of a man who deviates from the traditional male role by extending invitations to other males for emotional intimacy. This man, for many males, is likely to be perceived as highly suspect—"he may be alright but he seems homosexual." This is likely to occur even though subsequent information (e.g., the man shows no interest in sexual contact) invalidates the initial sex category-based stereotypes.

In sum, sex-role expectations affect males' perceptions of other males and have a halo effect on males' overall impressions of other males. Along with males' tendencies to perceive other males in terms of "masculine" traits described by Brannon (1976)—"The Big Wheel" (success, status,), "The Sturdy Oak" (toughness, confidence, independence), and "Give 'Em Hell" (aggressiveness, violence), his "No Sissy Stuff" factor contains a salient aspect of masculinity in the United States—the avoidance and/or denial of feminine aspects of self. While modern-day males may not have to meet all of the expectations associated with all four factors in fulfilling the male role (Brannon et al., 1981), I contend that most are unable to fulfil the male role in the eyes of many males if it is perceived that stimulus males have not established sufficient distance between themselves and femininity. The most salient factor in males' formation of impressions of other males is seen here as the extent to which stimulus males exhibit external cues consistent with males' expectations about the male sex-role. While subsequent information can alter male perceptions of stimulus males, the initial sex category-based information does tend to establish male impressions, and additional information about the male stimulus person is altered and becomes a part of earlier information. A common tendency among males exists, I feel, to perceive a "nice," "competent," "successful" man who has not established sufficient distance from femininity as "nice, competent, successful, but. . . . "

Male Impression Management: Manipulating the Perceptions of Other Males

We have seen how males control and manage the information revealed to females about themselves. In this section we will be concerned with males' controlling and managing the information they reveal to other males about themselves. While there is much evidence to support the idea that males engage in impression management when interacting with females, relatively little attention has been devoted to impression management in male–male social interaction. Yet it is likely that males try their hardest to control and manage impressions when they interact with other males. This is due to the possibility that while men seek validation of their masculinity from women, the ultimate validation of a male's masculinity comes from more "powerful" others—other males. Why? Because generally other males validate a crucial requirement for a particular male's masculinity—whether he has established sufficient distance from femininity.

As a result of males' concerns about other males validating this important aspect of their masculinity, males tend to give their most dramatic masculine "performances" in social situations where other males are present. Such "performances" can be seen in much male–male social interaction where men frequently exhibit competitively their mental and physical skills. The motivation behind these frequent exhibitions, in addition to male desires to compete and win male games, includes attempts by males to gain validation of their masculinity from other males.

Gaining validation of masculinity from other males usually means that a particular male who desires validation of his masculinity controls and manages the information he allows other males to have about himself. As stated earlier, males generally are thought to self-disclose much less than females and less intimately than females. This is a general belief, despite the fact that Maccoby and Jacklin's (1974) review of the literature on sex differences in self-disclosure revealed mixed findings. In fact, they concluded that men and women do not differ in self-disclosure. More recent studies such as the ones reported in this chapter also are mixed with some showing *sex* differences in self-disclosure and others showing strong relationships between *gender* and self-disclosure.

If males do tend toward minimum self-disclosure this would be consistent with our belief that many males are preoccupied with obtaining validation of their masculinity from others—especially other males. Since for any male some aspects of his "self" are likely to be perceived by other males as nonmasculine and/or feminine, it is logical to assume that he will tend toward minimum self-disclosure, especially in social situations with other males present. Findings from the Lombardo and Levine study mentioned earlier, however, indicate that sex-typed males (those males who should be somewhat concerned about managing and controlling information related to the self) report more disclosures and more intimate ones to *same-sex* friends, than do androgynous males. Overall, however, sex-typed males reported less disclosures and less intimate ones than did androgynous males. Androgynous males also, it should be recalled, self-disclosed equally to male and female friends.

The fact that sex-typed males disclosed more frequently and more intimately to same sex friends than to females or parents is interesting though and should be considered further. On the surface such a finding challenges our contention that because males value the opinions of other males about their masculinity, males tend to conceal aspects of themselves from other males. Do findings such as these from the Lombardo and Levine study suggest that our contention is in left field? *I think not* but before going further, let us digress for a moment.

Most of us have had the unpleasant opportunity to interact with persons who have been jilted in romances. In my experiences, my women friends have reacted to the loss of a loved one in qualitatively different ways than have my men friends. My women friends generally have seemed quite overtly emotional while discussing their losses. In contrast, my men friends who have discussed their lost loves with me generally have tended to establish distance between *themselves* and the faded romance situation. They typically have indicated the loss but attempted to make sure that I perceived that they were totally in control of their emotions and that I knew that they were resolved to get on with their lives. I believe that these are *not* atypical ways that men interact with other men on sensitive and intimate topics. Are men's feelings actually congruent with their behaviors when discussing with other men such sensitive and intimate subjects? No, but it is important to them that another man or other men perceive that their painful and/or sensitive self-disclosures are being handled by them in a "masculine" and "non-feminine" manner (no crying, no depression, in fact, little outward expression of emotions). Men may believe that for other men to perceive otherwise means for them to be perceived as "weak," "nonmasculine," and/or "feminine."

Returning to the topic of whether men tend to control and manage information about themselves that they give to other men, let us review findings from another recent self-disclosure study. Derlega, Durham, Gockel, and Scholis (1981) reported findings directly relevant to male self-disclosure to other males. They found that men tended to choose "masculine" content of topics for disclosure to their male friends but reduced their preference for "masculine" content of topics when disclosing to their female friends. Males also were less likely to choose "feminine" content of topics for disclosure than females. This tendency was even more apparent for males when the disclosure target was a male stranger. In discussing their findings specifically related to males, Derlega *et al.*, offer two interpretations consistent with our contention regarding male impression management when they interact with other males:

> Men may be very concerned about maintaining their masculine self-image. It may be threatening psychologically for them to be associated with traditionally feminine behaviors. The threat may derive from a concern about public ridicule or a violation of one's image as a 'male' . . .
>
> If men do not disclose personal information, other people cannot understand, predict or control their behavior. Men gain an advantage in reaching and maintaining positions of importance because they can keep their 'weaknesses' secret (pp. 444–445).

A final point on males' impression management in social interaction with other males deserves mention. Even when males engage in mixed-sex social interaction, they often do not reduce their efforts to manage impressions. When interacting with other males while in the company of females (friends, lovers, wives, etc.) males frequently exhibit extreme masculine behaviors while concealing their more "feminine" behaviors. In fact, other males frequently expect such behavior, and if a particular male fails to live up to such expectations, he may be castigated by other males for deviating from the "masculine" role Since most males are aware on some level of this role requirement, one motivating factor underlying much male behavior in mixed-sex social interaction is the manipulation of other males' perceptions.

The Implications of Male Perception for Ongoing Social Interaction

The precise nature of the relationship between perception and behavior is not known. Most social scientists agree, however, that a relationship between the two phenomena does exist. It is likely that perceptions affect behaviors and behaviors, in turn, affect perceptions—both are the essence of face-to-face interaction. If males tend to perceive that females expect them to be controlling in social situations, then, as we have seen, males are likely to exhibit controlling behaviors when interacting with females. Likewise, if some females tend to perceive that males expect them to be dependent in social situations, then those females are likely to exhibit dependent behaviors when interacting with males. Many of the problems in male–female relationships today, however, stem from the fact that both females and males perceive mixed messages coming from each other.

Many females in the United States complain that most males only pay lip-service to women's rights issues, and given the relatively stable underclass status of American women, they seem to be right on target. Numerous males, on the other hand, perceive that American women "really" do not desire equality, rather what they want is "choice." By "choice," these men mean a woman's choice to do precisely *what* she wants to do, *when* she wants to do it, and *how* she wants to do it! Most males find this unacceptable, and feel that this is not equality but rather *superiority*. Perhaps such perceptions are to be expected in a society undergoing some sex-roles transition. With expectations changing and being somewhat uncertain, a mild type of *anomie* probably exists.

Overall, however, male sex-role perceptions do not seem to have been modified as drastically as some believe that they should have. Males still hold certain kinds of expectations about females and many persist in perceiving females in sexist ways. Just perceiving women in sexist ways often influences women to behave in ways that conform to widespread sexist perceptions which are inimical to women's best interests. Efforts by the clothing industry to influence upwardly-mobile females to adopt more "masculine" dress is but one example of attempts made to influence women to accommodate to the expectations and perceptions of males *via* the subordination of "femininity." If males *perceive* that female executives become more professional when dressed in tailored clothing then female executives who dress in tailored clothing probably do become more professional because males interact with them in a more professional manner (self-fulfilling prophecy). Of course a similar process operates in male–male social interaction. If I perceive that other males are competitive in social interaction, then they probably are, since my communication strategy with them is likely to be based on perceived competition.

On a more general level, male social perception in the United States plays a powerful role in maintaining male dominance. It affects male–female social interaction and male–male social interaction. More important, however, is the fact that unless men begin to understand their worlds and think about their worlds less along strict gender lines, sex-role equality will remain a part of the distant future. Ironically, this will mean that males will be imprisoned for some time—locked within their own perceptions of the world.

CHAPTER 5

Male Social Roles

There is something rather special about a statement constructed by a group of men at the Berkeley Men's Center several years ago. This group of men felt that they wanted to become "human" and in essence, wanted freedom from what they perceived to be a highly restrictive sex-role in America. Among other things, these men said:

> We no longer want to feel the need to perform sexually, socially, or in any way live up to an imposed male role . . . we want to relate to both men and women in more human ways—with warmth, sensitivity, emotion, and honesty . . . we want to be equal with women and to end destructive competitive relationships with men (Pleck and Sawyer, 1974, pp. 173–174).

The significance of this statement, in addition to its contents, lies in the fact that a few modern-day men, over a decade ago, had raised their levels of consciousness regarding male sex-role obligations and expectations. In addition, they were brave enough to voice their resistance to a society whose norms imposed upon them specific obligations and expectations without due regard for individual differences among males. It would be misleading to say that the statement above has altered male sex-role obligations and expectations in the United States. Certainly the Women's Movement has been extremely influential in regard to male sex-role changes. Also playing significant roles in the modification of the male sex-role were the Civil Rights Movement and the anti-Vietnam War movement. Yet, I believe that these social movements and others were conditional variables related to male sex-role changes rather than direct independent ones. Men, themselves, have had to change. Some undoubtedly will question whether significant changes have occurred in the male sex-role. However, few can quarrel with the fact that thousands of men in America have begun to question, as did the Berkeley Men's Center, norms surrounding the male sex-role which indicate how males are to perform as well as what expectations they are to hold regarding the actions and role performances of other males and females. Such norms, obligations and expectations related to the male sex role are the foci of this chapter.

Included in our examination of male social roles are four roles assumed by most males in America at some point in their lives: married male, father, male friend and male worker. These roles are explored with full recognition that some sex-role changes have occurred in our society within recent years. However, it is also kept in mind that in the early 1980's, the male sex-role remains highly dysfunctional for many men and others in our society. A great deal of attention has been devoted to the hazards associated with the male role since the Berkeley Men's Center issued it's famous statement. Yet, as I write this chapter, UPI News Service issues the following report:

> Las Vegas, Nevada—Korean Boxer Duk-koo Kim remained alive Sunday only with the aid of a life support system after suffering a cerebral hemorrhage during a World Boxing Association lightweight championship fight Saturday against Ray Mancini.... "I am very saddened and very sorry," Mancini said Sunday. "I'll keep praying, hoping I'll get some answers to some of the questions I have been having the last couple of days . . ." Kim died November 19, 1982.

It does not take an in-depth analysis into present-day society to realize that the machismo syndrome is alive and well in the 1980's—that violence and destructive competition remain integral features of masculinity in America.

It is acknowledged that prescriptive roles for males in the United States have undergone some changes in recent years. Latitudes of masculinity have been broadened somewhat and specific expectations for many males, in a few instances, *do* take into account their competencies and characteristics (Perlman and Cozby, 1982). For example, some men have assumed homemaker roles, and, while this may have challenged social convention in the early 1970's, many more people have begun to feel comfortable with this "break from that traditional bastion of male identity, the nine-to-five job" (Holcomb, 1982). On the other hand, certain societal changes have inhibited alteration in the male role. We have already alluded to the inhibiting effect that the fundamentalist religious movement in our society is having on sex-role change. In addition, economic woes plaguing our society in the first years of this decade also may be having a negative effect on changes in sex-roles.

Aside from the fact that difficult economic times generally have tended to divert attention away from all kinds of societal inequalities (e.g., race, ethnic, sex), it also seems to have accentuated some of the more dysfunctional aspects of "masculinity." Male competition, aggression, and violence have all increased as life-sustaining resources have become more limited. Social-service agencies report increases in child abuse, wife abuse, homicides, and general male-influenced societal disorganization. Such reports typically explain these societal anomalies by saying that they are the result of the inability of many men to assume the traditional "breadwinner" role for their families. Such explanations, however, rarely explore why conditions beyond the control of individual males lead them to engage in acts destructive to others and themselves. Why have those more negative "masculine" traits surfaced increasingly in the face of economic trouble? One plausible reason for the societal dilemma is that it is inherent in the male sex-role, and may be just as American as apple pie, Chicano men, Native American men, and Black men. Our society teaches men to adhere to the "breadwinner" role. Men are supposed to hold certain attitudes, think in a particular way and above all, *perform* according to "manly" role prescriptions. When opportunities for "appropriate" "masculine" role performance are not available to millions of men (unemployment figures for June 1983 show 10,590,000 out of work) then inappropriate "masculine" role performances are likely to increase. Violence and aggression are just as much a part of the male sex-role as are competitiveness, rational thinking, and the work ethic. If men are blocked in their efforts to exhibit the latter three traits in order to "show" that they are men, then it is quite likely that there will be increased tendencies to exhibit the former traits. Succinctly, it is the male sex-role which produces the destructive and dysfunctional human beings so prevalent in American society today.

It is said that "a society reveals its concepts of gender through the social roles it assigns to each sex" (Popenoe, 1983, p. 170). If this is so, then some portion of America's conception of masculinity should become apparent as we explore the expectations and behaviors associated with the male sex. The first set of expectations and behaviors to be examined is related to males in marriage.

Men in Marriage

According to the United States Census Bureau, the percentage of married males decreased between 1970 and 1981. In 1970, approximately 64% (44,582,532) of all males (69,349,000) fifteen years and older were married with wife present while in March, 1981, only 60% (49,896,000) of the male population as defined (85,684,000) were married with wife present. During this same period, there was an increase in the percentage of single males from 26% in 1970 to 29% in 1981. A more detailed report of the marital status of males for 1970 and 1981 is shown in Table 6.

At a glance, one can discern relatively major differences between the time periods in three categories: married males-wife present ($-.04$), divorced males ($+.02$) and single males ($+.03$). Despite the changes that have occurred in the marital status of males in the United States during the last decade, the sheer number of married men in the United States today indicates that the male role in marriage remains a significant one for discussion. In other words, a majority of marriageable men in the United States still are willing to enter into marital relationships. Given this fact, what is the nature of the role assumed by men in marriage? Has the male role in marriage changed? If so what is the source of change in males' marital roles? These questions as well as others are answered in the discussion below.

The Male Role in Marriage and Sources of Change

Linda Haas (1981) contends that marriage today seems to be based more on equality between spouses, less rigid sex-based divisions of labor and husbands no longer being "undisputed patriarchs." If this is so, then

Table 6
Marital Status for Men (Age 15+) in the United States – 1970, 1980[a]

Male Marital Status	Numbers	% of Total
1970		
All Males	69,349,060	100
Married Males-Wife Present	44,582,532	64
Married Males-Wife Absent	2,401,723	3
Widowed Males	2,128,481	3
Divorced Males	1,924,776	3
Single Males	18,315,159	26
1981		
All Males	82,949,000	100
Married Males-Wife Present	49,896,000	60
Married Males-Wife Absent	2,287,000	3
Widowed Males	1,949,000	2
Divorced Males	4,393,000	5
Single Males	24,424,000	29

[a]Sources: United States Census Bureau, *Detailed Characteristics U.S. Summary*, 1970, No. PC-D1, p. 640; United States Census Bureau, *Current Population Reports*, 1981, p. 20, No. 372: Table 6, p. 35–37.

men's roles in marriages have changed. Traditionally, married men were expected to assume (and many did) breadwinner, handyman, and major decisionmaker roles, while their wives assumed domestic, childcare and minor decisionmaker roles. The former roles were considered men's domain and the latter roles were assigned to women, with rather rigid lines of demarcation culturally drawn between the two spheres.

Current thinking on sex-roles in marriage is that recent changes in sex-roles within our society have resulted in modifications of both the male role and the female role in marriage. Many feel that marriages are no longer characterized by sex-role segregation. According to this line of thought, men and women are increasingly beginning to "share" roles in marriage. Factors thought to be responsible for this change in the division of labor in marriage include *cultural sex-role changes* and *women's increased labor-force participation*. The first factor has its source in society's acceptance of the value of self-fulfillment and self-realization for all human beings along with the growing influence of the Women's Movement (Yogev, 1982). The source of the second factor is related to women's desires for self-fulfillment and the recognition that the traditional woman's role is not enough for many women; in addition, it is also related to the realities of modern day economic times which dictate either an atypically high sole family income or a dual family income.

These factors have influenced modern day sex-roles in marriage but whether there has been significant or (some feel) sufficient change is another matter. Societal change can be a slow process especially when such change involves a society's basic values. The values underlying most people's expectations about men's behaviors in marriage constitute part of the ethos of our society, which indicates, I believe, the difficulty faced by those who call for change in married men's roles. Let us explore more closely the nature of the male role in marriage and its effects on the institution of marriage.

Until relatively recently, married men were expected to be *heads of households*. Such a definition of the male role in marriage surely was congruent with our society's value system which emphasized individual success in a competitive world. Men were expected to internalize such a role and to perform in accordance with its prescriptions. This meant that *men* were not expected to, nor did they (and many still do not) assume domestic and childcare responsibilities. Instead, men assumed occupational-provider-protector roles somewhat external to the familial system. "Expressive" tasks (e.g., home-centered jobs) were thought to be part of the woman's role in marriage and men were expected *not* to be able to perform in this sphere. For a man to perform "expressive" functions in marriage meant for many men (and women) in our society that he violated the role that he was expected to assume. As we will see, remnants of such expectations for men remain in our society at the present time.

Over a decade ago, Balswick and Peek (1971) alluded to the inconsistency inherent in society's socialization of males into masculinity. They pointed out that while society teaches males that to be "masculine" means to be inexpressive, the marital role is defined in terms of sharing, affection, companionship, and the like—all of which require communication and expressiveness. More recently, Balswick (1981), in discussing what he calls the "cowboy role" some men play in their relationships with women, describes the role as a "feeling, nonverbal role." He states that men who assume this role relate to women *via* nonverbal messages of emotion. From this perspective, marriage for some men becomes an institution that relieves *them* of expressive expectations and requires their wives to surmise that "he married me and this is proof that he loves me." According to Balswick, this reduces "the requirement for him to continually demonstrate affection and tenderness toward her" (p. 114). Balswick states further:

> If together long enough, most couples develop shorthand symbols, such as an arm around the shoulder, a certain look, or a pat on the derrière, through which they express certain emotions and desires. The symbols come to represent the emotions which the husband has but is unable or unwilling to verbally express (p. 114).

That men in marriages traditionally have not been expressive and have viewed expressiveness as a woman's trait, probably provides one explanation for research findings showing decreased marital satisfaction in dual-income families. Such findings, though less common today, were especially prevalent in the 1950s and 1960s. During this period the male role within marriage was based on the model of the nuclear, conjugal unit with the man as head of household and the woman as homemaker, child-caretaker and nurturer of the husband. Women's labor force participation was viewed by laymen and social scientists alike as threatening to marriage and the family. Blood (1963), Nye (1963), Mischel (1967), and Epstein, among others, found correlations between wives working outside of the home and such phenomena as family disruption, marital conflict and lesser marital satisfaction. Many persons still hold this view regarding the effects of wives working on marriage and the family (e.g., the moral majority, other fundamentalist religious groups, anti-ERA groups, etc.). Social scientists, however, have questioned the applicability of these earlier research findings to marriage and the family today because of methodological deficiencies and more importantly, the fact that *the nuclear family is no longer the statistical mode* (Yogev, 1982).

Divorced parents, reconstituted families, dual-worker families, role-sharing families and other variant family forms have increased in the United States. This has affected the expectations held by men and women regarding their roles in marriage and commensurately, their sources of satisfaction within marital units. The issues are complex, however, and the effects of these changes on the male role also are complex, as we will see.

A Contemporary View of Men in Marriage

Several recent investigations of dual-career families (e.g., Campbell, Converse and Rodgers, 1976; Gross and Arvey, 1977; Staines, Pleck, Shepard, and O'Conner, 1978) do not find significant differences in marital satisfaction between dual-careers and one-career couples. Others (e.g., Burke and Weir, 1976; Bahr and Day, 1978) have found that marital satisfaction was affected when wives worked. Burke and Weir found that husbands were less satisfied; and Bahr and Day reported slightly higher satisfaction for couples when wives did not work. Such studies, which indicate a lack of clarity about the issue of wives working and marital satisfaction, have implications for the male role in marriage today. One line of thought is that husbands' marital satisfaction when wives are working is related to whether they are in the situation which they prefer (e.g., do they prefer a conventional marriage or a more contemporary marriage?) (Yogev, 1982). Obviously, if male preference is considered to be a legitimate determinant of marital satisfaction in dual-career marriages, the pattern of male dominance in such marriages remains. Thus, while more men may be willing to "allow" their wives to work, their wives engage in this role from a position of psychological subordinance rather than psychological equality.

Studies of family roles in the late 1970s offer some support for the contention that men are continuing patterns of dominance in marriage. The concept "role overload," for example, is one which applies mainly to working women who experience stress because while they are "allowed" to work by their husbands, they also must shoulder more than their responsibility in the home. Hunt and Hunt's (1978) contention that inadequate support systems which they feel characterize dual-career families may be inimical to both men's and women's careers does not help the matter. The point is, I contend, men have not altered their marital roles enough. Findings from several studies support this contention. Pleck (1978), Weingarten (1978) and Bryson, Bryson, and Johnson (1978) all report findings from studies which challenge ideas of role sharing, equalitarianism and the like in modern marriage. Pleck, for example, found that sex-role segregation is very much a part of married life and that husbands do not increase the amount of time they participate in family tasks when their wives work. Moreover, the men in Pleck's study were concerned about maintaining superiority over their wives with respect to earnings, prestige, psychological commitment to the job, and so on. Pleck's findings were consistent with those of Bryson, Bryson and Johnson (1978) who found that working women still had primary responsibility for childcare.

Findings from Weingarten's (1978) study further supports my belief that caution must be exercised when discussing changes which have occurred in men's marital roles. Weingarten found that while some dual-career couples may negotiate a division of labor, the result always tended to favor men. The wife is expected to make up (in terms of family tasks) for the time she spends working while the husband obtains the freedom to perform only those family-centered tasks that do not threaten his masculinity.

What all of this really means is that in many cases the *women's role* in marriage has been expanded; it includes paid employment outside of the home as well as primary responsibility for maintaining the home. Many men in marriage, on the other hand, with relatively minor adjustments, continue acting out the traditional male role with both its functional and dysfunctional consequences.

If the male role in marriage today remains essentially the same as it was ten or more years ago, then what about so-called changes in male parenting? Are there significant male changes in this domain? In order to answer these and other questions, let us examine males' participation in parenting.

Males as Parents

"Mother's baby and father's maybe ..." is the underlying theme that seems to characterize many males' social roles as parents in the United States. Supported by popular, religious and scientific perspectives on childrearing, male participation in parenting is at best minimal in the vast majority of households in America. This is so despite what some consider to be revolutionary changes in sex-roles in our society (of course, as we have discussed, many of these changes have been minor) within the last decade or so. In fact, given that in 1980 females headed 89% of all households with children under 18, excluding married couples (as reported in chapter one); and, that women and children are joining the ranks of the poverty-stricken in staggering numbers, the male-parent social role may be becoming even more minimal. Certainly it is to be recognized that some men have become more active in parenting; their numbers, however, remain relatively small compared with those male parents who still are only minimally involved in the parenting role. Additionally, recent conservative trends in the United States supporting the role of the female as child-rearer and the role of the male as bread-winner may operate against increased male parenting. Margaret Polat-nick's (1973–1974) analysis of minimal male involvement in parenting is instructive here.

Why Men Don't Rear Children

Polatnik's analysis rests in social power and she poses the idea that males gain a power advantage by not participating in the childrearing process. She begins her analysis with a discussion of biological beliefs about the childrearing process. Polatnik argues that sociological and psychological literature is replete with assumptions about the "naturalness" of women as childrearers. While women are commonly believed to be biologically tied to parenting, no such elemental biological connection between men and childrearing is thought to exist—mothers have "maternal instincts" but fathers do not have "paternal instincts." Even language is said to con-note that women are meant to rear children as when "mothering" means childrearing and "childrearing function" is referred to as maternal care. According to Polatnik this implies that only females can perform child-care social roles. In other words, the constant association of females with childrearing not only is descriptive (that is the way it is) it is also pre-scriptive (that is the way it should be). Moreover, the fact that women *have* children and can *feed* them in no way suggests objectively that they must assume the primary responsibility for rearing them . . . unless we go one step further and state that as a result of biology, women are pre-disposed toward child care (this is the line of thought favored by many, scientific-minded people as well as laymen). Discounting such biologi-cal-determinant models, Polatnick proposes a social power advantage model to explain the male parent social role.

　　Polatnick feels that men traditionally have participated only mini-mally in the childrearing process because "they don't want to rear chil-dren." Why? Simply because of the undesirability associated with the childrearing social role. Polatnick's position is that there are two general categories of the undesirability of childrearing. They are (1) the *advan-tages* associated with *avoiding* childrearing responsibility; and (2) the dis-advantages related to *assuming* childrearing responsibility. Under the first category, men are said to gain distinct advantages in earning money, achieving social status and gaining social power. As a result, it is to men's advantage to define childrearing as lying within the domain of women. Moreover, when men define childrearing as the woman's domain, this frees them to pursue achievement, responsibility and authority and the prestige and power that accompany such pursuits, all of which are translated into power within the home. "Fathers may default from the daily childrearing routines but . . . they still tend to wield the ultimate force and the ultimate decisionmaking power" (Polatnick, p. 224). This, in turn, results in maintenance of the status-quo where males have power and females are powerless, since male offspring learn that the proper role of paternity for a male is not to be too actively involved in childrearing because it limits one's achievement activities. After all, men *should assume* the primary breadwinning role.

Polatnick also points out that childrearing often involves parental subordination of personal objectives and putting other's needs ahead of one's own because of the demands of the role. Women as childrearers not only are expected to meet the demands of fathers and children but they also are expected to meet the demands of households—thus, men gain a double benefit "from the emotional indenture of women" (p. 228). Interestingly, this double benefit does not seem to diminish in times of social–economic crises when many women have to assume jobs outside of the home. In such instances, many women are encouraged by society to feel that their primary obligation is to manage home . . . and to *help* in breadwinning matters. Except in relatively few cases do such women feel that they have as much freedom from childrearing responsibilities as do men. Most women learn in America that the ultimate responsibility for rearing children is theirs.

As provocative as Polatnick's analysis is, minor changes which have occurred in the male parenting role have been neglected. In order to examine these changes, let us consider briefly the male parent role "some time ago," "in the recent past," and "now."

Men as Fathers Some Time Ago

The role of men as parents has been seen traditionally as one of providing for the family without direct involvement in child care. Polatnick's analysis, discussed earlier, handled the father role mostly from this traditional perspective. While men are seen as important to children as symbols of power and authority, they have little to do with the actual parenting of children (Fein, 1978, p. 123). From a traditional perspective, *fathers are breadwinners and mothers are childrearers.* Fathers generally are nonnurturant, nonexpressive and instrumental and in a sense, invisible parents—concerned primarily with interests external to the childrearing function.

The traditional perspective on male parenting predominated popular and academic discussions of the father role during the 1940s and 1950s. Fein, in reflecting on the traditional conceptions of males as parents, reports that traditional views of the father role reflected the social ideals and realities of the 1940s and 1950s. By and large, women during this period were not to be found in the labor force and men were to be found involved in interests external to the family. The 1960s, however, ushered in new lines of thought regarding the father role. Fathers were seen as important for the psychosocial development of children. This led many social scientists to begin to explore and examine the father role within the context of the father's participation in specific areas of child development. Let us briefy review these changes in the father role.

Men as Fathers in the Recent Past

Fein implies that the 1960s now led the period during which the modern perspective on male parenting began to emerge. Fathers were seen as directly influencing child development in three major areas: (1) the achievement of a socially appropriate sex-role identity; (2) academic performance; and (3) moral development. Children, especially boys, were thought to benefit from the presence of fathers in the area of "appropriate" sex-role identity establishment. In addition, academic achievement and positive social behavior were thought to be related to the father's presence in the home. Much of the research conducted by social scientists during the period centered on comparisons between father-present and father-absent families. As might be expected, researchers claimed that children (especially boys) from father-absent families were more likely to experience sex-role identity problems, academic failure and to engage in juvenile delinquency than children who were reared in father-present homes. Herzog and Saudia (1974), as Fein points out, in a review of the literature centered on such arguments, found that the effects of father absence on children's performances in school and proclivities for delinquency seemed slight; and, that there was a paucity of research support for the idea that children reared in father-absent homes were more likely to experience sex-role identity problems than those reared in father-present homes.

A major problem with studies of men as parents in the recent past is that the studies often dealt with the *consequences* of fathering rather than *fathering behavior* itself (Fein, p. 127). This means that much of what was viewed as men's roles as fathers actually was based on stereotypes and in many instances was speculation. The tendency for many to view the male parent role speculatively has continued. However, more recent studies have begun to shed light on actual male parenting behavior. We will be concerned with some of these studies as we examine the role of men as parents now.

Men as Fathers Now

In this section we deal with an emerging perspective of men as active participants in the childrearing process. Present day studies of fathering enable us to get a glimpse of men's experiences prior to the births of their children, the experiences of men immediately after the births of their children; and fathering in nontraditional social contexts (e.g., Wapner, 1976, Reiber, 1976; Hetherington, Cox, and Cox, 1976; Parke and O'Leary, 1976). Men are found to be active in caring for their infant children and some researchers have suggested that the early contact many modern day fathers have with their children may encourage the development of strong father–child bonds.

With more research being devoted to the relationship between men and their children, additional factors have been found to be related to male child-care activities. Factors such as sex-role orientation, education, mate's work-role pattern, sex of child, etc., all seem to influence the fathering role. While fathers historically have been seen as only minimally involved in childrearing, current research shows that "under certain conditions, in fact, father–child involvements exceed child-related activities performed by mothers" (Booth and Edwards, 1980).

The fact that many men are actively involved in childrearing activities does not obviate the fact that childrearing still is regarded by many as a woman's duty. Even as research studies show increased childrearing activities by males, women still dominate parent–child interaction and remain the primary childrearers. It would be easy to say that remnants from the traditional view of father's parental roles are responsible for greater female involvement in childrearing activities. In quite a few instances this may be true, but in some other instances emerging experimental findings offer an alternative explanation of greater female involvement in child-care-rearing activities. Robinson, Yerby, Fieweger and Somerick (1977) and Pleck (1978) report that women often tend *not* to express a desire for increased levels of participation by men in family related activities. Congruent with the works of Robinson, *et al.* and Pleck are the more recent findings by Baruch and Barnett (1981) that men who did more independent and joint childcare had wives who were less satisfied in their roles than the wives of men who did less independent and joint childcare. Baruch and Barnett suggest the possibility that those women who are more dissatisfied in their roles as mothers and spouses press their husbands for greater family involvement. Just as plausible, however, is the possibility that many women feel threatened by increased male participation in childcare and childrearing-related activities. It may be the case, then, that male participation in childcare activities to a certain point is perceived positively by women, but beyond that point is perceived negatively by women because of perceived loss of power in the expressive domain.

Among factors related to increased male participation in childrearing/childcare are sex of child, authority structure within the family, maternal work patterns and paternal sex-role expectations. Baruch and Barnett in their study found a significant positive relationship between parental nontraditional sex-role expectations and independent participation of fathers in childcare tasks. Independent father participation in childcare activities also was significantly related positively to the extent of wives' labor-force participation. Just as important is Baruch and Barnett's finding that independent participation of fathers in childcare activities seems to be negatively associated with father's self-perception of stereotypical masculinity. Is it the case that women who are likely to enter the labor force have husbands who are willing to participate independently in childcare activities or vice-versa? What about the direction of the relationship between fathers' self-perceptions of masculinity and father participation in childcare activities? Do fathers who participate more experience a reduction in self-stereotyping, or does reduced self-stereotyping on the part of fathers lead to their greater participation in childcare activities?

Booth and Edwards' findings on male participation in childcare activities are just as intriguing. For example, they found in their study of a stratified probability sample of Toronto families (462 parents from 13 census tracts) that, controlling for the amount of time available to spend with children, father involvement with children equalled mother involvement with children. Moreover, as mentioned earlier, father involvement with children exceeded mother involvement with children in Booth and Edward's study when the children were all girls, numbered fewer than three, and when one parent dominated the marital dyad. On the last point it does not seem to matter whether the authority structure is matriarchal or patriarchal. In other words, husband-wife egalitarianism does not appear to be a necessary condition for greater involvement of fathers in childcare activities. In fact, much of what is "known" about male participation in childrearing and childcare activities seems to be in need of revision given the empirical results emerging under closer scrutiny of the father-role.

Fathers' Influence on Children's Behaviors

That fathers play important roles in child development has been supported by empirical evidence from increasing numbers of studies devoted to fathering since the 1960s. However, as implied earlier, most studies of the fathering phenomenon have been indirect: researchers have attended to the impact of father influence on child development by comparing children's outcomes in father-present and father-absent families. Recent studies of this type show differential sex effects of father absence on child development. For example, Santrock's (1977) study of male youth in father-absent families indicate that boys who lose their fathers before the age of 6 tend to be more aggressive while boys who lose their fathers after age 6 seem more disobedient. Santrock's findings were consistent with Biller's conclusions from a review of the father-absence literature, but inconsistent with the conclusions drawn by Herzog and Saudia from their review of the father-absence literature. Generally, however, many researchers (e.g., Bannon and Southern, 1980) seem to accept the idea that father absence has an inimical effect on male youth personality development.

The effects of father absence on female youth personality development seems even less convincing and was the point of departure for a study by Bannon and Southern on the effects of father absence on adult women. Bannon and Southern controlled for three factors they felt were important in their study of father-absent women. The three factors were (1) cause of paternal absence (divorce or death), (2) age of women at loss of father, and (3) presence of an older male sibling. Reviewing the father-absence literature, Bannon and Southern contended that (1) paternal divorce and death may elicit different responses in children and thus different child-developmental problems; (2) many problems confronting father-absent females might emerge only in the heterosexual realm and therefore, when females began to interact with males; and (3) the presence of an older brother may lessen the effects of father absence in females. Using this line of thought, Bannon and Southern constructed three hypotheses indicating that father-absent women would differ significantly from father-present women in terms of adult self-concept; that father-absent women would relate to men differently than father-present women; and, that father-absent (divorce as the cause) women with older male siblings would be more similar to father-present women than to father-absent-divorce women with no older brothers on "self-concept" and "relating to men" measures. Bannon and Southern reported that "in regard to most aspects of self-concept, father absence in childhood does not appear to be associated with the self-concept of females as adults" (p. 80). Father-absent-divorce women obtained higher self-concept scores in the heterosexual realm than father-absent-divorce women with older brothers or father-present women. Father-absent-death women obtained the next highest score, leading Bannon and Southern to speculate that father-absent women with no male to rely on look within their peer groups for male reinforcement, support, and measures of self-validation. On the other hand, lower social self-scores showed that father-absent-divorce women with older male siblings were significantly different from father-absent-divorce women with no older male siblings and similar to father-present women. This result, according to Bannon and Southern, was possibly due to a decreased need to rely on extrafamilial sources for fulfilling interpersonal needs. Bannon and Southern did find that father-present women differed from father-absent women on the nurturance scale with father-present women being more nurturant than any of the other groups. The authors suggested that this finding lends support to the idea that fathers may influence their daughters' sex-role development. Bannon and Southern reason that fathers may tend to accentuate nurturance by reinforcing the trait in their daughters and/or by being reciprocal role models for their daughters. Succinctly, Bannon and Southern found that father absence *did not* adversely affect the self-concept of women and appeared to be related only to nurturance responses with age-peer men.

Perhaps as we learn more about the roles of males in parenting, the influence of fathering on child development will become less ambiguous. That there is a need for less ambiguity is apparent as another study shows. Slevin and Balswick's (1980) study of children's perceptions of parental expressiveness reveals that while fathers may have increased their participation in childrearing, images of them as parents leave much to be desired. In their study of 1245 high school students, Slevin and Balswick found that many stereotypes about fathers persist in the minds of children. Both sons and daughters perceive significant sex differences in parental expressiveness. Mothers were seen as more expressive of the emotion "love" than fathers, leading the authors to conclude that mothers carried the heavier burden of expressive behavior within families while fathers were relegated "to the onus of the physical punishment of children" (p. 298). Slevin and Balswick observe that when children differentially perceive their parents in the above manner, this has serious implications for family interaction and child development. Male children seem not to have an expressive same-sex model which may result in a self-fulfilling-prophecy pattern of behavior for males. Thus, males may act in accordance with definitions and perceptions of the male role . . . and the beat goes on . . . .

Empirical evidence shows that more males are taking an active role in parenting today than in past years. Women's increased labor force participation, the influence of the Women's Movement and men's consciousness-raising groups all are factors related to increased paternal parenting. Not only are more men engaging in shared parenting but a few divorced men have obtained custody of their children and have the primary responsibility of caring for them. Some others who do not have custody of their children are claiming their rights to parenthood through individual initiative and/or organizations (e.g., Fathers for Equal Justice) which have emerged to assist divorced men in their parenting efforts. Yet, by and large, children are still being reared primarily by women. This is so despite the estimate that more than half of all mothers with school-age children are employed outside of the home and more than one-third of mothers with children under three years of age work outside the home (Nordheimer, 1977). Findings discussed earlier in this chapter indicated that men do not greatly increase their involvement in home-centered tasks when their wives work. The obvious implication is that women are extending their roles in marriage and parenting. A recent study of the impact of maternal employment on children's perception (Rosenthal and Hanson, 1981, p. 598), revealed that "maternal employment has no significant effect on young adolescents' personal, educational or vocational development."

Given the above findings it is no wonder that many working women experience stress and role conflict. Early indications are that women have expanded their role within the family (e.g., working outside of the home, nurturing their children, and making sure they do not suffer emotionally) while men generally have made only minor adjustments in their role, and this includes the parenting aspect of the male role. This is unfortunate because current research shows that fathers who engage in active parenting can influence their children in significant ways. For example, Ihinger-Tallman (1982), using a simulated career game with parents and their children, found that sons with a high attainment value were more likely to solicit advice from their fathers and to have fathers who challenged their decisions but who did not either dominate them or defer to them. In other words, father–son socialization can be instrumental in fostering male youth attainment values. This is only one example of the ways in which male parenting can impact children. Perhaps just as imprtant, however, are the benefits which accrue to the entire family (whether intact or not intact) from paternal involvement in childrearing. Overall modification in the male sex-role will, I hope, mean even greater change in American males and more pronounced changes in the childrearing practices of men.

There is another line of thought, however, which states basically that modification in the male sex-role probably will occur more rapidly if women modify their rearing of males. According to Judith Arcana (1983), women have a major role to play in modifying the male sex-role. She feels that women, the primary childrearers of males, must confront and examine the pattern of male childrearing which produces non-nurturant, emotionally irresponsible, highly competitive, and materially oriented males who frequently verbally and physically abuse women and children. Arcana states:

> Mothers need to understand that we are creating and nurturing the agents of our own oppression; once we make them, their education as men in this misogynist society will pull them from our arms, set them above us, and make them the source of our degradation (p. 3).

Given the above comments, it is probably safe to say that before male childrearing patterns can change to any great degree, it may be necessary for men to cease their "masculine" behavior with other adults. It is indeed possible that their ways of interacting with adults bleed over into their relationships with their children. How men socially relate to other adults is the topic of our next section.

Men's Friends

In our discussion of male friendships during the childhood years, we noted that male youth generally have male friends and these friendships revolve around male youth organized or unorganized sports activities. Male youth friendships generally are diffuse and based on competitiveness, aggressiveness, dominance, and the like. It is quite common among male youth for the choice of friends and interaction with friends to be based on the dominant community sport of the season. For example, during baseball season a young male's friends are likely to be other young males on his baseball team. During football season, his friends are likely to come from his football team. In general, male youths' friends change as the sports seasons change. Not infrequently, then, male youth tend to form instrumental friendships, rather than ones based on emotional expressiveness. This pattern of friendship-formation for males continues into adolescence and adulthood, and actually leads to one of two patterns of friendship formation in male adulthood: diffuse and instrumental male friendships; or an absence of male friendships and diffuse instrumental female friendships.

There are several reasons why males tend to form diffuse and instrumental friendships with other males rather than emotionally expressive ones. The reasons lie in male sex-role socialization and include socialized competitiveness, dominance, and males' learned fears of emotional intimacy with other males. Early male youth friendships, as we have seen, are based on competitiveness, dominance, aggressiveness, and the like because these traits are ones male youth must learn if they are to become "men". These traits also are inimical to emotionally expressive friendships. Emotionally expressive friendships thrive on cooperation, sharing, and nurturant behaviors. The adult male who is "appropriately" socialized into masculinity is rendered incapable of forming close ties with other males. It is not unlikely that heterosexual males who enter into friendships constantly ask themselves "to be a friend, or not to be?" Now most men *are* aware of the fact that friends *should be* emotionally expressive with each other but they also are aware of the restriction that society imposes upon male friendships. Moreover, how does one reconcile intimate self-disclosing and being emotionally expressive with one's competitors who may attempt to use this in future competitive male games?

Yet, many males do, on the surface, appear to establish "friendships." Such friendships, though, seem to lack the spontaneity, warmth, and emotional closeness that many feel characterize the concept "friend." Just as male youth do, male adults form instrumental and diffuse friendships with other males. In addition, many adult males form friendships with other males through their female mate's friendships with *their* female friends. The results of such friendships maintain the emotional inexpressiveness of males and female dominance over males in terms of expressive power—*men continue to express their emotions vicariously through women in such situations and women continue to feel secure in their dependence.* Support for this contention derives from the extreme discomfort some women experience when their male mates attempt to establish friendships with males external to their relationship (e.g., other "unattached" males). Many women perceive such relationships as threatening and quite often the male acquieses and "returns to the fold." Of course this means that those males give up their chances to establish emotional intimacy with other males.

Why do men give up emotional intimacy with other men so easily? The answer to this question lies in males' socialized and deeply rooted feelings that men should not be emotionally close to other men—that somehow their masculinity is diminished if they allow themselves to become emotionally attached to other men. Lewis's (1978) "Emotional Intimacy Among Men" sheds light on the point being made here.

Competition, homophobia, an aversion to vulnerability and "closeness" are barriers to emotional intimacy among men according to Lewis. Competition, as mentioned earlier, makes it extremely difficult for men to be affectionate toward each other. Lewis echoes this point when he says that "it is hard to reach out affectionately to other males beyond a superficial level if one views all males as competitors in life" (p. 114). Examining two other barriers to emotional intimacy among men, Lewis suggests that the fear men have in our culture that their sexual identities will be colored "gay" prevents many men from establishing intimate relations with other men. This fear presumably derives from cultural norms against homosexuality; and, in addition, a failure by many to distinguish between sensuality and sexuality. Thirdly, Lewis notes that many persons buy into the male stereotype of males being stoic and unemotional. As a result, men are likely to feel that in order to present a masculine identity they must not reveal their weaknesses. Often this means that males maintain "fronts" of toughness, confidence, independence and the like. Moreover, as discussed in Chapter 4, males in America are likely to be rather "closed" regarding intimate details of their lives.

Given Lewis' comments as well as what we already know about men's socialization, men's selves, men's social perceptions, etc., it is probably apparent why men give up so easily emotional intimacy with other men. *Men do not really value other men's friendships.* The ability to restrict emotional intimacy with other men undoubtedly has implications for males' relationships with others. Often times it is difficult to keep the dysfunctions associated with barriers to emotional intimacy between men from bleeding over into relationships with women and children. If men learn the "ten commandments of manhood" as Dick Vittitow (1981, p. 193) contends, it is likely that they will be invoked in a wide variety of situations. The commandments are:

1. Thou shalt not be weak, nor have a weak God before thou.
2. Thou shalt not fail thyself, nor "fail" as thy father before thee.
3. Thou shalt not keep holy any day that denies thy work.
4. Thou shalt not love in ways that are intimate and sharing.
5. Thou shalt not cry, complain, or feel lonely.
6. Thou shalt not commit public anger.
7. Thou shalt not be uncertain or ambivalent.
8. Thou shalt not be dependent.
9. Thou shalt not acknowledge thy depth or thy limitations.
10. Thou shalt do unto other men before they do unto you.

Invoking such commandments in friendships render the relationships nonintimate, unemotional and in all likelihood, unfulfilling from
a human perspective. But the times are changing—increasing numbers
of men are rejecting the above commandments. Some men, according to
Vittitow, are beginning to *acknowledge* the male situation, explore the
effects of the commandments on their lives and to experience an intimacy with self. All of this, it is suggested, will lead to a greater capacity
for men to experience others genuinely and intimately. Additionally,
men no longer will be relegated to a "locker-room boy" role with men
which is dependent upon the existence of a "masculine subculture,"
where having established his masculinity, a male feels "free" to be
"expressive" without having his masculinity questioned (Balswick, 117).
Not only will men benefit from the changes in men's roles, but women
as friends also will benefit as well as our society in general. One area in
society which could benefit from changes in the male sex-role is the institution of work as discussed below.

Men at Work

William Liss-Levinson (1981) remarks in his article, "Men Without Playfulness," that "work may be the area in which it is most difficult for a
male to be playful in our society" (p. 24). One reason for this is that society conceptualizes work and play as opposite poles on a continuum.
Males, if they are to be "masculine" in America, must internalize the
work ethic and incorporate it in their work-role performances. This alone
does not negate playfulness but other aspects of internalization and
incorporation of the work ethic do. For example, males also are expected
to be "successful" and this goes beyond simply internalizing and acting
upon the work ethic. To be successful in America often requires males to
be "winners" in competitive work games with other men. Therefore, little time can be devoted to play in work situations since "winning" also
implies "masculinity" and a masculine identity plays a crucial role in
most males' feelings of self-esteem, self-worth, self-concept and so on.

What do men win in competitive work games? They certainly do not
win satisfaction in their jobs as Daniel Yankelovich (1974) implied when
he estimated that about 80% of the males in our society experience overall job dissatisfaction. However, males (usually White males) do win
something: *they win the opportunity to accept gracefully their role as provider
for others, feelings of personal sacrifice, and the resultant enhanced image of their
own masculinity.*

Not all social scientists would agree that explanations for men's work behaviors lie in differential sex-role socialization. Instead, it is argued, male work attitudes and behaviors are functions of location in organizational structures (e.g., Kanter, 1976). This structural perspective attributes male work behaviors (and female work behaviors) to such factors as the opportunity structure, the power structure, and the sex-ratio. In making her case for a structural analysis of the work behavior of men and women, Kanter states:

> It becomes important to understand how women and men get distributed across structural position and how this differential distribution affects behavior—not how women differ from men.

One problem with the above statement is that men and women do not *get* distributed, they are *distributed,* and usually by men who "distribute" people in a particular way because they *are* men who enact the "masculine" role and different from those women who would enact a "feminine" role in distributing people. Explaining female behavior in work situations as different from men's behavior because females lack system-wide power diminishes the importance of sex differences but does not consider adequately the "halo" effect of sex on work behaviors in men and women. The effect, I feel, stems from *differences* between many men and women as a result of sex-role socialization.

That men and women generally behave differently in work situations is not surprising from a social-psychological perspective. Male youth socialization, with its emphasis on aggression, competition, and the like (as discussed in Chapter 2), prepares male youth for the adult male work role. Women generally have not been socialized to assume "masculinist" work roles in our society. Yet, some apparently do, and this challenges the assumption that sex differences are responsible for differences in the work behaviors of men and women. The assumption becomes even more suspect when one hears women charging other women with competitive, aggressive, and generally "masculinist" behavioral strategies. This leads some to conclude that *indeed,* hierarchical structures shape the behaviors of persons in the work situation. Such an explanation, I believe, *includes* the fact that upwardly mobile women often feel they *have* to assume "masculine" roles in work if they are to achieve any measure of "success," but *overlooked* the fact that some upwardly mobile women "identify with their captors."

Many women in work situations come to internalize precisely those work values which devalue "femininity" and thus, aspects of themselves. A relatively recent study (Kutner and Brogan, 1981) of problems faced by women entering the medical profession revealed that women medical students were just as likely as their male peers to hold unfavorable attitudes toward other women medical students or to be unsure of how they felt. In other words, these women seem to have internalized similar "work" values as men regarding the medical profession. Internalization of these and other work values (e.g., competitiveness, aggressiveness, the "success" ethic) leads many women to lessen their commitment to femininity and thus strengthen their commitment to masculinity. The result of such a process is a tendency for such women to "identify with their captors." This is usually manifested in women's exhibitions of extremely "masculinist" behaviors toward others—and especially toward other women and men who exhibit "feminine" behaviors. Moreover, men (who usually are in even more powerful positions relative to upwardly mobile women in such situations) reinforce these behaviors by rewarding such women with small amounts of power over other women and "weak" men. The fact remains, however, that work in America is based on a masculine sex-role identity paradigm and those in power resist attempts to feminize (and therefore, humanize) the work institution.

However, the masculine sex-role-identity paradigm that characterizes many aspects of the work institution in American *can* be altered. With the increased labor-force participation of women, it is possible for women to influence work values and initiate changes in many professions—if they, themselves, resist acceptance of traditional masculine work values. For example, Lesserman (1980) found that the professional orientations of men and women first-year medical students differed on health-care issues and such issues as physician's autonomy, income, and status—the latter being related directly to dominance aspects of the male work role. Lesserman concluded from her study that women students were oriented more to humanizing relationships between physicians and patients and bringing about political, economic, and social status changes in the medical profession. Whether these women will maintain such orientations or whether they can achieve their goals while maintaning such "feminine" orientations is not known. What *is* known, however, is that a greater commitment to such values would surely de-masculinize one profession in the male sex-role-influenced work institution.

De-masculinizing the work institution would have positive consequences personally for both males and females. Pines and Kafry (1981) in a comparative study of stress in the lives of working men and women, report that men feel almost as torn between their work and their lives outside of work as women. The conflict for women, however, appeared to be external and based on other people's demands. For men, the source of the conflict was not as apparent since men in the study had more positive work features, and perceived life outside of work as more important (and with more positive features). Yet, the fact that men, relative to women, did describe their life outside of work as significantly less important than did women may provide a clue. Perhaps men's greater commitment to work despite the fact that life outside of work was perceived more positively was responsible for men's conflicted state. If men *are* driven in their quests for achievement, success, and so on, then even minimum demands outside of work can produce work-life–outside-of-work conflict. The problem for men is that upward mobility and advancement are the sole criteria for men's success in the work place; and, as we have discussed, these criteria imply other masculine traits which often are inimical to men's functioning personally and socially. Lewin and Olesan (1980) offer an alternative career pattern which may be useful for many men to consider, especially those who do not strive (or want to strive) to "get ahead." They explore what is called "career lateralness."

Suggesting that vertical mobility may be an inadequate description of the occupational lives of males and females, Lewin and Olesan feel that lateralness must be considered a viable and meaningful career pattern. They feel that the concept of "lateralness" allows for the full range of human motivation. This is seen as important since all persons do not necessarily strive to get ahead but rather enjoy contentment and work satisfaction by *maintaining* work situations in which they find themselves. The authors feel further that "lateralness" has important implications for clarifying the concept "motive-to-avoid-success," redefining women's lack of progress in work in terms other than "victim of discrimination," and for going beyond analyses of work behavior that departs from "normal" male patterns as failure or deviation (p. 627).

While Lewin and Olesan applied lateralness to working women (postbaccalaureate nurses), they felt that lateral movement rather than vertical movement may also more closely characterize men's work patterns. Admittedly, much work remains to be done by social scientists who analyze work, achievement, and success. However, not all of the work to be done is academic. Possibly, society should be informed that career lateralness is a respectable alternative career pattern to competitiveness, aggressiveness, and efforts to "move upwards" in the workplace. One thing for certain is that a large number of men in America would benefit from such a change in society's values and its definition of masculinity. Sattel (1976) has written that much of the male sex-role is constructed to maintain positions of power and privilege for men and implies that fundamental social change will be difficult to accomplish. I agree with his observation but I also agree with Lewin's (1981) position that the evolution of a new male role is "ultimately worth the difficulties encountered in achieving it."

A Modified Definition of the Male Role: Beyond Androgyny

Basic sex-role concepts such as sex, gender, gender identify, and so on, have been defined, examined, and proposed throughout this volume. In most instances, the assumptions underlying the conceptualization also have been discussed. In this section, an emerging definition of the male role is examined which is couched in a traditional continuum view of masculinity and femininity with reformulated assumptions. The basic source for this emerging conceptualization of the male role is Freimuth and Hornstein's (1982) provocative work entitled "A Critical Examination of the Concept of Gender."

The concept of gender has been explored in previous chapters in terms of three categories: androgyny, femininity, and masculinity. In our discussions of masculinity and men's enactment of "masculine" behaviors, it has been pointed out that many men attempt to establish distance between themselves and femininity. This can be interpreted to mean that most males in their everyday activities behave as though gender-role is a continuum with masculinity representing one pole on the continuum and femininity representing the other pole. It should be mentioned, however, that if all males in the United States were asked to conceptualize gender, it is quite likely that most would conceptualize masculinity and femininity as two dichotomous categories. Freimuth and Hornstein believe that conceptualizing gender in this way stems from popular beliefs that males and females can be clearly distinguished on the biological level and that a similar distinction exists on the psychological level paralleling that on the biological level.

Most males, however, are rarely questioned regarding their conceptualization of gender. Instead, males are expected to *behave* in certain ways deemed "appropriately" masculine; and as we have discussed, often this means behaving in a nonfeminine manner. I believe, though, that if men were asked why they engaged in a particular kind of behavior commonly associated with masculinity rather than another kind commonly associated with femininity (e.g., a rough slap on the shoulders rather than a hug and kiss upon greeting a friend one has not seen for some time), most would give replies that meant "because I am a man and the other behavior is too feminine." Still, other men, somewhat more "enlightened" by changes in sex-role expectations in our society, might very well resist behaving in an "appropriately" masculine manner upon greeting a friend. Instead, these men might behave in an "androgynous" manner and exhibit traits commonly associated with femininity. An interesting point here is that it is hard to conceive of many modern day males who do not, in some situations, exhibit "feminine" traits, especially after they have firmly established their masculinity" (e.g., the male football player who cries when his team loses a game). In a sense, then, male *behavior* tends toward a continuum view of gender, especially if we speculate about what goes on behind closed doors (away from public view).

Perhaps Bem (1974), Spence and Helmreich, and others' views of gender-role deserve mention at this point. They have suggested that masculinity and femininity are qualitatively distinct. Because a male football player cries when his team loses (exhibits "feminine" behavior) says nothing about his masculinity. From their perspective, the hypothetical football player could simply be *very* masculine and *very* feminine (androgynous). Put simply, Bem, Spence, Helmreich, and others suggest the conceptual independence of masculinity and femininity. Aside from the fact that most American males probably do not construct their personal definitions of masculinity and femininity along two independent nonpolar dimensions, Freimuth and Hornstein's criticism of this view also is important. They state:

> To the extent that masculine traits such as aggressiveness are defined in our culture in terms of a contrast with feminine traits such as passivity, conceptual independence between masculine and feminine characteristics is not possible . . . Thus, in our view, it does not follow conceptually to define some gender-role characteristics as masculine and others as feminine. Each characteristic represents a continuum which ranges from clear masculinity at one end to clear femininity at the other (p. 526).

Freimuth and Hornstein dismiss the likely criticism that their continuous view of gender makes it impossible to distinguish between androgynous types of persons (those who are high on femininity and masculinity) and "undifferentiated types" (persons who are low on both masculinity and femininity). They feel that few persons would fall into the undifferentiated category and that those who do probably are generally depressed. Moreover the authors do not advocate a return to using traditional gender-role scales because such scales are not limited to behavioral/trait characteristics, nor are they defined in terms of social construction.

An inescapable conclusion that one reaches when discussing "masculine traits" with men today is that few define themselves in the manner in which scholars talk about men. As stated in the last chapter, men do not view themselves quite as "masculine" as the prototypical male

(Cicone and Ruble, 1978). Indeed, males *and* females vary in their definitions of self as masculine and feminine (Storms, 1978). Perhaps this is why numerous males resist the stereotypes so casually associated with them. Now this is not to be interpreted to mean that males do not have privilege in our society. Males do have privilege, but much of the privilege is based on a model which has been socially constructed and sustained. In discussing the gender concept, often we make the mistake of measuring it nominally when in fact an interval level of measurement should be used. We have known for some time that much information is lost when a nominal level of measurement is used with continuous data. Gender, as we have seen, involves much of which is "continuous" and therefore more accurate measures of the concept should be along the lines of interval levels of measurement. Such measures would make it more difficult for individual men to define characteristics often associated with men as inapplicable to them personally. The obvious advantage such men have would then be removed since when men define stereotypical characteristics as inapplicable to them personally they are saying "there is no reason for men to change."

How, then, can the male role be defined generally in our society? I believe that Freimuth and Hornstein offer some possibilities for defining the male role on a general level. Such a definition, however, does not negate the fact that many specific role performances by most men today continue to be dysfunctional to men, women, and society overall.

Let us begin by examining Freimuth and Hornstein's work. Freimuth and Hornstein point out first of all that differences between males and females on a *hormonal* basis are differences in degree rather than kind. Both males and females possess androgens, estrogens, and progestins. For males, however, the androgen hormonal level is higher relative to the estrogen/progestin levels. Females' estrogen/progestin levels are much higher than their androgen levels. Because both males and females possess all three hormones, maleness and femaleness becomes a matter of degree and is handled best when viewed as a continuum.

A second aspect of gender proposed by Freimuth and Hornstein is *gender-related physical characteristics.* Including, but going beyond the genital/reproductive structure of persons, the authors note the irony in most judgments of persons' genders. We judge persons' genders often on the basis of, at least in part, secondary sex characteristics but we describe our judgments in terms of the two typical gential- and reproductive-structure categories into which most people fall: male or female. Yet, we do *not see* most people's genitals, but we *do* make gender attributions based on secondary sex characteristics and even on other physical characteristics. Because some of these other physical characteristics are culturally defined arbitrarily as masculine or feminine, additional variations in persons' masculinity and/or femininity can be expected. Freimuth and Hornstein feel that when judgments are made about a particular person's masculinity and/or femininity based on physical appearance, comparisons are made with some prototype of physical masculinity and/or femininity. Their view is that the above gender-related physical characteristics "constitute a continuum dimension, ranging from clear cases of masculinity at one end to clear cases of femininity at the other" (p. 524).

The third aspect of gender, according to Freimuth and Hornstein, is *gender-role* which they limit to include behaviors and social traits associated with masculinity and femininity. Arguing against a dualistic view of masculinity and femininity, the authors propose a bipolar view with some individuals (typically called "androgynous" persons) falling at the midpoint.

Gender preference as an aspect of gender is also seen from a continuum perspective. Pointing out that the conceptualization of gender preference is limited to genital structure, Freimuth and Hornstein, note that a reliance entirely upon genital structure to define a person's gender choice is inappropriate. Such a reliance does not take into consideration the fact that other gender-related characteristics are related to choices of persons' sexual partners. In a provocative manner, Freimuth and Hornstein state that the preference of a masculine male for a feminine female is different from a preference of a masculine male for a masculine female. If we go beyond genital structure and thus are able to say that individuals are *more or less* heterosexual, homosexual or bisexual, we conclude axiomatically that the latter "masculine" male above is more homosexual or bisexual than the former "masculine" male.

The final aspect of gender considered by the authors is *subjective gender identity* which refers to how persons view themselves overall in terms of masculinity and femininity. This view of self, according to Freimuth and Hornstein, involves more than a person's knowledge of his or her genital structure; it involves also a person's organized conception of those continuously distributed physical and psychological characteristics of self which he or she believes relevant to gender. This means that subjective gender identity is "a statement about one's relative masculinity or femininity" and, like the other aspects of gender, can be thought of as existing along a continuum ranging from clear masculinity to clear femininity (p. 529). Given Freimuth and Hornstein's observations, let us propose a definition of masculinity that may conform more closely to persons who are highly "masculine" and those who are low on "masculinity."

Determining Male Gender

Given the aspects of gender mentioned above, determining a particular male's gender is extremely complex. "Masculine" physical characteristics are likely to be highly correlated with high levels of androgen hormones relative to female hormones in a particular male. However, the psychological components of gender (gender role, gender preference and subjective gender identity) are likely to be less highly correlated with each other and with the hormonal and physical characteristics of a particular male. Moreover, as Freimuth and Hornstein have implied, a male's stage in the life cycle may affect the relationships between his gender components (i.e., whether some components are highly correlated with each other).

Most persons in our society recognized as males probably possess an "appropriate" level of androgen hormones relative to estrogen/progestin hormones. Often this is manifested in their physical appearance (e.g., facial hair, breast size, and so on). On the other hand, many males have physical characteristics that are nebulous from a typically "masculine–feminine" perspective. This results in judgments of males' masculinity being subjective on the parts of observers and varying from one observer to another along bipolar prototypical masculine–feminine/masculinity continua.

Masculinity for a particular male also is determined by whether he is perceived to enact "masculine" gender roles. Judgments regarding the enactment of masculine gender roles are made on the bases of cultural and subcultural definitions of masculinity. In addition, such judgments also derive from judges' subjective comparisons of a particular male's behavior with some prototypical male. This means that a male, in enacting social roles, is judged by others in terms of conformity to the "masculine" ideal and whether his behavior is sufficiently distinct from prototypical feminine behaviors. Of course, the judgments of others depend upon their interpretations of the male's performance of the behaviors as well as their interpretations of the behaviors along a masculine–feminine continuum.

For many people, the single factor determining a male's masculinity more than any other is his choice of a sexual partner. Ordinarily, however, people think of a male's choice as limited to either "male" or "female." Thus, if a male chooses another male as a sexual partner, many people will automatically question his masculinity. Given the model under consideration, a male's choice of a sexual partner is much more complex, as far as gender preference is concerned. Because a person's gender involves much more than his or her genitals, a male's choice of a female with external female genitals is not sufficient to say that his choice is completely heterosexual. This means that if a male's masculinity in part depends upon his heterosexuality (choice of a sexual partner opposite in gender), then all aspects of the chosen person's gender must be opposite to his aspects of gender in order to conclude that the male is totally masculine. What often happens in reality is that little distinction is made between sexual and gender preference. This is interesting, since a male who chooses a masculine female sexual partner may differ only minimally from a male who choses a masculine male sexual partner following Freimuth and Hornstein's reasoning.

A final aspect of gender that is important in determining a particular male's gender is subjective gender identity. Despite an "appropriate" androgen hormonal level, other male's physical characteristics, "masculine" gender role and "heterosexual" gender choice of a sexual partner, a male's perception of himself is critical in determining his gender. Does he think that he is highly masculine, moderately masculine, or minimally masculine? Interestingly, as pointed out earlier in this chapter, most men tend to rank themselves somewhat below their prototypes of masculinity but with sufficient distance from femininity. If, however, a male perceives himself as feminine then this may set in motion numerous behaviors by himself and others that will refute the initial categorization of the male as masculine.

The difficulty of determining male gender should be obvious. However, if a definition of masculinity is continuum-based, the difficulty diminishes. The definition of masculinity offered below is derived from the following illustration of Freimuth and Hornstein's model

A person can be said to be masculine to some degree if that person is found to have the following characteristics: *a higher androgen hormonal level relative to the hormonal level of estrogen/progestin; a proportionately greater number of masculine physical characteristics than female physical characteristics; typically exhibits more culturally defined masculine behaviors than feminine ones; generally prefers and chooses a sexual partner who possesses opposite gender-related characteristics; and, defines oneself somewhere from the midpoint to the masculine pole on a masculine-feminine continuum.*

It is not possible at this time to discuss the relationships between the aspects of gender described above, although Freimuth and Hornstein feel that an individual's gender can be adequately characterized only if all five aspects are taken into consideration. This means, as they point out, that "it becomes important to know whether an individual's position on one dimension can be predicted from information about his or her position on another" (p. 529). At the present time the issue remains to be explored and while some correlations among aspects of gender probably

Table 7
An Illustration of Freimuth and Hornstein's Aspects-of-Gender Model

---

1. Gender-Related Hormones

Androgen hormonal level relative to estrogen/progestin level	Androgen hormonal level relative to estrogen/progestin level
High	Low
Masculine ━━━━━━━━━━━━━━━━━━━━━━━━━━━	(Feminine)

2. Gender-Related Physical Characteristics
(Genitals, body size, hip size, facial hair, etc.)

Physical characteristics associated with males	Physical characteristics associated with females
(Masculine) ━━━━━━━━━━━━━━━━━━━━━━━━	(Feminine)

3. Gender Role
(Culturally defined behaviors)

(Masculine) ━━━━━━━━━━━━━━━━━━━━━━━━━━━━ (Feminine)

4. Gender Preference
Basis of Choices of Sexual Partner and Frequency of Such Choices

---

All gender-related characteristics the same as one's own	All gender-related characteristics different from one's own
A (Homosexual) ━━━━━━━━━━━━━━━━━━	(Heterosexual)

Relative Frequency of Choice Above

B   (Always) ━━━━━━━━━━━━━━━━━━━━━━━ (Never)

5. Subjective Gender Identity
(One's conception of one's own gender overall—both in terms of physical and psychological characteristics)

(Masculine) ━━━━━━━━━━━━━━━━━━━━━━━━━━━ (Feminine)

---

exist (e.g., biological and physical aspects), one-to-one- correspondence probably does *not* exist (e.g., physically masculine homosexual men are cases in point, as are men in advanced stages of the life cycle). Just as Freimuth and Hornstein's model is intended as a stimulus for theoretical formulation and empirical research, this application of the model to the male sex role is intended likewise. In addition, it is intended to help many males today in their individual efforts to rethink and reconstruct their roles in American society. Table 7 illustrates Freimuth and Hornstein's model.

CHAPTER 6

Male Interpersonal Attraction

Captions on the covers of women's magazines frequently read some version of "What Do Men Want?" Several avid feminist women in my "Social Factors in Male Personality" course confronted me with such a magazine cover in October, 1982, and wanted to know "how do you feel about this magazine's attempt to cater to men?" My response was that I did not see the caption as an attempt by the magazine to cater to men. "Well, what do you see the caption as?" one of the women asked. I replied that I saw the caption as an attempt by the magazine to delve into an area of interest to many people—academic people as well as those outside of academia. The area of interest I was referring to, of course was *interpersonal attraction*. In other words, the October 1982 issue of *Ms.* magazine, from my perspective, addressed issues such as why do we like some people and why do some others like us? What are the factors which promote interpersonal relationships and what factors cause such relationships between men and women as well as promote more harmonious relationships between them. In a sense, this is what this chapter is all about. What is it in a man that attracts others and what is it in others that attracts a man?

Berscheid and Walster's (1974) findings that physical attractiveness is related to sexual attraction and that the relationship is stronger for males than for females indicate that *physical attractiveness* plays an important role in male attraction (especially sexual) to females. Determining the importance of physical attractiveness in male attraction to females is confounded, though, by the fact that judgments of physical attractiveness are subjective and vary among males. What one male considers a physically attractive trait another male might find physically unattractive. Because of these variations in male judgments, it may not be useful to consider physical attractiveness alone as a general determinant of male interpersonal attraction. It is recognized, of course, that persons' external characteristics are important at least during the initial stages of interpersonal attraction. Persons possessing desirable physical characteristics often are thought to possess certain social characteristics such as kindness, warmth, sexiness, arrogance, and so on, as discussed in Chapter 4. As a general interpersonal-attraction framework, however, it seems more useful to consider Levinger and Snoek's (1972) stages of interpersonal attraction. First, let us review Levinger and Snoek's model and then apply it to male interpersonal attraction.

Levinger and Snoek's Model of Interpersonal Attraction. In what they considered as a "new look" at interpersonal attraction, Levinger and Snoek presented four stages through which persons pass in social relationships. In each of the stages certain factors are postulated as determinants of interpersonal attraction. The first stage is labeled the *zero contact stage*. As the label implied, this stage is characterized by the lack of a relationship between two or more persons although they may be in physical proximity to each other. Perlman and Cozby (1982) feel that the influence of physical proximity (propinquity) on interpersonal attraction is due to several things; physical proximity increases the likelihood that persons will meet each other; the likelihood is greater that persons in physical proximity will show similar attitudes and values and therefore will like each other; and, the fact that persons are exposed to each other increases the likelihood of interpersonal attraction.

A second stage proposed by Levinger and Snoek is *awareness* which is couched in person perception as discussed in Chapter 4 and involves no interaction between persons. One person becomes aware of another and while they do not interact, mutual awareness is possible. Persons during this stage first observe characteristics of other(s) such as physical features, clothing, body movements, nonverbal messages of emotion, and then form impressions of other(s).

Following the stage of awareness, two persons typically enter into an exploratory contact stage which Levinger and Snoek have labeled *surface contact*. Surface contact characterizes initial interaction between persons. It involves persons testing and evaluating bits of interaction with other(s). During this stage, persons find out what they have in common, and whether the interaction produces rewards in the forms of social approval, equal exchange and the like.

Given that two persons "pass" successfully through the "evaluative" stage of social interaction, they may enter into what is called the continuum stage of *mutuality*. This stage begins with a minor overlapping of persons involving factors such as increases in the amount of time spent together, increasing self-disclosure and increasing expressiveness. All may become more intense if persons continue to find their association rewarding and the result is progression from minor overlapping of persons to *moderate* overlapping to *major* overlapping.

Application of Levinger and Snoek's Model to Male Interpersonal Attraction. If physical proximity is related to interpersonal attraction, then male interpersonal attraction is affected by the amount of space men assume in their surroundings. This effect is due to the positive relationship between space and dominance. Walum (1977) has implied that women have lower status than men in American society and that this is reflected in the greater amounts of space men use when they are in physical proximity to others (especially women, since men resist invasions of their spaces by others). If men do use greater amounts of space when they are around others this has direct implications for Levinger and Snoek's *zero contact stage* as it applies to males. Males, simply by their appearance in social situations, have a greater likelihood of being interpersonally attractive to women and of being seen as a "threat" by other men (Walum, in discussing Willis' findings, points out that males tend to "fight" when other males attempt to invade their personal spaces).

The second stage, when applied to men, also places them at a distinct advantage with respect to heterosexual interpersonal attraction. Undoubtedly *awareness* is related to the amount of space persons use in situations with others. If males use relatively large amounts of space, then the likelihood is increased that their personal characteristics will be observed by others. The awareness stage for males, however, is affected by the sex of the observer and the observed. As stated above, men resist other men's invasions of their personal spaces and this certainly affects the *awareness* stage. Moreover, men often are careful to *observe* each other's personal characteristics only in instrumental social situations. In addition, it must be remembered also that males tend to reveal only partial information about themselves to other males, for homophobic and homosexist reasons. Thus, while men often have an advantage in the heterosexual awareness stage, they may be at a disadvantage in the awareness stage during male–male social interaction.

Because of awkwardness that characterizes male–male *awareness*, surface contact between males often does not occur. In other words, many men do not even enter into initial interaction and thus explore interaction with each other. Those who do often test and evaluate only limited amounts of "instrumental" information that they are able to gather from other males—thus, the tendency for many males to avoid self-disclosing conversation with other males. Interestingly, the tendency for men to be extremely instrumental with other men during the surface contact stage also carries over into their initial relationships with women. The reason men seem to be affected more than women by the "physical attractiveness" variable and to perceive women in terms of stereotypes, then, may be due to men's tendencies to be more instrumental than women during the surface contact stage.

If Levinger and Snoek's stage of mutuality is applied to males, according to some authors, only minimum to moderate levels of the stage are reached. Regardless of the reason for males' minimum to moderate self-disclosure and expressiveness, the fact remains that the stage of mutuality is characterized by *increasing* amounts of each with continuing association. If men resist increasing self-disclosure and expressiveness in their relationships with others (both females and males), major overlapping of their lives with others cannot occur. In essence, then, the fourth stage of interpersonal attraction is only partially entered by many men. That this is what occurs for many men is the major thrust of the arguments presented by Blakeley (1982) and others who are concerned about men's deficiencies in the area of interpersonal relations.

Their arguments center around the idea that men (and some women) who internalize the masculine gender role in our society are attracted to those persons whom they can dominate. Even well meaning "masculine" men—those who feel that they are "enlightened" on the topic of sex-role equality—often have not undergone the self-learning necessary to live freely and to allow others to live freely. The problem, according to Blakeley (1982) is that men have not cultivated their empathic abilities. In addition, she states, few men learn to accept sex-role equality without exhausting some woman in the process. Blakeley goes on to say that men exhausting women are the terms of changes in men's behavior because men have not grasped fully the total picture of the women's movement. One reason for this, she reasons, is that many men have *changed* their behaviors because of a desire to please women but men have not changed for themselves. As a result the women's movement represents nothing more than a set of rules to many men—every new issue that arises is a surprise to men and drains women's energy. Blakeley laments the present where men, while undergoing external changes, have not evolved invisible, internal consciousness which would enable them to understand and see women's issues as a gestalt.

While it is questionable that men are incapable of empathic understanding, it is probably true that men often do not engage in empathy in order to maintain power in our society. If men use inexpressiveness to maintain power (Sattel, 1976), in all likelihood, their nonempathic ability also has its source in power maintenance. This is seen when Levinger and Snoek's model is applied to male interpersonal attraction. I submit that men's attraction to others is based on instrumentality regardless of the sex of others. It is not that men are not empathic (able to assume the role of others and feel as others), they are; their empathic ability, however, is used for their own (instrumental) advantage rather than to promote more harmonious interpersonal relationships

Varieties of Male Interpersonal Attraction

Williamson, Swingle and Sargent (1982) have stated that "the bases for interpersonal attraction or liking rest in interpersonal perception" (p. 399). Such factors as persons' needs to affiliate with others, persons' dependence on others for certain rewards, and interpersonal similarity may result in interpersonal attraction. In other words, persons are attracted to others who can fulfil their needs, their dependencies, and who are similar to themselves. Williamson, *et al.*, discuss interpersonal attraction as a unidimensional phenomenon as reflected in their synonymous usage of the concepts "interpersonal attraction" and "liking." Others who work in the area of interpersonal attraction (e.g., Segal, 1979) discuss "liking" as only one type of interpersonal attraction among several. As male interpersonal attraction is explored in this section, varieties of male interpersonal attraction are discussed. The specific varieties discussed are male *liking*, male *friendship*, male *respect*, and male *love*. Because male friendship has been discussed at length in Chapter 3, male liking and friendship (as they relate to interpersonal attraction) are combined in the discussion below.

Male Liking and Male Friendship

In the late 1970s Mady W. Segal (1979) made a distinction between liking and friendship and suggested that they were different varieties of interpersonal attraction. She noted that while liking may be necessary for friendship, it was not sufficient for friendship. Friendship, according to Segal, can be seen as a structural relationship which has a more important component of actual behavior than does liking. For example, it is difficult for persons to be close friends with many others but persons can be liked by and can like many others. In addition, Segal hypothesizes, there is a greater probability of mutuality in friendship than in liking.

An interesting feature of Segal's work is the fact that her findings are especially applicable to male interpersonal attraction since her research involved 703 Maryland state policemen and 101 college football players (from two teams). One problem, however, does arise with respect

to the sex-role implications of the study. The 703 state policemen participated in the research in 1966, several years prior to the modern day
women's movement in America. On the other hand, the college football
player data were collected in the middle-1970s during the height of the
women's movement. The significance of these dates of data collection
should become apparent as we reflect on Segal's findings as they relate
to present day male interpersonal attraction. However, because data on
friendship, liking and respect were obtained only from the football
groups, much of our discussion is devoted to findings from those groups.

Segal presents several findings related to friendship and liking
which are important to consider. They are as follows: (1) friendship is
more mutual than liking; (2) the ratings given on friendship were lower
than those on liking; and (3) friendship was more strongly related to
joint participation in leisure activities than liking. In discussing these
findings, Segal concluded that "friendship is a social relationship
whereas liking is a feeling and therefore, friendship is more strongly
related to spending time together than is liking" (p. 260).

Given our discussion of males thus far in this volume, an alternative
interpretation of Segal's findings seems even more plausible. The interpretation offered revolves around a basic assumption that much male
behavior is instrumental. This assumption, if true, has implications for
the types of friendships males form, as pointed out in the last chapter.
Based on Segal's findings it may be possible to say that men tend *not* to
form friendships with other men they *really* like. If male friendships are
more mutual than liking; and, if male friendships are related more
strongly to joint participation in leisure activities than is liking, then it
certainly seems plausible that men may not form friendships with other
men they really like. Moreover, men may not spend time with men
toward whom they have strong positive feelings.

That men tend not to form friendships or spend time with other
men they really like should not be surprising, since cultural norms tend
to mitigate such relationships between men. Thus homophobia and or
homosexism may be responsible for relationships between male liking,
male friendships, and males' joint participation in leisure activities. If we
will recall, Segal suggested that friendship is a social relationship,
whereas liking is a feeling; therefore friendship is more strongly related
to joint participation in leisure activities. The interpretation of her findings offered here is that because liking is a feeling, men may be "afraid"
to spend time with those men they really like because of homophobia
and/or homosexism. Such an interpretation seems possible because
males who follow the pattern of not forming relationships with those
men they really like can always provide an instrumental explanation to

self and others for "why they spend time with other men." It is not so much because they have positive affect for these men, rather it is because they enjoy participating in similar leisure activities. This kind of explanation removes much of the need for an "expressive" explanation of many men's relationships.

As Segal's interpretation of men's interpersonal attractions and mine are reflected on, it is important to remember the time period of the research and the fact that liking and friendship are explored in work and work-like natural groups. Kulik and Harackiewicz's (1979) findings on males in their opposite-sex interpersonal attraction also may be important for us to review. Males were found to prefer androgynous females slightly more than feminine females for platonic liking but reversed their preferences for romantic liking (p. 449). The authors interpreted this finding to mean that while men may value some women's "masculine" characteristics in some situations, these same characteristics may prove threatening to some men in romantic situations. A modification of their interpretation is that many men may find it "inappropriate" to become romantically involved with women who exhibit gender characteristics similar to their own. Interestingly, this is a form of homophobia and/or homosexism which derives from Freimuth and Hornstein's (1982) model discussed in Chapter 5. Because Freimuth and Hornstein's model considers gender characteristics *preference* to be more than *genital* characteristics preference it is indeed possible for some men to exhibit homophobia toward persons who possess female physical characteristics and male other gender-related characteristics.

Another point deserving mention is that romance is a very expressive form of interpersonal attraction. This means that while it is possible for some men to form instrumental platonic relationships with "masculine" and "androgynous" females, it may be much more difficult for them to form expressive romantic relationships with such females. Based on Freimuth and Hornstein's model, this should be a logical outcome in "heterosexual" men. The reason these men are not romantically attracted to "masculine" and "androgynous" persons with female genitalia is similar to the reason why such men are not attracted romantically to masculine and androgynous persons with male genitalia. These heterosexual men prefer members of the "opposite" sex in romantic relationships and this means more than "opposite" genitalia; it also means "opposite" physical and other gender-related characteristics. On the other hand, these same men may prefer to form friendships with masculine and/or androgynous women who can share similar attitudes and values and who can participate in joint (nonfeminine) activities—all of which requires only an instrumental orientation.

Male Respect

Perhaps more than any other variety of interpersonal attraction, male respect has its source in social power, which implies at least initial violation of reciprocity on the part of an actor or actors in social relationships. Male respect as a type of attraction is some function of the possession of rare and valued attributes: it is related to the perception of contributions (expressive and instrumental ones) to the goal of a relationship (Segal, 254). Segal states " . . . in a group, people who are perceived as contributing to the goals of the group are respected by other group members" (p. 254). However, a crucial ingredient which must be present in groups and/or relationships for respect to flourish is consensus regarding group and/or relationship goals. For example, since numerous relationships males form appear to be more instrumental than expressive, male respect is more likely to be related to contributions made to instrumental "goals" of a relationship or a group.

Peter Blau, in his classic book *Exchange and Power in Social Life* (1964) discussed respect almost entirely from a male perspective. Now some will surely point to the tenor of the times as the reason for Blau's masculinist orientation. I suspect, however, that the reason goes deeper. Respect, as a concept, seems much more applicable to interpersonal relationships men form than to those formed by women or ones formed in mixed-sex groups. Most discussions of respect are couched in concepts such as competition, authority, unilateral approval and the like (Blau, 1964; Segal, 1979). In fact, Blau's early ideas on respect (which, incidentally, remain the major source for contemporary explanations of the concept, as reflected in Segal's usage of the term) were illustrated using only hypothetical male relationships. For example, Blau (p. 63) states:

> Without men to strengthen a union or to organize a gang, to assist fellow workers or score for a basketball team, the members of these groups would be deprived of valued benefits. The obligation of group members to these who make such benefits possible are discharged by according them superior status. They command respect and compliance, which serve as rewards for having made contributions in the past and as incentives for continuing to make them in the future.

Given the above quote, one cannot help but recognize that respect implies a type of interpersonal attraction characterized by dominance. Blau states further:

> Respecting a person means looking up to him, and if his standing requires others to look up to him, theirs cannot require him to look up to them, too, although he may admire their skills in debating, while they admire his as a

quarterback. Finally, the term respect denotes a positive evaluation of a person's ability in a given area or his abilities in general . . . (p. 63).

Another characteristic of respect not mentioned by Blau and other writers is that it is the one form of social attraction most acceptable in male–male relationships in the United States. While many men might find it difficult to give "liking" and "love" *to* other males or accept "liking" and "love" *from* other males, few experience problems when the attraction given or accepted is labeled "respect." The reason, of course, is obvious. If my attraction to another man is labeled "respect," then the source of my attraction is instrumental and based only on the contributions that individual makes to my personal goal attainment, without any expectations of further reciprocity or mutuality. My positive evaluation of another man's abilities in a given area (and thus, my respect for him) eliminates the need for me to further reward him which may be reflected in "liking" and "loving" him. Liking and loving, as is respect, are *types of interpersonal attraction* and *types of rewards* given to others in social exchange. In social exchanges between males in the United States, however, respect rather than liking/loving more closely approximates the norm for male–male relationships.

Not only is it culturally more *acceptable* for men to respect other men than it is for men to like/love other men, it is in all likelihood *easier* for men to respect other men than it is for them to like/love other men. After all, men learn to compete with other men, to aggress against other men, to try to dominate other men and to behave in general toward other men in ways contrary to liking/loving. To expect men suddenly to cast aside these traits and become expressive, warm, human and so on toward other men is in all likelihood, expecting too much. This may be especially the case if a concommitant change in male socialization has not occurred.

Respect as a type of interpersonal attraction in male–female relationships also is important to consider. Interestingly, only recently have men been confronted with the issue of respect in male–female relationships. As women have increased their participation in previously male dominated groups (e.g., occupations, organizations, clubs), men increasingly have been confronted with intersex respect. How men have dealt with intersex respect, though, is debatable, given the widespread sexual harassment to which women have been subjected. In many instances, unilateral approval of women's abilities as judged by objective standards has not been forthcoming for women entering male-dominated professions, organizations, occupations and the like. Instead, women have frequently been subjected to types of interpersonal attraction other than respect. One specific type of interpersonal attraction that has been imposed on many women is *sexual harassment* in the workplace. In fact, some feminist writers contend that sexual harassment in the workplace has nothing to do with interpersonal attraction (e.g., Taylor, 1981). Rather, sexual harassment is thought to be simply a form of coercion that derives from male domination and female subordination. Taylor (p. 675) contends that "sexual harassment involves sexual advances that are not mutual, but are imposed, in most instances, upon a woman by a man who directly or indirectly holds power over her, more often than not the direct power to hire and fire her." Specific behaviors which connote sexual harassment, according to Taylor, include verbal abuse, indecent suggestions, propositions for dates, requests for sexual favors, demands for sexual intercourse, physical touching, rape, and the list goes on.

In contrast to the perspective that sexual harassment has little to do with interpersonal attraction (McKinnon, 1979; Farley, 1978), I believe that it has much to do with interpersonal attraction, albeit cruel and inhumane. In fact, the pervasiveness of sexual harassment (a 1976 survey of nine thousand women by Redbook magazine found that 88 percent had been sexually harassed on the job) gives a hint of its relationship to interpersonal attraction. Sexual harassment of women (disrespect) is the other side of the respect coin. It is a form of disrespect which is substituted for respect in male–female relationships, and is associated closely with men's conceptions of women and their "place" in the social structure. Moreover, as Taylor indicates, sexual harassment is not a new problem: "It is a form of sexual coercion that women have faced and endured throughout history" (p. 673). Still, despite its coercive nature, sexual harassment *is* a type of interpersonal attraction. Let me explain why.

Prior to women's entry into America's male-dominated organizations and institutions in large numbers, male respect for females had little to do with females' abilities—unless women's abilities included not being overtly sexually promiscuous. Indeed, most men today do not equate respect for women with unilateral approval of women's abilities as judged by some objective measure. Instead, male respect for a woman generally means that he feels that the woman is of high "moral character" and stays "in place." On the surface, there appears to be little association between this meaning of respect and Blau's definition of respect mentioned earlier. How do women's "high moral character" and "staying in place" get translated into women's skills and abilities in a given area? They do not—unless men's conceptions of women exclude them from full participation in American society and relegate women to the domestic domain. That this is precisely what occurs seems to be substantiated by the observation that many men who show "respect" for women display the same kinds of inexpressive and deferential behaviors in their presence that are displayed in the presence of "respected" males. However, the source of the respect is different. Men "respect" other men for their superiority, while men respect women for their inferiority; that is, women's "abilities" to allow men to maintain their "masculinity" by not challenging the *status quo* with respect to sex roles in America.

Support for the belief that men do not respect women for their abilities even in the 1980s comes from relatively recent work by Alperson and Friedman (1983). Using an interpersonal phenomenological technique to study sex-role attributions in heterosexual dyads, they concluded that women who attempt to adopt instrumental aspects of the male role are likely to be met with considerable resistance. In fact, in the dyads they studies, women were less likely to be validated for socially "mature" behavior and more likely to be validated for socially "immature" behavior. Alperson and Friedman state:

> Since our society values instrumental behavior more than social immaturity (women were found to be less likely validated than men on the single "instrumental" cluster of items which was also a part of a similar cluster called "masculine"; and more likely to be validated on a different cluster called "social immaturity"), it is not an unreasonable inference that women are less likely to be validated for socially desirable behavior than men, and more likely to be validated for socially undesirable behaviors than men (p. 472).

Because many men do not perceive women as potential contributors to "group" goals, they also are incapable of using objective standards to judge women's contributions and thus give women positive evaluations on their abilities (respect). The mere presence of a woman in the nontraditional social role violates many men's bases for "respecting" her since her presence attests to her non-inferiority. Thus, instead of men responding to women in such situations on the basis of "respect" (recognition of the degree to which they contribute to group goals), many respond to women on the basis of "disrespect" (i.e., by expressing power over women—sexual harassment). In both instances, bases for the behaviors reside in social power. However, the male sex-role orientation of most males in America promotes unilateral attraction in the form of male "respect" in male–male social interaction. Obviously, personal, organizational, social, and legal methods must be employed to remedy the problem which I feel lies in male sex-role socialization and is manifested in inappropriate male responses to females such as *sexual harassment*.

Most scholars would agree that respect for another person is based on the perception that the other has rare and/or valuable qualities (e.g., Blau, 1964; Segal, 1978). This means that respect is a type of instrumental attraction and may not be related to other forms of interpersonal attraction such as liking, friendship, love, or to their manifestation in the forms of expressiveness, joint participation in leisure activities, and the like. For example, Segal found that male instrumental-leadership nominations among football players were more strongly related to respect than to either friendship or liking. Moreover, when group harmony was defined as a group goal (an expressive group trait translated into an instrumental group trait), expressive leadership nominations were more strongly related to respect than to either liking or friendship. Thus, not only does male respect seem to be instrumental but it also seems quite easy for men to substitute instrumentality for expressiveness—respect for liking and friendship in their interpersonal choices.

On the other hand, respect as a form of interpersonal attraction seems awfully difficult for men to give women in social relationships. The source of the difficulty lies in men's persistent beliefs that "femininity" in itself consists of "rare" and "valuable" qualities that are incompatible with "contributions to group goals" except traditional feminine ones (e.g., childrearing, domestic chores, nurturing men). The obvious dysfunction of this perspective for women, though, is that such "rare" and "valuable" qualities associated with femininity contribute significantly to the maintenance of male dominance and female subordination.

Male Love

Of the varieties of interpersonal attraction discussed in this chapter, love more than any others requires mutuality, Usually one person does not remain in love with another person very long if the other is not perceived to return the love on some level. Blau (1964) has stated that love is the ultimate instance of intrinsic attraction. He contends further that while exchange processes characterize love relationships, their dynamics are different since specific rewards are exchanged in love relationships only to produce the ultimate reward of intrinsic attraction between lovers. According to Blau, only when two lovers' affection for and commitment to one another expand at roughly the same pace do they tend mutually to reinforce their love. His analysis of love is similar to Berscheid and Walster's (1978) description of love as a relationship involving the intertwining of the lives of persons where there is intense affection. Put simply, love is a deep interpersonal relationship.

Because love is a deep interpersonal relationship we may be likely to forget that it also is a type of exchange relationship. However, elements of social exchange, as noted earlier, do characterize love relationships. Blau feels that persons in such relationships furnish rewards to each other not necessarily to receive proportionate extrinsic benefits in return, but rather to express and confirm their own commitment and to promote each other's commitment to the relationship. Blau states:

> The repeated experience of being rewarded by the increased attachment of a loved one after having done a variety of things to please him may have the effect that giving pleasure to loved ones becomes intrinsically gratifying (p. 77).

Recognizing that there may be "sex role differences in specific practices," Blau, in discussing men's orientations to women, refers to the preciousness of costly possessions in love and hypothesizes that *a man's intrinsic attraction to a woman* (and hers to him) *rests on the rewards he expects to experience in a love relationship with her* (pp. 78–79). Herein, I feel, is where male dominance enters into heterosexual love relationships in America.

If a man values dominance in a romantic relationship with a women, then a woman's subordinance in that relationship is rewarding to the man . . . and based on Blau's analysis, her subordinance can foster further the man's intrinsic attraction to her. But, do modern day men value dominance in their heterosexual love relationships? Two recent studies suggest that despite so-called sex-role changes in American society, many men continue to value dominance in their heterosexual romantic relationships. Moreover, one of the studies suggests that some women may *prefer* a romantic relationship characterized by male dominance. Kulik and Harackiewicz (1979) found that while females preferred androgynous males to sex-typed males on both platonic-liking and romantic-liking measures, male preferences differed. Males, according to their findings, preferred androgynous females slightly more than sex-typed females for platonic liking but preferred sex-typed females more for romantic liking. They concluded that "some men probably experience ambivalence stemming from the potential threat that androgynous women will not be "suitably deferential" in romantic relationships.

A more recent study (Orlofsky, 1982) of males' and females' ideal dating partners/potential spouses suggests that even in early relationships when "love" may not be full-blown, males like to assume dominant roles. Orlofsky found that 66% of the women in his study preferred androgynous males while only 32% of the men preferred androgynous females. Some women in Orlofsky's study did prefer men who were slightly more masculine than feminine but most preferred partners who were both highly masculine and highly feminine. Men in Orlofsky's study, on the other hand, wanted feminine-typed dating partners/potential spouses. While androgynous males did express some desire for androgynous female dating partner/potential spouses, they preferred

feminine females just as frequently and nearly all masculine males preferred feminine-typed females as dating partners/potential spouses.

Based on the findings from the above two studies, it appears that
many men still prefer male-dominant romantic relationships with
women. Changes in men's and women's societal roles may not be carrying over as readily into changes in sex roles that affect heterosexual
romantic relationships. While the studies examined above substantiate
such a conclusion, Hill, Rubin, Peplau, and Willard's (1979) contention
that men who are willing to participate in research on interpersonal relationships may be less traditional than those who choose not to participate
also gives us reason to believe that many men may continue to prefer
traditional coupling (where the man is dominant and the woman is subordinate). Succinctly, much male love in heterosexual relationships
seems to be based on male dominance.

To say that male love is based on male dominance means that even
in love relationships, men constrain women and restrict them to only
those role performances that meet men's needs and maintain men's dominant positions. The finding by Hill, Rubin, and Peplau (1976) that
women are more likely to initiate dissolution of a romantic relationship
may be an indication of some women's resistance to male dominance in
romance. That males desire to be dominant in their romantic relationships should not be surprising, since it only means that males are just as
instrumental in their love relationships as they are in their other relationships (e.g., liking and friendship). We must remember Davidson's
(1981) finding that men often pretend more love and affection than they
really feel. Obviously this pretense is constructed by men for their own
purpose . . . to get what they want . . . accomplish a goal (for example,
sexual favors, exclusive commitment, and so on). If, and when, men's
goals are realized, as many women discover, men tend not to continue
the pretense. What often occurs is that the romantic relationship, from
the woman's viewpoint, becomes even more inequitable and intolerable
(as the man often displays increasingly dominant behaviors). This may
be reflected in the finding that women are more likely than men to initiate the dissolution of dating relationships (Hill, Rubin, and Peplau) and
the fact that increasing numbers of women are fleeing marital situations.
Such withdrawal on the parts of women in inequitable romantic relationships are to be expected since strong interpersonal relationships
rarely survive extended periods of unfair social exchange.

Given our foregoing discussion of male love, it is possible that the
seeds for the dissolution of romantic heterosexual relationships lie in
most romantic relationships between men and women because most men
value dominance. This means that in most romantic involvements, unless
a particular woman allows a particular man to be dominant the romantic

relationship will dissolve. In a review of divorce research, Kitson and Raschke (1981) concluded that divorced couples may have different views of marital roles than do those samples who remain married. While they do not say so, in all likelihood, the basis for men's and women's divergent views of marital roles probably lies in their different conceptions of men's and women's roles in American society in general.

Why Men Are Attracted to Others: What Men Want

It has been recognized for some time that certain rewards others provide frequently result in interpersonal attraction (Berscheid and Walster, 1969). Rewards such as reduction of anxiety, stress, loneliness and insecurity; propinquity, which increases the probability of rewards; reciprocal liking; similarity of attitudes; need complementarity; need completion; and cooperative behavior, singularly or in combination, foster interpersonal attraction between men and others. In this section, we will discuss not what men *ought* to want or who they *should* like but rather, what men today seem to *actually* want and who they seem to *actually* like. Quite simply this section discusses traits in others (both men and women) that attract men. We will begin by exploring traits in men that attract men.

What Men Like in Other Men

To begin with, the discussion in this section is limited to nonsexual relationships between men. Sexual relationships between men will be explored in the next chapter on male sexuality. The discussion to follow does, however, include homosexual men who have same-sex interpersonal relationships that do not extend to sexual relations. The rationale for the inclusion of homosexual men in these nonsexual relationships is simple: they are men most of whom are indistinguishable from the heterosexual male population in all respects with the exception of sexual preference.

In a recent survey of 181 men and women (70 men and 111 women) in an introductory sociology class at Ohio State University 84% (59) of the men listed physical attractiveness among the three traits which most attracts them to women. While this percentage was expected given the findings from previous studies (e.g., Berscheid and Walster, 1974; Janda et al., 1981), the fact that 36% of the males (25) listed physical attractiveness among the three traits which most attracted them to other males was surprising. Further inquiry into why physically attractive males were preferred by those men listing the trait clarified the finding. Over three-fourths of the men who indicated that they were attracted to physically attractive men reported either that such men could be assets in their relationships with women or that such men would be more likely to enjoy participating in the same sports activities. The other men gave no reason for their attraction pattern. In essence, many of the men felt that physically attractive male associates would perform important instrumental functions for them. As expected less than 10% of the men in the survey listed traits associated with emotional intimacy such as warmth, kindness, understanding, and so on.

Much controversy has existed regarding male–male relationships. For example, some have suggested that men form lasting friendships while women are incapable of such lasting bonds (e.g., Tiger, 1974; Donelson and Gullahorn, 1977). Others (e.g., Bell, 1977; Wheeler and Nezlez, 1977) contend that women's friendships are characterized more by intimacy and emotionality than men's friendships. A recent study by Caldwell and Peplau (1982) on sex differences in same-sex friendships among college men and women reported that men's friendships were qualitatively different from women's friendships. Both men and women in the study reported valuing intimacy in friendships but objective measures of intimate interaction used by Caldwell and Peplau indicated that men's interactions with a best friend were less personal and intimate than women's (p. 731). In fact, men were found to prefer engaging in specific activities with their friends rather than conversing with their best friends. When men did talk with "best friends" the conversation centered around shared activities and interests rather than their feelings, problems, personal relationships, etc.—topics that dominate women's conversations with their best friends. Caldwell and Peplau conclude, as suggested earlier in this chapter, that emotional sharing plays a lesser role in men's than women's same-sex friendships.

That a male's attraction for another male is not based on the other male's ability to reduce his anxiety, stress, loneliness, insecurity and the like should be expected. While most men may be attracted to women whose presence reduces their anxiety, stress, loneliness, and insecurity, it is unlikely that they will be attracted to other men who have the same effect on them. To the contrary, most heterosexual men experiencing such an effect in the presence of other men probably would be unsettled by the experience. Indeed, in all likelihood their stress and/or anxiety would be exacerbated by the "discovery" that other men can arrest their anxiety and/or stress.

What *are* some characteristics in men that other men find attractive? Generally, men are attracted to other men who share similar ideas, values, attitudes and who like to engage in certain similar activities (e.g., sports, clubs, etc.). Since liking is not as expressive in male–male relationships as in others (like male–female relationships and female–female relationships), mutual expressiveness does not seem to be necessary in male–male interpersonal attraction. In fact, because emotional sharing plays a lesser role in men's interpersonal relationships, joint participation in activities seems to be the magnet that draws men together, Succinctly, men are attracted to other men because of specific instrumental qualities, such as shared interests in sports and work (Pleck, 1975). This means also that men's initial attraction to other men may largely depend upon perceived similarity in attitudes and values. Regardless of whether increasing association results in perceived similarity or vice-versa, men who perceive themselves to be similar in attitudes are likely to be attracted to each other. Now this does not mean that they are or will be intimate friends. Yet, if they show similar instrumental and nonempathic attitudes and values, they may very well be able to form the bases for social organization.

What Men Like in Women

As mentioned above 84% of the men in the survey listed physical attractiveness among the three traits which most attracts them to women. Yet, as we alluded to earlier, factors other than physical attractiveness seem more useful in determining interpersonal attraction since perceptions of physical attractiveness vary considerably among men. In addition, there is no dearth of physically attractive women in American society and few men seem to be attracted to all of them. Instead, most men tend to be attracted to specific other women for reasons which go beyond their physical characteristics. The reason can be lumped into one category: the rewards women provide for men which may include anxiety and stress reduction, reciprocal liking, need complementarity, etc. What is interesting about the specific rewards women provide for men that attract men is that the rewards are valued by men because they reinforce male dominance. Ninety percent (63) of the men in the survey mentioned "feminine" traits such as "warmth," "ladylike," and "feminine" as ones which attract them to women. Traits like "intelligence," "assertiveness," and "strength" appeared on only 14 % (10) of the men's lists. In addition, over one-half (56%) of the men reported that they preferred a male-dominated relationship with women; roughly 39% (27); and 5% (3) preferred egalitarian and female-dominant relationships respectively. Of the men (40) who preferred male dominant relationships with women 98% (39) listed physical attractiveness among the three traits which most attracted them to women. Only 70% (19) of the males preferring egalitarian relationships (27) listed physical attractiveness among the three traits which most attract them to women; and, two of the three men who preferred female-dominant relationships listed physical attractiveness. These findings support a position that many males continue to resist sex-role changes in American society; and feminist claims that many men's preoccupation with women's physical features may be a form of male dominance appear to be true, although physical attractiveness seems to be important for males with various preferences.

Quite a few men in American society today are attracted to those women who reduce their anxiety, stress, loneliness, and insecurity. In practice this means that the majority of men are attracted to women who are not perceived as threatening—women who validate their masculinity by allowing them to be dominant in relationships. While reciprocal liking is important for men in their heterosexual interpersonal relationships, most men interacting with women tend to do so from positions of dominance. Goffman (1952) once made a statement about marriage that seems to apply to less intense interpersonal relations between men and women in American society. Goffman (p. 456) stated that "a proposal of marriage in our society, tends to be a way in which a man sums up his social attributes and suggests to a woman that she is not so much better as to preclude a merger or partnership in these matters." This seems to be the precise strategy used by men during the initial stages of interaction with women. Women during the initial stages of interaction are expected to display "appropriate" submissive behaviors, which men find rewarding. It is not that a particular woman should hold attitudes and values *similar* to a particular man's but rather, she should hold attitudes and values which, to a large extent, *agree* with the ones held by that man. More often than not this means that women's attitudes and values should be complementary to men's—women must be willing to assume roles that allow men to be dominant in relationships. Most men in American society are not capable of enjoying the rewards that can accompany heterosexual interpersonal attraction unless such rewards are predicated on the assumption of male dominance. Stated another way, men are attracted to women to the extent that women's attitudes and values are in agreement with theirs regarding a man's "place" and a woman's "place" in society. While some men relax these requirements somewhat for platonic relationships, the requirements for romantic relationships tend to remain intact. Further changes in the roles of men and women and sex-role socialization consistent with such changes, will, I hope, alter the role that male dominance plays in male interpersonal attraction.

Characteristics in Men that Attract Others: What Women Like in Men

Orlofsky's findings that males preferred dating partners/wives who were more feminine than themselves and that although females preferred androgynous dating partners/husbands, they wanted them to be somewhat more masculine, led him to draw the following conclusion:

> ... heterosexual attraction patterns may also be governed more by societal stereotypes and norms than by individual differences in sex-role personality traits. According to a norm which may be on the decline but is still probably quite prevalent in the society, husbands should be more masculine and less feminine than their wives (p. 1069).

Orlofsky's findings are similar to those obtained by Kulik and Harackiewicz as discussed in this chapter. The message is clear: heterosexual women appear to be attracted to men who are high on masculine qualities but who also exhibit some feminine qualities. Perhaps qualities such as warmth, emotional expressiveness, kindness and the like are seen by women more as human qualities than masculine ones. Moreover, women may perceive such qualities as necessary in harmonious relationships between members of either sex since same-sex friendships between women have been found to be more intimate and emotionally expressive than those between men. Whatever the reason, many women today express a preference for those men who possess some characteristics traditionally associated with femininity.

Data from the survey mentioned earlier reflect that many of these women prefer androgynous males. For example, 89 percent (99) of the women listed traditionally "feminine" characteristics (e.g., warmth, kindness, tenderness) among the three traits which most attracts them to men. At the same time, 92% (103) listed traditionally "masculine" traits (e.g., athletic prowess, intelligence, assertiveness, confidence) as attracting them. Another interesting finding from the survey was that 77% of the women listed physical attractiveness among the three traits that most attract them to men; and, all of the women (12%—13) who preferred a male-dominant relationship listed physical attractiveness as a trait that attracts them to men. Eighty-four % (93) of the women perferred an egalitarian relationship and 4% (5) wanted female dominant relationships. Indeed, 70% of the women *expected* their actual relationship to be egalitarian.

What these data seem to imply as well as do women's articles, books, public statements, and so on is that women today are increasingly resisting male dominance. While women's voices may be more muted now than they were in recent past, women still are demanding mutual expressiveness, empathy, authority, and power in their relationships with men. This means that we will have to continue freeing ourselves from the shackles of societal sexism if we expect initial attraction between ourselves and women to develop into long-lasting and harmonious relationships.

CHAPTER 7

Themes in Male Sexuality

Undoubtedly persons hoping to learn something about male sexuality in the United States get a distorted picture from films such as *48 Hours*. Nick Nolte and Eddie Murphy, portraying a policeman and a convict respectively, successfully present a "wham, bam, thank you ma'am," inborn-sexual-impulse perspective of heterosexual male sexuality—a perspective that is insulting to many men *and* women in American society. Unfortunately this does not mean that many men in American do not hold sexual attitudes and exhibit sexual behaviors of the kind presented in *48 Hours*. Indeed, too many American men *do* display these kinds of sexual attitudes and behaviors, despite the fact that sexuality is a much more complex issue. In addition, the position taken here is that the source of such attitudes and behaviors lies in socio-cultural conditions rather than in innate tendencies. A basic assumption underlying this chapter, then, is that *male sexual behavior is largely acquired through experience and socialization* (Gross, 1978). This perspective contends that male sexuality is more than the sexual act and involves more than the biological component of sexual response. Male sexuality consists of *affective, cognitive, behavioral*, and *physiological* components which interact, become defined, and are experienced by men as sexual events.

To begin with, it is safe to say that one aspect of masculinity in American society is the sexualization of men's relationships with others. Not only are men's relationships with women sexualized but their relationships—or lack of relationships—with other men also are sexualized. It is because men's relationships with other men are sexualized that much homophobia exists among males in our society. Moreover, as we will discuss, even when sexual relationships exist between men, these relationships are often similar to heterosexual relationships and suffer from similar dysfunctions. As male sexuality is explored, we will examine general ideas about males and sex; men's levels and patterns of heterosexual involvement; men's homosexual involvements; men's ambisexual involvements; men's asexuality; and, the relationship between men, sex, and violence.

Men and Sex

Upon reaching adolescence, Julius Lester (1973) recalls, the pressure to prove himself on the athletic field lessened but the overall situation worsened "because now I had to prove myself with girls" (p. 112). Lester was referring to the fact that much male adolescent peer pressure is directed toward the male youth's sexual "accomplishment." His account of these pressures is strikingly similar to Bill Cosby's (1975) memories of his experiences with the girls in his neighborhood and the imagined pleasure to be derived from their bodies. Such pressures and conversations among young American males are commonplace and to a great extent expected by society. In fact, if boys do not display these sexually oriented behaviors upon reaching adolescence, parents (especially fathers) are likely to become extremely concerned that either the boy suffers from some physiological disability or, worse yet, that an emotional or psychological problem exists which has caused a "disturbed sexual identity."

Males in our society are expected to be interested in sex, have a greater need for sex, and to know about it at a relatively early age. Gross has pointed out that sexuality becomes a central part of masculine identity for male youth early in boyhood because of combined social and biological forces. He contends that easy access to the penis coupled with boys' erections probably result in earlier masturbatory activities for boys than girls. Early masturbation establishes a link between sexual desire/ feeling and the penis. Thus, boys tend to develop quite early a genital focus which is supported overtly by male youth peer groups' emphases on "seeking sex" and adult society's (especially adult men's) covert acceptance *and* encouragement of such activities. These activities include "proving oneself with girls" games, "circle-jerk" games, and the like. What all such games have in common is a preoccupation with sexual climax and the idea that sexual climax is an indicator of sexual accomplishment. Gross feels that this attitude leads many men to isolate sex from other social aspects of life. As a result, men more than women are not likely to combine sex and intimacy which is thought to be incompatible with the sexual orientation of many women. Women are thought to have more extensive social and affectional needs than men (Reik, 1960).

Do great numbers of American men really have genital foci and do they tend to isolate sex from other aspects of their lives? The answer to this question appears to be an unqualified "yes" based on the fact that numerous men require only minimal involvement with a sex partner in order to enact the sexual role. While men do *select* their partners, their criteria for acceptability of sexual partners admit a wide range of partners. For example, most men find acceptable as potential sexual partners many persons with diverse characteristics and this violates a necessary condition for relationships characterized by *deep involvement.* "A necessary condition for achieving deeper levels of engagement with the partner is that the sex partner must meet more narrow and stringent requirements for becoming an acceptable sex partner" (Mosher, 1980, p.17). Men, in contrast, generally have wide latitudes of acceptance of sex partners which is related directly to men's preoccupation with sexual climax and the tendency to isolate sex from other aspects of their lives. Evidence for this contention is seen in higher rates of sex offenses among men ranging from heterosexual rape and including sex offenses with children to homosexual acts in public toilets. As Mosher has suggested "chance or the opportunity to engage in sex seems to be more important than the sex partner's appearance or personal qualities." Many men learn sexual attitudes and strategies consistent with such a casual acceptability of sex partners. Using Mosher's dimension of sexual involvement, it seems likely that internalization of masculine traits in America predisposes men toward a particular kind of sexual involvement that is generally discrepant with women's sexual involvement. Let us consider these dimensions and their implications for male sexuality.

Mosher contends that effective physical sexual stimulation is a function of the extent to which a participant is psychologically involved in the sexual act. Psychological involvement in the sexual act refers to the degree a person during the sexual contact episode is characterized by (1) expressive action; (2) focused awareness of sexual sensations and emotions, excluding all other aspects of the sexual environment; and (3) interpersonal engagement with the partner. Psychological involvement is seen further as varying in depth from *shallow* to *deep*. Depth of psychological involvement in the sexual act *specifies the levels to which a person is absorbed in expressive action, focused awareness and interpersonal contact.* The deeper the participant is psychologically involved in the sexual act, the greater the likelihood that the experience will be both emotionally satisfying and meaningful.

Depth of psychological involvement is seen further by Mosher as consisting of three distinct dimensions: (1) involvement in sexual role enactment; (2) involvement in sexual trance; and (3) involvement with the sex partner. When a person *enacts a sexual role,* he or she actually plays a sexual script that is complementary to that of his or her partner's during a sexual contact episode. In other words, a sex role is assumed that involves demands and expected behaviors in an appropriate sexual environment. Involvement in sexual-role enactment ranges from disinterest or avoidance on the part of a person (zero involvement) to what Mosher calls "ecstatic sexual role enactment," wherein the person loses a sense of self and union with the partner is complete. Six levels of depth of involvement in sexual role enactment are proposed by Mosher and described in Table 8.

A second dimension of a participant's psychological involvement in the sexual act, according to Mosher, is *the degree to which a participant becomes involved in sexual trance.* Sexual trance refers to *a person's altered state of consciousness as a result of absorption in a special sexual orientation.* The process is described as one where there is a gradual fading of a person's generalized reality orientation accompanied by the gradual construction

Table 8
Depth of Involvement in Sexual Role Enactment

0.	Zero Involvement	Avoidance or disinterest; complete segregation of self and role; no effort or effect.
1.	Casual Sexual Role Enactment	Detached or perfunctory motor behavior; imagines self in another role; inappropriate or angry affect.
2.	Routine Sexual Role Enactment	Routine, mechanical action; consistency between role enactment and expectations; façade of efforts and affects; critical spectator.
3.	Engrossed Sexual Role Enactment	Concern with style, tempo, motility, and duration of action; becomes role and complements role enactment of partner; heated self-expression.
4.	Entranced Sexual Role Enactment	Action flows without conscious deliberation or direction; self merged into role; nonvoluntary and intense affects.
5.	Ecstatic Sexual Role Enactment	Person possessed by overpowering need and preoccupation; no volition but self is transported and transformed; peak experience.

of a special sexual orientation—"the person begins to filter sensations, emotions, and meanings through the emerging special sexual orientation" (p.13). When a man, for example, becomes totally absorbed in the special sexual orientation, reality is what is occuring at the moment. He focuses on his specific sensations and actions as well as those of his partners. The only thing that is important for him, for example, is the extreme pleasure being derived from the warm, lubricating and satiny feeling of his partner's genitals surrounding his penis. Mosher's six levels of depth of involvement in sexual trance are listed in Table 9.

Mosher's third dimension of psychological involvement is *depth of involvement with the sex partner*. Pointing out that persons have varying latitudes of sex partner acceptance (which include casual acceptability, general acceptability, selective acceptability, affectionate acceptance, and unique acceptance), Mosher feels that the deepest involvement with a sex partner requires narrow partner acceptance. When a person becomes union-oriented in sex he or she experiences a spiritual and/or mystical sharing (the ultimate sexual union) and a loving merger where the self and partner are transcended. This means that the depth of involvement with the sex partner goes beyond the past and the present; does not include the individual's ego, a concern with the partner's appearance, or a concern with the partner's core self. In other words, the union itself becomes paramount. As Mosher describes such unions, "sex is timeless and eternal, a symbol of union, death, and rebirth that is ageless yet fresh and newborn . . . Feeling blessed, the person feels humble and in awe at

Table 9
Depth of Involvement in Sexual Trance

Fading of the Generalized Reality-Orientation (GRO)	Construction of the Special Sexual-Orientation (SSP)
0. Inability to give up GRO.	1. No development of SSO.
1. Partial relaxation of critical attitude; vulnerable to situational distraction.	2. Partial orientation to sexual experience and meanings.
2. Partial fading of GRO; vulnerable to interruption through spectatoring.	3. Predominant focus of attention on SSO.
3. Abandonment of GRO.	4. Establishment of SSO; interest captivated.
4. Urgent distraction arouses GRO.	5. Concentration in SSO through deliberate awareness.
5. Urgent meaningful distraction recalls GRO.	6. Involuntary fascination in SSO.
6. Emergency reawakens GRO.	7. Total absorption in SSO.

Table 10
Depth of Involvement with the Sex Partner

1. Past-Oriented, Ego-Centered Involvement.	Hostility overrides sexuality; fantasy of revenge to reverse past sexual trauma; partner as prop.
2. Present-Oriented, Ego-Centered Involvement.	Present sensory, genital experience; fantasyless; partner as necessary genital.
3. Self-Oriented, Surface-Centered Involvement.	Self-appraisal of appearance and performance; fantasy as secret pornography; partner as necessary 'alter' to ego.
4. Partner-Oriented, Surface-Centered Involvement.	Appreciation of partner's appearance and performance; partner's pleasure as important as own pleasure; fantasy as shared pornography; 'alter' is equal partner to ego.
5. Partner-Oriented, Care-Centered Involvement.	Appreciation of partner's core potentialities; self-disclosure and acceptance of partner's self; loving synergy; fantasies are romantic and poetic; partner is love.
6. Union-Oriented, Care-Centered Involvement.	Consciousness of self and partner is lost in experience of mystical union; human act of living is a spiritual sharing that celebrates life itself; partner and self become universal man and women.

the reverence of this celebration of life" (p. 22). Table 10 describes the depths of involvement with the sex partner as proposed by Mosher.

Patterns of Men's Heterosexual Involvement

As suggested earlier, if men internalize traditional definitions of masculinity they may not be able to become deeply involved in sexual relationships. Using Mosher's model, let us explore American men's sexual involvement along the suggested dimensions. Regardless of the sex of men's sexual partners, men in the United States generally bring with them into the sexual arena certain traits or characteristics that may impede deep involvement in sexual activities. While relatively few men (although the numbers are said to be increasing) seem to avoid sex or express disinterest in the activity, many more only casually enact the sexual role, as reflected in the tendencies of some men to have unusually wide latitudes of partner acceptance. Men who rape, have sex with children, engage in sex with willing partners in public facilities (e.g., parks and restrooms), visit prostitutes and the like can be thought of simply as engaging in a detached and perfunctory motor sexual activity. Basically these men are not concerned with pleasing their partners and many are actually hostile toward them (e.g., the rapist). In such instances, the sex partner is only an instrument used to accomplish sexual release. Men engaging in such sexual-contact episodes remain in touch with reality, never constructing a special sexual orientation. In essence, the depth of involvement for men who engage in these sexual acts is ego-centered, filled with hostility, post-and present reality, and is simply a physical act. What is important about this shallowest of sexual involvements is that men as a rule seem more capable of engaging in sex on this level. Sex-role socialization may be responsible for men's greater, albeit unfortunate, capabilities in this area. If males in our society learn to isolate sex from other aspects of their lives and also have genital foci, then it is axiomatic that many adapt patterns of shallow involvement in sexual activities. Mercer and Kohn's (1979) finding that sexuality is more integrated into the overall personality for females than for males; and, their argument that a reported greater male sex urge is central to understanding sex differences in sexuality integrations are instructive. For females, *sexual urge* better predicted *frequency of sexual contacts* while *attitudes and values* better predicted *number of sexual partners*. For males, attitudes and values did not predict frequency of sexual contacts nor did they predict number of sexual partners; however, reported sexual urge predicted both. In terms of sex-partner selection for males, then attitudes and values play a relatively minor role for many once they feel the sexual urge. Certainly this reflects men's tendencies to isolate sex and also their propensity toward engagement in shallow sexual relationships.

The link between sex and masculinity for American men surely is important but some choose *not* to engage in the most casual of sexual encounters described above. Quite a few men do construct general classes of acceptable persons for recreational sexual involvement. These classes may be along racial, age, ethnic, religious, and physical-attractiveness lines, separately or in combination. Men who engage in recreational sex may be *routinely* or more *engrossed* in their sexual role enactments. The latter depth of involvement for men probably characterizes those more spontaneous recreational sexual encounters characteristic of many premarital and/or extramarital relationships. During such sexual contact episodes, men may be either present-oriented, ego-centered, or self-oriented, ego-centered. The partner is viewed simply as necessary for the experience and often men at this level of involvement are concerned with their performances during the sexual-contact episode. During such encounters, most men relax their orientations to reality and may even experience partial fadings of their generalized reality-orientations. This is accompanied by minimum-to-high interest in a special sexual orientation. Many American men are capable of such a relationship.

When men display more selectivity in partner acceptance by being concerned about their partner's physical qualities, and by feeling that it is necessary to have a personal bond between them and their partners (which may range from pleasure to affectionate investment), the depth of involvement with the sex partner usually will be at least partner-oriented, surface-centered and may approach partner-oriented, core-centered. The sex partner's pleasure in such encounters is deemed important by men. Concern with the partner's pleasure is manifested for these men in their concern with the technique, style and duration of the sex act. Men involved in sexual acts of this kind frequently give up their reality orientations and firmly establish their sexual orientations, often through deliberate concentration and awareness, but occasionally without conscious deliberation. This kind of male sexuality is probably characteristic of a wide variety of males who have internalized the sexual norm of men pleasuring their sex partners.

Another male sexuality pattern is seen in the behaviors prior to sexual contact. Sex, for these men, is an affectionate adventure and involves self-disclosure and acceptance of the sex partner as a love object. The sex role is enacted spontaneously and the man does not think of himself as distinct from the role he is performing. During the actual sexual episode, men's reality orientations tend to disappear and there is total and unconscious concentration on their emergent sexual orientations. Often, however, the male sex role interferes with men's sexual involvement to further depths. After all, men learn not to place themselves in such vulnerable positions—they are to be strong, in command, powerful, and dominant. To become more deeply involved in sex, for many men, would mean to give up portions of their masculinity. Men involved in this sexuality pattern do remain partner-oriented and in a real sense, psychologically in control. To go further means to give up the last vestige of male dominance. Admittedly, few men today seem capable of taking the final step.

The final step of involvement has been reached by a man in a sexual relationship when his latitude of partner acceptance is unique—when there is a single, specific person and they are enveloped by a bond of love and the two persons participate in loving sex. The male sex role, though it presents barriers to such partner acceptance, may not inhibit such an involvement in men's *romantic* relationships. The male sex role does, however, inhibit further development of male sexual involvement along other dimensions. In order for a man to become totally absorbed in his special sexual orientation, the male self has to be transformed and transported. The man must experience a feeling of complete oneness with his partner, with no self-boundaries. In a heterosexual sexual encounter, maleness and femaleness must become unimportant so that full absorption in the special sexual orientation may occur. In a very real sense, as the man becomes united with the woman, he must experience that aspect of the union that is feminine as well as the aspect that is masculine. Sex-role socialization frequently renders men in our society incapable of such an experience which requires imaginatively taking the role of the female sex partner—a requirement that is opposed to the socialization experiences of men in our society.

Women's Freedom and Men's Sex

The advent of the birth-control pill for females in the early Sixties and the subsequent free-love movement of the late sixties and early Seventies led to what is commonly called the "sexual revolution." In addition to changes in the sexual roles of males and females, the concept "sexual revolution" implies that *sexuality* has been altered for American men and women. Current sex surveys reveal that, indeed, change has occurred in American sexual attitudes and values. Most of the change, however, has occurred in women's sexual attitudes, values and behavior. Current sex surveys indicate that, in contrast to women of twenty years ago, women today are quite similar to men in the variety of their recreational sexual practices. Janet Lever (1982) of Northwestern University, who was hired along with several other researchers by *Playboy* magazine to conduct a sex survey of the "veterans" of the sexual revolution, states that "men and women have mutually benefitted from a change in attitudes toward sex."

Results of the analysis of more than 100,000 responses which have received the most publicity, however, deal with the responses from approximately 20,000 women. Aside from the finding that men, like women, are looking for "love," most attention has been directed to such findings as "women in the survey, more than men, indicated that they talked dirty during sex; a greater proportion of women than men under 29 said that they lost their virginity before the age of 16; and that 43% of the 80,000-plus men wanted to marry a woman with sexual experience. Such findings led the team of researchers to suggest sexual prosperity for

American men and women. Lever states "the good news is that people are happy, healthy, and more satisfied with each other."

Equally optimistic about the sexual health of American men and women were findings from a sex survey conducted by *Ladies Home Journal* magazine in June, 1982. Ellen Frank (1983) of the University of Pittsburgh (who analyzed the results of responses from 83,000 married women) reports that 80% of the respondents rated their sexual relationships as satisfying and their marriages as happy; 70% reported that they were sexually active before the age of 20; 83% had engaged in sexual intercourse prior to marriage; 95% said that they sometimes initiated sex with their partners; and 21% indicated that they had experienced an extramarital affair. Frank concluded that "the vast majority of our respondents see a healthy, active sex life as a natural and important part of being married."

Disregarding the questionable generalizability of the findings from the two surveys because of the "accidental" nature of the samples obtained, results of the research actually tell us little about male sexuality—or female sexuality for that matter. To be sure, some married women seem to be enjoying sex both within and outside of marriage. Also, women responding to the surveys seem to be experimenting more and earlier than men (according to one of the surveys); and, some men (43% in one survey) do not indicate that they are "turned off" by the fact that women in general, hold sexually liberated views and behave in a sexually "free" manner. In other words, the two surveys corroborate Bonnie Allen's (1983) contention that women are now able to "initiate one-night stands" and say "wham, bam, thank you, mister." I contend, however, that a larger part of the story remains untold. Women's exhibition of sexually "free" behavior does not mean that there has been any real alteration in male sexuality or in the female sexual role. Men in America still remain in charge of the sexual arena, and as long as male dominance in sexual matters persists, male sexuality and female sexuality will be unalterable. A quote from Allen's essay in a recent issue of *Essence* Magazine states succinctly the thrust of the sexual revolution and the results for women:

> The way things changed to me is all about boredom. I've been through everything at least once. I don't have the energy to repeat myself. The sexual revolution showed me that men and women are equally fucked up. Before, I could get a piece because my body wanted a piece. I thought I could separate my body from me. Now I know I can't.

The lamenting theme of the above quote implies that one woman recognizes that while the sexual revolution might have changed women's behaviors, it did *not* rewrite the sexual script. The sexual script basically says that men assume powerful roles in sexual relationships and women assume submissive roles. Recent exhibitions of sexual freedom by many women have not altered this power-dependence relationship as Jack Litewka (1979) illustrates in his essay, "The Socialized Penis." Litewka relates three personal sexual incidents that have implications for socialized male dominance in the sexual arena. Quite simply, Litewka found himself unable to have erections on three different sexual occasions and on each occasion he was with a different woman whom he really liked, respected, admired, and so on. In Litewka's own words, having resocialized himself and being "liberated" he was "able to accept these women on all levels as equals" . . . except for one level: "I was not capable of accepting females as sexual equals. I hold onto this last bastion of male supremacy with a death-grip" (p. 106). Just as revealing as Litewka's personal account is a Black man's account of his response to a sexually liberated woman, as reported by Bonnie Allen: "The first time a woman told me how she wanted sex, I fell apart. This was supposed to be my territory. I realized if she could tell me what she wanted, and how she wanted it, she might be judging my performance" (p. 118).

Men's Dominance and Men's Sex

A common theme of male sexuality in America underlies both of the above accounts—*male dominance*. This trait in male sexuality is so firmly established in most heterosexual men's identities until it is nearly impossible for them to engage in sex unless the traditional sexual script characterizes the sexual-contact episode. How do men get this way or as Litewka would say, how do men become so sexually damaged? The answer seems to lie in the socialization experiences of men which involve, for most, internalizing an *achievement orientation* (Slater, 1976) to sex and the development of certain elements necessary for sexual stimulation and response such as *objectification, fixation* and *conquest* (Litewka, 1979).

An achievement orientation has been mentioned as one of the traits most men in the United States are expected to internalize and exhibit in social interaction. Slater believes that men's obsessions with achievement pervade their sexual lives leading them to strive for perfect orgasms while ignoring the pleasures that can accompany leisurely love. Such obsessions are thought to be related to men's preoccupation with technical mastery. When translated to the sexual arena, women become objects to be manipulated and men become preoccupied with the *end* (climax) of the sexual act. This aspect of many men's sexuality suggests that not only may a particular man not be interested in a particular woman, but he really may not be interested in sex; rather, he may be interested simply in releasing tension, since he cannot tolerate pleasurable stimulation "beyond a minimum level and wants it to end as rapidly as possible within the limits of sexual etiquette and competent performance" (Slater, p. 87). The fact that quick sexual gratification apparently has become more plentiful for men with increasing sexual freedom for women has not meant that men have become less goal-oriented in their sexual behavior. In fact one might find that men may be having sex *more*, but enjoying it *less*, especially with more emphasis being placed on their "performances" and no accompanying increases in the depths of their sexual involvements.

Slater poses some interesting male "attraction" questions which have further implications for male sexuality. He asks: "Does the fact that men are so easily turned off—by age, weight, and sundry other departures from some narrow *Playboy* ideal—mean that they really don't like women much?" Are men's heterosexual desires so weak until they need a specialized feminine ideal to help them "get it up?" Do women really like men more than men like women? Noting that women seem far more nonspecific in their attractions to men than vice-versa; and also, the fact that homosexual men are just as specific in their requirements for sexual partners as heterosexual men are in theirs, Slater implies that this sexual orientation may be a result of sex-role socialization and the dysfunctions associated with the isolation of feelings and the sacrificing of emotions in men's goal-oriented strivings.

The Socialized Penis and Men's Sex

The sexual handicap that many American men bring with them to sexual encounters with women center around their "socialized penises" which are taught to perform only when men have the opportunity to *objectify, fixate on,* and *conquer* women (Litewka, 1979). Having objectified, fixated on and conquered their penises and having made them central to their definitions of masculinity, men become self-contained sexual systems. As Litewka says, having a penis and getting an erection is equated with maleness and ego and anything that causes erections is to be used (p. 105). Females do not even have to be physically present for this to occur. But, when they *are* physically present, men can enact the socialized sexual script and thus hopefully reestablish and affirm their masculinity through sexual climax. The first step of enacting the male sexual script most men learn in early childhood is to objectify women. Once the male child is able to distinguish himself and other males from females and rationalize that the distinction rests on female attributes (e.g., females do not have penises, females have breasts, females have rounded hips, and the like) male objectification of females begins. Further sex-role socialization regarding appropriate behavior for males and females nurtures males' tendencies to objectify females. Litewka feels further that male sexual initiation involves males' learning to fixate first on externally visible parts of the female body (e.g., breasts, legs, waist) which become associated with pleasure, being a man, getting an erection, and so on. In this way, men become socialized to the role of fixation in male sexual response. Males learn that they can imagine females, and portions of their bodies and cause erections. The final development of male sexuality occurs when males achieve some form of sexual gratification as in heavy petting, sexual intercourse and the like. This is done through conquest, with men awarding the "trophy" to themselves when they are able to say that they are men and share this knowledge with other men. Such scenarios mean that males are socialized to respond sexually to no specific female but with the ones they happen to be with at a particular time. As Litewka states: "Any number of lips or breasts or vaginas would do— as long as we can objectify, fixate, and conquer, an erection and (provided there is some form of penile friction) ejaculation will occur" (p. 105).

Men and Homosexuality

Homosexuality and Men's Power

There are few names an American male can be called which will result in greater and more emotionally violent responses in him than "fag," "queer," "fruit," or a synonymous name. This is true for both homosexual men *and* heterosexual men. However, in this section we will be concerned with *homosexual men's responses* to themselves, others, *and* others' responses to homosexual men. In general, the responses many homosexual men have to sexual-orientation slurs are similar to the responses other minority group members (e.g., Blacks, Italians, women) have to racial/ethnic/sexual epithets. But, why do heterosexual men seem to respond so negatively to being labeled "fag"? A tall, blonde, blue-eyed, straight-haired, chisel-featured white male who can trace his lineage to Anglo-Saxon families in Europe would probably be only amused at the most if he were called a "nigger." Why is it that a "straight" male who is aggressive, athletic, independent, responsible, and woman-loving can respond so violently to being called "queer," "fag," or "sissy"?

Undoubtedly if such a male is questioned regarding his negative reaction he will say that he is responding to how "fags" are and he is not like "them." He would point out that unlike "fags" he possesses the following characteristics and/or exhibits the following behavior: he is not afraid of women; in fact he "screws" women; he does not act like a woman; he is muscular and does not "look" like a fag; he is married or plans to get married; he has children; he does not molest little kids; he does not aspire to be a beautician, artist, dancer, or the like; he is upwardly mobile; and the list goes on. Ironically, part of the explanation of our hypothetical "heterosexual" male's violent response to being called "fag" lies in his list of characteristics describing himself. Most homosexual men possess the same characteristics; and, in terms of behavior, either exhibit similar behaviors now or have exhibited such behaviors in the not-too-distant past.

Lehne (1974), in a survey of early 1970s studies on homosexual men makes the following observations: around 20% of self-labeled homosexual men are married; approximately 75% of homosexual men have engaged in petting with women; 50% have engaged in sexual intercourse with women; 50% have at some time been involved in a relationship with a woman lasting more than a year; only 15% of homosexual men are suspected of being "gay"; there is no evidence that homosexual men avoid characteristically "masculine" occupations; there is no demographic research to support the belief that homosexuals often molest children (there is a tendency on the part of many to confuse pedophilia with homosexuality); and, some studies do show that homosexual men appear to be more upwardly mobile than comparable groups of heterosexual men.

Returning to our hypothetical male's violent response to being labeled "fag," not only are his characteristics and behaviors similar to many male homosexuals characteristics and behaviors, but many "heterosexual" men engage in homosexual sex at some point in their lives after adolescence. The surprising report (for many Americans) nearly three and a half decades ago that 37% of the American male population had experienced homosexual sex to orgasm (Kinsey, Pomeroy, and Martin, 1948) indicated that homosexual sex is not an alien act to many American males. Why, then, do men respond in "characteristically" negative ways to being labeled homosexual and why do heterosexual men respond so negatively to homosexual men? Lehne feels, and I concur, that persons who are homophobic are not really threatened by *homosexuality*; rather, they are threatened by alterations in the male role that could mean less male dominance, less male power, and so on. He suggests further that male devaluation of homosexuality supports maintenance of men's power. Since the male role is maintained largely by men, a homophobic norm controls men in their male roles. Any man is subject to this control because any man has the "potential" for homosexuality and therefore can be made to "fear" being labeled "homosexual." This fear, according to Lehne, is used to ensure male conformity to "masculine" role expectations. Those men, for example, who do not use power for their own benefit; who do not participate in the process of male power maintenance by defining and enforcing women's sexual roles (e.g., sexual harassment or sexual exploitation of women,); and, who do not exhibit other sexual and nonsexual dominance traits can be labeled or threatened with being labeled "homosexual." By labeling or threatening to label such men "homosexual," it is implied that they do not support the dominant male role, nor are they likely to use their male "power" to further the interests of males. This, in itself, justifies excluding some men from positions of power, since they constitute a threat to the continuation of male power (Lehne, pp. 79–80). Research findings (e.g., Hooberman, 1979) actually show that homosexual men tend to be more androgynous (exhibiting a greater tendency to both highly masculine and highly feminine traits) than heterosexual men but that homosexual men portray great variety in their sexuality, gender and gender identity. If such findings are applicable to larger populations of homosexual men, then the belief that homosexual men are a threat to male power maintenance is unfounded, albeit noncomplimentary to women.

Another point that can be made regarding the labeling of some men as homosexuals is that the labeling process is also beneficial to other men. It is beneficial to some other men because it decreases the number of males who can compete for highly prestigious positions *within* the powerful male group. Certainly this increases the probabilities of "success" for other "capable" men not labeled. Rodney Karr (1978) found in his study of the homosexual labeling process that men who are labeled "homosexual" are devalued by other men and that other men maintain social distance. Moreover, those men who were found to hold more negative attitudes toward homosexuality exaggerated their reactions to the presence of a homosexually-labeled man. Thus, many reactions men have to homosexual men may have little to do with the behaviors of homosexual men at a particular time but rather, may be some function of already existing dispositions on the part of heterosexual men. Also consistent with our contention of the homosexual labeling was a finding Karr referred to as perhaps the most intriguing. The male subject who told other men in an experiment that one of the men was homosexual was perceived by other men in that phase of the experiment as more masculine and more sociable than when the same man did not publicly identify a male subject as "homosexual" in another phase of the experiment. In essence, the labeler received an increase in power and status when he "helped" group members conform to societal expectations by "labeling" a "homosexual." This does not mean that homosexual men are not to be found in powerful positions in our society; indeed, they are; however, their homosexuality is generally kept secret even with today's changes in sex roles. If such men *are* "discovered," the usual pattern is for other men to strip away their power, as has occurred with political, religious, and educational figures in recent years. Some of these men have fought to keep their positions of power and have tried to prove their loyalty to "masculinity" by saying that they are victims of severe "personality disorders." Obviously such claims represent acquiescence to the powerful norms other men established for males. However, usually it is too late for such men, because they are perceived now and forevermore as unworthy and untrustworthy of protecting male power. Regarding the homophobia theme that permeates American society, Lehne writes:

> Homophobia is inevitably used to support the *status quo;* it is an effective technique regardless of the nature of the *status quo* which it supports as long as women and homosexuals are considered to be inferior and devalued. Homophobia must be evaluated independently of whatever personal feelings you may have about homosexuality, because the main social function of homophobia is not primarily directed toward homosexuals (although it certainly affects them). If homosexuals could be granted civil rights, including the right to marry, their lives would improve. Little would be gained by most men and women, however, unless the prejudice against homosexuality were also eliminated (p. 81).

Despite our society's powerful norm prohibiting sexual attraction and relations between men, such attraction and relations occur. Men in America follow the patterns of males in other societies and males in most species of animals, with a majority engaging in nearly exclusive heterosexual activity, but a substantial minority engaging in nearly exclusive homosexual activity (estimates for the latter group range from 5 to 10% of the American male adult population) and an even greater proportion engaging in ambisexual behavior.

Diversity Among Gay Men

Studies (e.g., Bieber, 1962; Weinberg and Williams, 1974; Bell and Weinberg, 1978) of gay males' descriptions of themselves on the homosexual–heterosexual continuum reveal that a substantial majority (about three-quarters) consider themselves to be exclusively homosexual in their sexual behavior. While most have engaged in heterosexual intercourse at least once in their lives, relatively small percentages continue to engage in heterosexual intercourse once they have become members of the gay subculture. Reasons given for lower incidences of heterosexual intercourse among gay men include greater emotional expressiveness with males, more comfortable feelings with males, more satisfaction and fulfillment with males, and the like. Sexuality for gay males, then, tends to involve much more than sexual release. This is substantiated by the fact that gay males are much less likely to report having exclusively homosexual feelings (Bell and Weinberg), yet many do not appear to act on such heterosexual feelings. On the other hand, the variety of sexual partners that most gay men experience during their lifetime does give credence to the idea that homosexual men regard sex in the same isolated way as do their heterosexual counterparts. This idea is explored further later in this section.

One of the more interesting myths about gay men is that they are all the same and that their levels of involvement in the sexual act can be characterized at most as one of routine sexual enactment. This myth probably persists because many people perceive gay men simply as "perverts" who cruise public parks, public toilets, certain streets in a city, etc. In actuality there are numerous dimensions to the gay experience. Some gay men do cruise public facilities but many others enjoy quite different experiences and are in fact quite different from other gay men. Bell and Weinberg offer a typology of gay experience that I feel is instructive at this point. They constructed the following typology: (1) closed-coupled, (2) open-coupled, (3) functional, (4) dysfunctional, and (5) asexual. The authors used five highly discriminating variables *via* further analysis to categorize gay men. The five variables were: (1) whether the respondents were coupled, (2) how much they regretted being gay, (3) how many sexual partners they had during the past year, (4) the amount of cruising (looking for sexual partners) they did, and (5) the level of their sexual activity. Fourteen percent of the men were characterized as close-coupled, which means that they were low in terms of sexual problems, number of sexual partners, amount of cruising, and had few regrets about being gay. Twenty-five percent of the men were characterized as open-coupled—they lived with another man but were high on one of the following variables: number of sexual partners, number of sexual problems, and amount of cruising. Twenty-one percent of the gay males were defined as functional, which meant that they were not coupled and, while they might have been involved in an affair, they were high on the number of sexual partners and levels of sexual activity. Bell and Weinberg also found that these men had few regrets about being gay, few sexual problems, and cruised frequently. The eighteen percent of gay males defined as dysfunctional scored high on the number of sexual partners, and the level of their sexual activity. They regretted being homosexual and they had sexual problems that stemmed from not being able to find suitable sexual partners, not being able to maintain affection for their partners, and being sexually inadequate. A fifth type categorized by Bell and Weinberg was the asexual. Twenty-three percent of the gay males were considered relatively asexual. They were not coupled and were low in sexual activity, number of partners and amount of crusing. Asexuals also had more sexual problems, could not find suitable partners, had low levels of sexual interest, and regretted being gay.

A striking point about Bell and Weinberg's typology is that it allows all types to have high numbers of sexual partners with the exception of close-couples, and even with close-couples some variety of sexual partners and some amount of cruising are allowed. In all likelihood, the typology allows for high numbers of sexual partners because gay men, regardless of type, tended to report high numbers of sexual partners. This is primarily where the general male sex-role affects gay males. Gay men, like heterosexual men, tend to internalize attitudes toward sex which allow them to isolate sex from their other social experiences. This has implications for the depths of their sexual involvement which are similar to those of heterosexual men.

A common question posed frequently of homosexual men is "What causes you to be homosexual?" A legitimate response increasingly being given by homosexual men is "what causes me to be 'gay' probably is the same thing that causes you to be heterosexual . . . what causes you to be heterosexual?" Many such responses include also a distinction between "being gay" and "being homosexual." Following Weinberg's (1972) distinction, many contemporary men sexually attracted to men will indicate that they are characterized by more than a simple erotic preference for men (homosexuality); they also reject the negative societal stereotype associated with this sexual orientation and therefore, they are "gay." Being "gay" thus becomes a political statement as well as a statement of sexual preference; and in addition, being gay means being "healthy" while being "homosexual" means being "unhealthy" (Morin and Schutz, 1978). While such a response might seem flippant to some, it is appropriate because the causes of gayness, like the causes of heterosexuality, are unknown.

Both gay and heterosexual adults engage in same-sex and opposite-sex sexual behavior before puberty. Saghir and Robbins (1973) report findings corroborating Kinsey, *et al.* that 60% of adult males engage in same-sex activities before puberty and 39% have same-sex sexual relations following puberty. Moreover, gay males tend to begin dating females earlier than heterosexual males. Riddle (1978) concludes that both gay males and heterosexual males engage in same-sex and opposite-sex sexual behavior prior to adulthood; and that, if anything, gay males are more heterosexually active and at an earlier age than heterosexual males. Her conclusion is in line with Kremer, Zimpfer, and Wigger's (1975) contention that adolescent sexuality has little, if anything, to do with adult sexual preference.

The Politics of Gay Men's Sex

That gay men, as do heterosexual men, internalize values that devalue femininity is reflected in their overwhelming partner preference for gay men who present a stereotypically "masculine" image (Bell and Weinberg, p. 92). This is carried even further when gay men are asked to describe what they like in a sexual partner. While many will mention special facial, hair, or eye features, practically none are interested in "feminine" physical characteristics, substantial numbers are interested in the "size" of their partner's genitalia, the body hair, muscular build, and so on (p. 86). Gender 'political statements' often are made even further when the issue of sexual technique is raised.

It is commonly accepted in the gay world that some men prefer to assume the active role in sex while others prefer to assume the passive role. In actuality, research studies show that gay men tend to be rather diverse in the roles they assume (Saghir and Robbins, 1973; Weinberg and Williams, 1974). Nevertheless, there does seem to be an interesting political game that gay men play with sexual technique. While there are variations within techniques, such variations seem to be based on the following: (1) fellating a partner, (2) being fellated by a partner, (3) masturbating a partner, (4) being masturbated by a partner, (5) performing anal intercourse, (6) having anal intercourse performed, and (7) body rubbing to orgasm. Politically, in terms of gender, techniques 1, 3, and 6 are submissive "feminine" roles; techniques 2, 4, and 5 are active "masculine" roles; and body rubbing is perhaps the most "equalitarian" role. While performing and receiving fellatio seems to occur more frequently among gay men, with masturbation next most frequent, followed by anal intercourse, and finally, body rubbing, gay men's favorite techniques are receiving fellatio and performing anal intercourse (Bell and Weinberg, p. 108). Such a finding is consistent with a belief that gay men, too, internalize "masculine" attitudes toward sexual techniques. In the gay world, men who perform fellatio and receive anal intercourse are less valued than those who have fellatio performed on them and who perform anal intercourse—the inserter is valued since his role is "masculine" and the insertee is devalued since his role is perceived as "feminine." While such politics are often worked out in long-standing relationships (a diversity of techniques are employed) because most homosexual relationships are brief, the gay world as a whole mirrors the heterosexual world, where masculinity is prized and femininity is devalued. In addition, race and age are political factors that are also thought to affect gay men's functioning in the gay world. Let us consider further the impact of sexism in the gay world as well as that of racism and and ageism.

Sexism and Gay Men

Hooberman, using the Bem Sex-Role Inventory (BSRI), found in his comparative study of two groups of gay and heterosexual men that while the gay men's group had greater numbers of men who endorsed an androgynous sex-role orientation, approximately 16% endorsed a near-masculine-to-masculine sex-role orientation. Approximately 41% could be labeled androgynous and 44% had near-feminine-to-feminine sex-role orientations. Furthermore, Hooberman found that self-esteem was positively related to masculinity, provided that expressive traits commonly associated with femininity were not rejected. No overall difference between the homosexual and heterosexual groups on self-esteem were found. The findings from this study are interesting from a gay male sexual politics point of view in that there clearly appear to be political games played in the gay world.

Gay men in the gay world frequently organize themselves into political camps and use their memberships to engage in political "sexual games" that mirror those in the heterosexual world. Blumstein and Schwartz (1977) relate comments of one of their respondents which define the political camps rather graphically and somewhat accurately. He said, "There are four kinds of men: men who screw women, men who screw men and women, men who screw men, and then there are the queers" (i.e., the ones who *get* screwed) (p. 43). That the political camps may not reflect accurately sexual relationships between men is given support by the observation that sexual partners involved in a long-standing relationship are apt to employ a diversity of techniques; and to engage in whatever reversals of role are prompted by their sexual inclinations of the moment (Bell and Weinberg, p. 106; Hooker, 1965). In addition, Bell and Weinberg reported that practically all of the gay men in their study had engaged in five or more of the techniques within the year prior to the study. The significant point here is that age seemed to have been the chief determinant of sexual technique, with older men basically performing fellatio while younger men were most likely to have engaged frequently in a variety of the sexual techniques (p. 108).

Yet, gay men do play sexual politics related to gender with each other and perceived preferred sexual technique is the determining factor in the game, along with race and age. Regarding perceived preferred sexual techniques, the gay man who is perceived to prefer "passive" sexual techniques is devalued in the gay world in an even more denigrating manner than women are in the heterosexual world. The perceptions of such men's preferred sexual techniques are usually based on gender characteristics such as style of walk, word-pronunciation, pitch of voice, other body language, clothing, and so on. Men whose traits are thought to fall along the feminine end of the "masculine–feminine" continuum in the gay world are responded to by more androgynous and masculine gay men in condescending and oftentimes hostile ways. It is as if such men "remind" the more "he-man" types who they really are. The irony, of course, is that many gay men, despite their purported acceptance of gay and more androgynous identities and behaviors, cling tenaciously to traditional stereotypes of masculinity—at least in the eyes of the public. This is so even if the public is "selective," i.e., other gay men.

Because "masculine" gay men are more preferred as sexual partners (Bell and Weinberg, 1978) by other gay men, they are also valued more in the gay world. Such differential valuation often plays havoc with gay men's relationships when one partner publicly exhibits masculine traits and the other exhibits feminine traits. The "masculine" gay man may receive a great deal of attention from other gay men who in various ways attempt to show him that he can do much better than being coupled with an "effeminate" man—the man who holds low status in the gay hierarchy. The problem is enhanced if the division of labor within the gay men's relationship is congruent with the public image presented in the gay world. For all purposes, the "feminine" partner's status becomes synonymous with many females' status in American society. He becomes a subjugated person dominated by a "masculine" partner. The message is clear: changes in the definition of masculinity can benefit not only heterosexual relationships but also gay relationships that are also rooted in prevailing cultural attitudes, values, and norms about masculinity. Sexism, though, is not the only cultural trait that permeates the gay world. Racism also assumes a role of critical importance.

Racism and Gay Men

Given the degree of tension that exists between racial and ethnic aggregates in the United States, it would not be surprising to find explosive relations between men from these aggregates in the gay world—especially between White gay men and Black gay men. There is no documented evidence that such negative relations exist. However, this does not mean that all is well on the racial front in America's gay "society," since at least one organization has emerged within the gay culture to combat racism. Black and White Men Together (BWMT) was formed in 1980 to promote more harmonious relations between the races. While only scattered, *overt* incidents of racism have occurred in gay communities throughout the nation (as frequently reported in gay newsletters) by and large, Black gay men have been (and still are) subjected to *covert* prejudice and discrimination.

In all likelihood race relations within the gay world would be much more negative if it were not for one overriding factor: *Black gay men tend to assume deferential postures in the gay world relative to White gay men.* The gay world, like other facets of American society, is characterized by prejudice and discrimination directed toward its Black population as well as members of other racial and ethnic groups. Because Blacks are the most visible minority group, they receive most of the prejudice and discrimination. Unlike Black men today in straight society, Black gay men seem more willing to assume the inferior status assigned to them in the gay subculture. Perhaps it is the double "stigma" of being Black *and* gay which contributes to Black men's apparent acceptance of their "lot" in the gay world. Whatever the reason, Black gay men seldom are to be found in policymaking positions in the gay world; Black men seldom own gay establishments (even Black-oriented ones); Black gay men are often the targets of discriminatory admissions policies for gay activities and establishments; and, Black gay men are underrepresented in the gay mass media. In essence, Black gay men's status in the gay world equals the status of Black straight men in the heterosexual world—and if anything, may be slightly lower.

The racism which characterizes institutions in the gay world bleeds over into intimate relationships between Black gay men and White gay men. Bell and Weinberg report that relatively few of their white respondents indicated that their sexual partners were Black, but two-thirds of their Black respondents claimed that *more than half* of their sexual partners had been White. It is impossible to know if Bell and Weinberg's White respondents underreported their interracial sexual contacts and Black respondents overreported theirs. However, if White respondents did underreport their interracial sexual contacts, this would be consistent with several patterns of interracial interaction which can be observed in gay establishments.

Generally, one observes two separate "societies" in the gay world— a White one and a Black one. While those patterns basically are supported by "predominantly Black" gay establishments and "predominantly White" ones, the pluralistic pattern is often reflected within a single gay establishment. For example, often White gay men can be found in one section of a gay bar and Black gay men can be found in another, with only a few individuals moving between the two sections. When there is movement between the two groups, it usually involves a person who is "known" to like "White guys" (in the case of a Black "mover") or one who is "known" to like "Black guys" (in the case of a White "mover"). An interesting point here is that most of the movement, as status theory would dictate, occurs from the White group to the Black group, usually when it is near closing time for the establishment and one "needs to find a trick." Basically, this characterizes patterns of interaction between Black gay men and White gay men in the gay world, although there are exceptions.

The most common exception to the above one-night-stand interracial interaction is one where an interracial couple defies gay norms and becomes "romantically" attached. Usually such affairs are relatively short-lived because of the dynamics that emerge when a Black man and a White man couple. Aside from the curiosity aroused outside the gay world when an interracial male couple is seen frequently together, curiosity also is aroused within the gay world. More than curiosity, though; perceptions of the men are altered in the gay world generally and *within* the two "separate societies." Each man is seen by certain members of the opposite racial group as "fair game." in addition, each man acquires an "untouchable" label assigned to him by members of his own racial group. The label is acquired either because the man is perceived as "tainted" or because the man is perceived as only interested in members of the opposite group. The result for the couple is usually disastrous, and it is not uncommon for the men to find themselves uncoupled and passed from one "interested" person to another within the opposite group, never establishing a long-term lover relationship. In the gay world, then, race takes on the same significance as it does in the straight world. Race and sex are powerful discriminatory factors in gay society along with another factor—ageism.

Ageism and Gay Men

It is commonly believed that the gay world, more than the straight world, emphasizes youth. In fact, as Kimmel (1978) has pointed out, "Fears about aging as a gay person have been used to dissuade young people from accepting their homosexuality, further hindering self-acceptance" (p. 114). Older gay men are frequently depicted in novels, movies, and other mass media as lonely, depressed (if not depraved), and sexually frustrated. This view of the aging gay male has led some to conclude that the effects of aging on gay men rival the effects of aging on movie stars. Needless to say, most of the negative views of gay aging are speculative and not based in fact. Certainly gay men, as do heterosexual men, experience special problems and disadvantages which accompany aging. There is reason to believe, however, that gay men's aging problems are basically similar to and may be slightly *less dramatic* than those faced by heterosexual men. Yet, there are some problems associated with gay aging. Let us explore some possible sources: the emphasis on youth in the gay world; the loneliness around holidays; and the death of a long-term lover.

Because sexual preference does not guarantee protection against loneliness on holidays or the death of a mate, it is questionable whether gay men's aging problems on these issues are significantly different from those of aging heterosexual men. While such problems undoubtedly exist for many aging gay men, the problem seems to be due to a dysfunctional cultural aspect of American society which does not hold its elderly population in high esteem. Even so, aging gay men seem to experience less dramatic changes than their heterosexual counterparts. Kimmel, in discussing this phenomenon, alludes to Francher and Henkin's (1973) conclusion that gay men's major life crises seem to occur in their adjustments to their sexual orientations rather than with aging. The fourteen older gay men studied by Kimmel reflected this pattern although the "aging" and "adjustment to sexual orientation" variables tended to interact. Interaction between the variables occurred because of the "lateness" of gay involvement for many of the men.

Yet, there is one aspect of aging that is said to be ubiquitous in the gay world: ageism. Ageism refers to the discrimination that occurs when people are assigned different privileges and opportunities on the basis of their ages without regard to their individual capacities (Spencer, 1983, p. 150). Ageism, as a problem for gay men, is reflected in gay newsletters, magazines, and handbooks that decry the tendencies for the gay world to isolate its older gay members. These are legitimate concerns, but, as stated earlier, the basis of the concern is cultural and not simply gay world-bound. In fact, gay activities and entertainment centers seem much more likely than "straight" ones to include older gay men. Moreover, love relationships and affairs frequently exist between older and younger gay men, To be sure, older gay men do seem to perform fellatio much more than younger men in brief sexual encounters (Bell and Weinberg, 1978); however, no one knows if this is the sexual technique preferred by these men or if they are relegated to this technique because of age. Moreover, assigning value to the various techniques in such encounters may be inappropriate since time, situation, personal preference, and so on must be taken into consideration.

The ageism problem, while existing to some degree, seems to be overestimated for the gay world. This probably stems from gay men's apparent concern with their external appearances. A simple observation of patrons in a gay bar often gives the impression of an emphasis on youth. One notices, upon visiting many gay establishments, that middle-age paunches, wrinkled faces, elderly postures, and other accoutrements of aging are conspicuously absent. Oftentimes, however, age is not the factor contributing to the external appearances of youth in gay establishments. Rather, gay men have gone to great lengths to remain physically attractive and have usually followed rigorous physical and dietary programs. The emphasis in the gay world may not be so much on youth as it is on presenting a physically attractive "self." Physical attractiveness seems to be a more crucial discriminating factor in the gay world than simply age itself. As Kimmel has stated, the stereotypes of the lonely, depressed, and sexually frustrated gay men do not hold valid for the majority of older gay men studied to date. However, older gay men do have special needs, as do older straight men. Increasing visibility of gay communities throughout our society portend the addressing of the needs of older gays. Given the long-standing struggles such communities have wagered, no doubt the gay community will once again bond together to solve a serious problem.

Ambisexual Men

Male "bisexuality" refers to the ability for a man to eroticize both males and females under some circumstances (Blumstein and Schwartz, 1977). Current usage of the term "bisexual" varies in that some persons perceive "bisexuals" as individuals who are equally attracted to males and females; others, however, allow individuals greater latitude in their sexual attraction to both sexes. This means that a person who only occasionally engages in heterosexual or homosexual behavior during some point in his life is also thought of as "bisexual." Still others feel that self-labeling is a crucial variable to take into consideration, as is sexual behavior, when categorizing persons as "bisexual." Perhaps many of the different perceptions of "bisexuality" that exist are related to the confusing nature of the concept itself. As Blumstein and Schwartz write:

> Bisexuality gives a misleading sense of fixedness to sex-object choice, suggesting as it does a person in the middle, equidistant from heterosexuality and from homosexuality . . . (p. 32).

The authors go on to say that while they are indebted to Kinsey for insisting on a heterosexual–homosexual continuum, Kinsey's viewpoint also had a misleading element. The misleading nature of the continuum viewpoint emerges when there is a focus on the individual's "sexual place" as a unit of analysis rather than on sexual behavior. Blumstein and Schwartz, nevertheless, finally decide to use the concept, "bisexuality," because of its entrenched nature in English language. I have elected, instead, to use their more preferred "ambisexual," as the nominal concept describing men's sexual behavior with both men and women.

For several decades now, researchers (e.g., Kinsey, Pomeroy, and Martin, 1948; Kinsey, Pomeroy, Martin, and Gebhard, 1953; Humphreys, 1970; Kirkham, 1971; Ross, 1971; Donte, 1974; Weinberg and Williams, 1975; Blumstein and Schwartz, 1976; Bell and Weinberg, 1978) have consistently reported relatively high incidencies of ambisexuality among both gay and heterosexual men, While it is practically impossible to obtain reliable estimates of ambisexual behavior, there is reason to feel that it is far more common than many might believe. Beginning with Kinsey's estimate in 1948 that 37% of the American male population had experienced homosexual sex to orgasm, and including Humphrey's sample of tearoom participants, of whom 54% were married, as well as several other studies indicating male participation in sexual activity with both men and women, ambisexuality among American men has been well-documented. Our exploration here will center on the nature of male ambisexuality, factors conducive to the phenomenon and men's adjustment to this sexual-preference orientation. Major sources for our discussion include the work of authors mentioned earlier, and especially the research and conclusions of Blumstein and Schwartz (their work in the area remains among the most important to date.)

The nature of men's ambisexuality in the United States seems to come from men's socialization experiences. As stated often in this volume, men are socialized to isolate their sexual experiences from other aspects of their lives. Moreover, many internalize the popular notion that the male sex drive is overwhelming. However, men also internalize the idea that it is shameful and deviant to be erotically attracted to members of their own sex while simultaneously receiving society's message that they *must* be erotically attracted to women. As stated earlier, many men respond to society's directives regarding their sexuality by constructing their sexualities along ambisexual lines. If men's ambisexual orientations were congruent with their behavior, an explanation of the nature of men's ambisexuality would be less difficult. As Blumstein and Schwartz discovered, however, this often is not the case. Some men claim to be ambisexual while only engaging in heterosexual sexual activities; others say that they are gay but periodically have sex with women; and, still others indicate that they are heterosexual but occasionally move into the gay world or engage in tearoom sex. A point that is crucial to mention here also is that a relatively great number of men are ambiguous about their sexual orientations because of heterosexual, gay, or ambisexual experiences at some point in their past lives.

For our purposes, it is useful to conceive of the nature of ambisexuality in terms of men's present sexual experiences. It does not seem feasible, for example, to speak of men who were emotionally attracted to men and participated in ambisexual sex during adolescence or at some point in their past as ambisexuals. For this reason, further discussion of ambisexuality in men will be limited to those men who routinely or periodically engage in both heterosexual and homosexual sexual activities and not one or the other exclusively. This should not obviate the fact that presently heterosexual men, if placed in certain settings (e.g., prisons) for long periods of time can (and many probably would) develop sexual relationships with other men. It also does not preclude the possibility, although much less likely than the above, that some gay men, after years of exclusively gay sexual experiences, engage only in heterosexual sex. Succinctly, ambisexuality defines the behavior of men who label themselves ambisexual and presently engage in ambisexaul behavior; those who label themselves homosexual but presently engage in ambisexual sex; and those who label themselves heterosexual but presently engage in ambisexual sex.

Blumstein and Schwartz (1976) found several common patterns among self-labeled ambisexual men who "presently" engage in ambisexual behavior: (1) broadened involvement with sexual partner(s), (2) past socialization experiences were not anti-gay, (3) ambisexual phase during adolescence followed by a hetereosexual phase which was followed by an ambisexual phase, and (4) early sex experience.

Self-Labeled Ambisexual Men

Self-labeled ambisexual men who engage in ambisexual sex probably are the most "liberated" groups among ambisexuals. From all indications, such men do not experience the shame, guilt, or ambiguity regarding their sexuality as do men from the other two categories we will discuss. While their past sexual patterns vary, there does seem to be a pattern of rather extensive past sexual experience with male and female sexual partners. Group sex experience, while mentioned by some ambisexuals in Blumstein and Schwartz's study, was rather rare. Those who did indicate that they had experienced group sex felt that the experience enabled them "to learn to enjoy behavior they would never ordinarily have considered" (p. 351). One rather common feeling among these ambisexual men reported by the authors was the existence of "moods" for both heterosexual and gay sex. It appears, for example, that many ambisexuals can be attuned erotically and behaviorally to women for a period of time, followed by being attuned erotically and behaviorally to men for some time and vice-versa. Though some of these men's behavior may appear to be similar to other men's behaviors who engage in ambisexual behavior, there are important differences as we see in the next section.

Predominantly Gay Ambisexual Men

While many people believe that men who engage in gay sex do not engage in heterosexual sex, results from several studies indicate that this is not necessarily so. Even among men who are predominantly gay in their sexual preferences, some also engage in heterosexual sex. Blumstein and Schwartz, in discussing gay men's heterosexual sexual activities, make five important points: (1) the women involved usually are personal friends who are aware the man is gay, (2) the men usually have become comfortable with their gayness, (3) having defined themselves as gay, the men involved do not experience anxiety about the heterosexual sexual encounter, (4) the men do not feel pressured to form lasting relationships, and (5) the experience, while enjoyable, is not highly eroticized.

We have seen earlier that gay men tend to begin their sexual activity with women earlier than heterosexual men. Yet, the interesting thing about predominantly gay men who have ambisexual experiences is that these men seem *not* to have been heterosexually active as adolescents. It is possible that once such a gay man becomes comfortable with a woman who knows about his sexual preference, this developed inhibition toward women is defused. Because he does not perceive that she holds certain expectations for him, the gay man becomes less anxious and feels less pressured to "prove" his masculinity and as the saying goes "nature takes its course." Also important is the fact that such men are not experiencing difficulties with their sexual identities. This is salient since predominantly gay men generally indicate that their sexual contact with women is not nearly as exciting and/or erotic as it is with men.

Perhaps just as important for a predominantly gay man is that his female sexual partner understands that he is not prepared to, nor does he want to, form a lasting relationship. Most predominantly gay men who become sexually involved with women do so only if they are able to perceive that the above point is clearly understood. There are some exceptions which recently have been publicized. Because of a variety of reasons (e.g., desire for companionship, deep emotional attachment, disillusionment with love relationships) some predominantly gay men decide to marry or live with women who "understand" their predominant sexual preference. Referred to often in the mass media as the "new couple," such relationships may be highly satisfactory for the gay man who in essence is the prime beneficiary. Since such relationships are extremely difficult to research, given the stigma associated with them, a dearth of information exists about the "success" and "failure" rates of such "arrangements." Speculatively, if the woman in such a relationship is willing to "hold up her end of the bargain," the arrangement probably remains intact. The rarity of such a relationship is obvious given the awesome "burden" women in these relationships must shoulder. Not only must these women understand their secondary sexual status with gay men, but they must also be willing to accept it. While these women surely are in "disadvantaged" relationships, their position may be more enviable than those women in relationships with men who are predominantly heterosexual but who *do* engage in sex with men.

Predominantly Heterosexual Ambisexual Men

"Sexual outlet" seems to be the most important factor accounting for ambisexuality among certain "heterosexual" men. "Driven" by what they perceive is an extremely high sex urge as well as a "need" for a "variety" of sexual acts, these men identify themselves as heterosexual but do participate in sexual activities with men. These are the men who may become involved in homosexual activity in prisons or engage in tearoom sex, go to gay baths, gay bars, and the like. Such men generally have only one purpose in mind—sexual release. They do not identify themselves as gay men, nor do they allow themselves to become more than genitally involved with their sexual partners.

In identifying such men, Blumstein and Schwartz imply that it is essential to know the length of time that they have been involved in ambisexual activities. If such men have "histories" of this kind of behavior, they undoutedly fall into this category. On the other hand, as Miller has shown, for many heterosexually involved men, furtive gay sex is the beginning of the social construction of a gay identity. Yet, some heterosexual men do not progress beyong this "trade" stage. While it is tempting to discuss factors responsible for this nonprogression, such as "nondiscovery," "feelings about family," etc., I am convinced that those factors are of little importance. For some heterosexual men, occasional movements into the gay world is all that are wanted, and their predominant sexual identity and preference is heterosexual. In other words, even "discovery" or family disruption would not push such men into the gay world, nor would their sexual preferences be appreciably altered. Certainly men in "male total institutions" often have sufficient times for their sexual careers to progress from Miller's "trade" man to "faggot" man. For large numbers of men, this does not happen, as evidenced by their return to predominantly heterosexual activity once they leave such institutions.

Of the types of ambisexual men, the predominantly heterosexual ambisexual is probably the most anxious and guilt-ridden. Because many are married or involved in long-lasting relationships with women, and due to the fact that such men accept their behavior only as a genital urge, most of their gay sexual experiences are clandestine, impersonal encounters in public faciities, or ones they can "arrange" driving around gay establishments at night looking for furtive gay sex. These men, when they are husbands with children, often view alternatives to their situations as extremely limited. The gay world is not a viable alternative for them:

> Frequently, they describe it as "superficial," "bitchy," "shallow," "unstable," "full of blackmail and violence." When asked what they see for the future, the typical response is "to go on like this, I guess" (pp. 215–216).

Because many men who can be labeled predominantly heterosexual–ambisexual are married, it is important to devote special attention to these men. In addition, since some "predominantly heterosexual" men do gradually construct gay identities, we will also view this process.

Being Married and Ambisexual

Being heterosexually married and being ambisexual are not necessarily incongruent social statuses. Nevertheless, many people believe that the two statuses are mutually exclusive phenomena (Miller, 1978). In addition, the degree to which married men consider themselves gay varies. This is consistent with McIntosh's (1968) idea that in some societies, a great deal of gay sexual activity occurs, but there are no gays. In such societies, other persons' reactions to gay activities have not been organized and thus no status has been constructed to stereotype persons who engage in gay sex. In the United States, this is certainly not the case. However, on an individual level, many men do continue to construct heterosexual identities as we have stated, despite the fact that they engage in gay sex. It is practically impossible to know how many such men there are in our society because they are basically indistinguishable from the male heterosexual population in terms of their participation in heterosexual social activities and in terms of their self-labeling. Studies have reported varying estimates of the percentage of gay men who are married heterosexually. The Kinsey Institute for Sex Research found that 20% of their gay bar patrons were married (Bell, 1972). Humphries (1970), in his study of tearoom participants, found that 54% of the men were married. In other studies (e.g., Dank, 1974; McNeill, 1976; Saghir and Robbins, 1973), the percentages of gay men who report having been married range from 18 to 25%.

Regardless of the actual figure, there is good reason to believe that there is no dearth of married men who participate in gay sexual activities. In addition, many of these men live with their wives and function publicly as heterosexuals throughout their lives. Others, as we will see, gradually become more and more absorbed in a gay world, as did Zack in the remarkable movie "Making Love." Bell and Weinberg imply that while it might seem that the psychological strain resulting from fear of exposure would probably contribute to many married gay men moving totally into the gay world, this often is not the case. More than anything else, it is the guilt, shame and/or anxiety that probably result in many married men moving out of the heterosexual world and into the gay world. Miller offers still another reason, as we will see.

While many gay men who live with their wives are ambisexual, many are not. Thus, within the gay married male population, we can expect to find men at various points on the homosexual–heterosexual continuum. In general, gay married men seem to fall into three categories: married men whose wives do not know that they are gay; married men whose wives do know and "accept" the gay "trait" in them; and, married gay men who have left their wives. Admittedly, these are crude categories, and they do not, moreover, capture the process many ambisexual married men undergo. They do, however, specify the statuses which numerous married men have in "heterosexual" unions. Brian Miller, in his brilliant article on adult sexual resocialization, discusses the "process" of married ambisexual men's entry into the gay world. While some ambisexual married men do not complete the process, many do, as statistics on gay men's prior marital statuses show. Let us review Miller's work. Miller studied 30 self-labeled gay men who had been or currently were heterosexually married. Basing his findings on 2–4 hour audio-recorded interviews, Miller developed a typology of gay husbands which addressed a crucial issue: "How do gay husbands structure a reality that allows them to solve their contradictory statuses?" (p.207).

Miller proposes four types of married men who engage in same-sex sexual behavior. They are the *trade husband,* the *homosexual husband,* the *gay husband,* and the *faggot husband.* The *trade husband* is the label given to married men whose public and private identities are heterosexual but who, nevertheless, engage in impersonal and furtive gay sex. Most of the men's sexual-contact episodes occur in tearooms, public parks, and so on. The *homosexual husband*, like the trade husband, is marginal to the gay world, even though he admits his gayness to himself and may even admit it to close gay friends. To the public at large, however, he is heterosexual. Miller suggests that this type of husband is the most guilt-ridden and ambivalent about his gayness. The homosexual husband frequently contemplates divorce, since his marriage either is conflict-ridden or one of near-total disinterest to him. Some of these men may remain married, however, because of their commitment to their children and/or the failure to perceive viable alternatives to their situations. Needless to say, these are perhaps the most vulnerable of the "gay" husbands, and may be the group which contributes significantly to married gay male suicides. Miller's *gay husband* is much more involved in the gay world. He has learned his way around the gay scene. Usually the gay husband, upon leaving his wife, has told her and maybe even his children and other close relatives of his sexual preference. To the public at large, especially his employer, he remains heterosexual although the gay husband is likely to have numerous gay friends. The *faggot husband*, in Miller's scheme, has made the transition to the gay world. His identity is totally gay and he is highly visible in the gay world. Publicly, the faggot husband has "come out" and his world is organized around his "gayness."

According to Miller, despite the increased public stigma experienced by men as they move from trade husband to faggot husband, these men also experience enhanced feelings of psychological well-being as their careers progress from "trade" to "faggot." Gradual movement through each stage reduces cognitive incongruence for married gay men, They no longer have to compartmentalize their worlds or neutralize the homosexual label to reinforce their heterosexual identity. On the latter point Miller contends that trade husbands' negative views of the gay world are a result of restrictions they place on their own activities within the gay world so that they can continue to view themselves as heterosexual. Despite this "adjustment," trade husbands often realize that their behavior is inconsistent with heterosexuality. Miller states:

> Trade and homosexual husbands find successful integration of the two institutions, traditional heterosexual marriage and impersonal gay sex, to be problematical without radically altering their intrinsically incompatible structures. They experience a no-win situation where they feel damned if they cannot have their families and damned if they cannot engage in homo-

sexual behavior. Far from having the best of both worlds, they tend to have the worst of both worlds (pp. 225–226).

What moves the trade husband or the homosexual husband to the gay world? Miller contends that the single factor that initiates cell progression from trade husband or homosexual husband to the gay world is the experience of *falling in love*. Falling in love is thought to intervene with trade husbands' construction of unfavorable images of the gay world. Falling in love makes it difficult for trade husbands to continue constructing their realities of the gay world as bitchy, shallow, violence ridden, and so on. But how does the trade husband fall in love when his relationships are shallow and impersonal? It may happen, according to Miller, when a trade or homosexual husband repeatedly encounters a former "trick" at a cruising place or when he goes to a trick's house and meets his gay friends. In other words, whenever a trade or homosexual husband broadens or extends his knowledge of a gay contact beyond genital foci, the opportunity for initial progression into the gay world is present.

An initial move toward the gay world for a gay-oriented person can culminate in a gay identity because the gay world has a seductive pull. Miller states:

> It may appear strange that anyone relinquishes heterosexual status and privilege to enter the stigmatized gay world. One must not forget, however, the ironic fact that the gay world, being disvalued and secretive, has for the homosexually oriented a seductive pull. This dynamic, first described by Georg Simmel, is applied to an analysis of homosexuality by Warren (1974). Coming out in the gay world offers a clear-cut identity, a close-knit community, and it fosters the sense of an elite, chosen-people status. These factors serve to increase the salience of the gay world to the individual entering it, to facilitate a positive social construction, and to make it a viable alternative to heterosexual marriage.

Once a homosexual husband becomes a gay husband, reconstruction of his sexual identity tends toward positive lines with support from newfound gay friends and associates. In those instances where homosexual husbands have undergone the breakup of marriages, Miller contends that they are equipped with a militant stridency for the process of gay identity construction. These men, in every sense of the word, become converted to the gay world. Finally, it should be mentioned that progression from trade husband to faggot husband may be characterized by movement back and forth between cells at any point until the final move to faggot husband is made, where the person fully develops a positive and constructive gay image of himself.

The "Silent Killer" and the Gay Community

Developing a positive and constructive gay image may be becoming extremely difficult for many gay men to do in the early 1980s, given the existence of a "silent killer" which has caused panic in the gay community—indeed, in the nation at large. Known by the acronym AIDS, this relatively "new" disease in the United States (Acquired Immune Deficiency Syndrome) destroys the body's immune system, leaving a person vulnerable to debilitating and fatal diseases. At this time, there is no known treatment for AIDS and relatively little is known about how persons contract the disease. It is thought, however, that sexual contact between homosexual men is a major source, along with blood transfusions and intravenous drug use. Most of the victims of AIDS have been homosexual men (homosexual men account for approximately three-quarters of the cases), Haitians, hemophiliacs and intravenous drug users.

Of critical importance for gay men is the fact that they are the principal targets of hysterical and insensitive fear about the disease. Such fear has threatened to set gay men even further apart from other members of American society. This is so despite the fact that AIDS is much more than simply "a gay men's problem." Lending support to all of this are some religious and political conservatives who voice the idea that AIDS is God's vengeance heaped on a sinful people.

The implications of AIDS for gay men's sexuality and social relationships are not clear at this time. It is probable, however, that many gay men have begun to exercise extreme caution in their selection of sexual partners. In some instances, gay men's social relationships, especially with heterosexuals, probably have been beyond their control since fear about the disease is rather widespread. Succinctly, many social relationships between gay men and heterosexuals have, in all likelihood, been curtailed. This is unfortunate since slow but gradually increasing understanding between homosexuals and heterosexuals seemed on the horizon. As Patricia O'Brien who writes for the Knight-Ridder newspapers states, quick containment of AIDS is imperative—"not just to quell fears for our own safety, but to put a lid on other fears that can be just as poisonous and destructive."

Asexual Men

Of all male sexual alternatives, asexuality probably is the least understood. Just as some men respond erotically to women and/or men, still others respond erotically to neither sex. Not only do these men fail to respond erotically to neither sex, but they also do not engage in sexual relations with any "other." If anything, such men engage only in self-sexual behavior.

While asexual behavior may seem to be somewhat rare except for the elderly (many persons erroneously perceive older persons as sexually inactive), it is in fact quite common among a significant minority of persons in our society. Like heterosexual, homosexual, and ambisexual behaviors, asexual behavior is characterized by malleability and temporal unpredictability. Most people are asexual for significant periods of time in their lives, usually during childhood and at least part of adolescence. These are not the people being discussed in this section. This discussion is devoted to those males who have passed through adolescence but for one reason or another do not engage in sexual relationships with others. These men, too, I believe, are not so rare in American society.

We have already discussed the fact that men in America internalize norms which encourage frequent, albeit minimum depth of involvement in sexual encounters. Why then do certain men violate these norms associated with masculinity by not engaging in sexual relations with others? Is it the case that such men are devoid of sexual urges? Are these men malfunctioning physiologically? Probably some are characterized by physiological malfunctioning, but many others experience structural, social and psychological barriers to self–other sexual interaction.

For our purposes, asexuality refers primarily to nonsexual contact with others since persons can respond erotically to others and still fail to *act* upon their responses. Moreover, erotic attraction in itself is an extremely private and complex phenomenon which usually involves not only a sex object but also a view of the self as a sex object. For most men, the sex object assumes a primary role in sexual imagery while the self, although present, becomes secondary. For other men, however (i.e., asexual men) the self *remains* the primary focus and the sex object is secondary. These men have learned a pattern of sexual behavior that is opposite to the pattern of behavior frequently practiced by the vast majority. Instead of pursuing the sex object for possible sexual gratification, many asexuals, I contend, pursue themselves for sexual gratification. From this perspective, instead of asexuality implying nonsexual gratification, it implies non-self–other sexual gratification. Let us explore some factors conducive to asexual behavior.

Three factors conducive to male asexuality are structural factors, social factors and psychological factors. Structural factors include those perceived barriers to sex-object choices such as prisons, mental institutions, or the military. Social factors conducive to male asexuality refer to others' negative sexual responses to a male based on their definition of him as an undesirable sexual partner. Many asexual men with physical handicaps, congenital defects, obesity problems, unattractive physical characteristics, and so on, fall into this category. These men, like those facing structural barriers to sex-object choices, actually may not be voluntarily asexual. Nevertheless, circumstances have defined their sexuality along asexual lines. A third set of factors responsible for male asexuality is psychological. Many men experience phobias related to the sexual act. These phobias can stem from a variety of sources including a fear of being ridiculed because of the perceived smallness of the penis, fears related to threats to male dominance, fears related to sexual preferences and numerous others. However, phobias are not the only source of male asexuality; males sometimes construct their realities along asexual lines after the loss of a loved one or even after they have been disillusioned by a loved one. Whatever the psychological reason, some men opt to refrain from sex with others while simultaneously engaging in self-sexual behavior.

The need for more research into the area of asexuality and self-sexuality is obvious. Men defined as asexual are not only considered deviant in American society but they are also frequently thought to be lonely, depressed, and unhappy. Whether or not this is true remains an open question. It may be that men electing not to have sexual relations with others are *not* characterized by the dysfunctions often associated with being sexually inactive with others. Instead, such men may have found for themselves their most viable sexual alternative—asexuality. In addition, we are reminded of the fact that asexuality need not imply that a man receives no sexual gratification. It only implies that he receives no sexual gratification through self–other participation in sexual-contact episodes.

Males, Sex, and Violence

> The sexuality of most men shows an admixture of aggression, of a desire to subdue. (Sigmund Freud, 1938.)

Freud's explanation for the link between sex and many instances of violence in the United States that men direct toward women and other men is couched in biological determinism. While erotic and aggressive instincts are fused together in Freud's framework, they are seen as functioning independently. Violence, then, can be thought of as a component of the sexual instinct in men which is exaggerated and functions independently.

Current thinking on the topic of violence and sex eschews Freud's linkage between sex and violence. Instead, sexuality is seen as a social act having important cognitive components as well as biological acts "that may take many different forms and are comprised of several states and elements" (Malamuth, Feshbach, and Jaffe, 1977). Violence refers to destructive behaviors, which often are expressions of hatred and anger with hostile and injurious components. Many (e.g., Fromm, 1973) feel that violence is incompatible with sexual arousal for the vast majority of men from an evolutionary perspective.

> From an evolutionary perspective, it may be conjectured that the elicitation of the forceful, uninhibited pursuit of sexual ends served survival purposes, but that evolutionary forces favored the inhibition of hostile, destructive tendencies during the close physical proximity and associated vulnerability involved in copulation (Malamuth, Feshbach and Jaffe, 1977).

Heim, Malamuth and Feshbach (1977) offer support for the assertion that sex and violence may be incompatible for most men. In their study, "The Effects of Violent Aggression in Erotica on Sexual Arousal," the authors found that male and female undergraduate students were less sexually aroused when reading an erotic passage that depicted a hostile rape than when reading an erotic passage that depicted a mutually desired sexual episode. Heim *et al.* concluded that their data supported the idea that "as far as 'normal' subjects are concerned, hostile, aggressive behavior inhibits sexual arousal." Yet, male rapists have been found to be highly sexually aroused (as reflected in self reports and direct physiological measures of erection) when they have been given descriptions of a rape scene (Heim, et al.). For these men sex appears to be more intimately linked with violent aggression. Heim, *et al.*, in examining their research techniques and materials, further report that when the female in the rape scene is seen as becoming sexually aroused during the course of the rape and thus enjoying the experience, both male and female subjects become "quite aroused sexually" (p. 127). The social nature of sexual arousal seems apparent here. If this is so, however, why are there numerous instances of linkages between sex and violence in our society?

I contend that sex-role socialization is responsible for most of the linkages between sex and violence in the United States. Men, in our society, learn certain traits associated with masculinity which include both sexual aggression and sexual dominance. In addition, most men also "learn that cues associated with permissible sexual arousal also cue the disinhibition of aggression (McConahay and McConahay, 1977, p. 136). Most men are taught that while assertive aggression is permissible— indeed, expected—in possible sexual encounters, violent aggression is taboo. However, it is also necessary for the male socialization process to include recognition of cues that are associated with nonpermissible sexual arousal. Needless to say, the male socialization process often fails at this point. This is not to say that all violent sexual behaviors directed toward women and men by men are consequences of inappropriate male socialization. It is to say, however, that the often-seen linkages between sex and violence are related to the male sex-role in the United States with all of its accoutrements, including the devaluation of women.

As reported often in this volume, violence, aggression, and forceful behavior are traits of masculinity which most American males are encouraged to internalize. Unfortunately, many American males also learn the link between sexuality and violence, which often means inaccurately empathizing with women in our society. That some men are taught to inaccurately take the role of women in America is substantiated by findings on rape and near-rape incidents on college campuses where men have assumed that when women said, "no," they actually meant "yes." Kanin's (1965) findings nearly two decades ago that 25% of the male college students studied admitted at least one incident of sexual aggression probably still holds up. Just as revealing are the findings from several studies (e.g., Malamuth, Haber, and Feshbach, 1980; Malamuth and Check, 1980; and Tieger, 1981) showing that 35% of the males studied, if assured that they would not be discovered and punished, *would* commit a rape act. While these males were college students, there is also evidence that even high school male youth have positive attitudes toward rape in some instances. When Giarusso, Johnson, Goodchilds, and Zellman (1979) asked high school males in the Los Angeles metropolitan area if they condoned rape in certain situations, 76% indicated that it was "okay." Reasons given included, "if she gets him physically excited," "if he has spent a lot of money on her," "if she is sexually promiscuous," and so on. Thus, while only a small percentage of men actually commit rape, many more men in our society have inclinations to rape women.

Russell believes that males' inclinations toward rape are related to their socialization—the fact that men are taught aggressive behavior and that rape is one type of aggressive behavior. Malamuth (1981) has found that men who report high likelihoods of rape also choose more severe forms of punishment for women who reject and insult them. The message is clear in this instance. Women are supposed to be passive and accepting with men. If they are not, then they must be prepared for men's vengeance, which may include, among other acts of aggression, physical violence. McConahay and McConahay's findings from their cross-cultural study that sex role rigidity and violence are positively correlated is instructive here.

The male sex-role that teaches men that the masculine norm to become a conqueror, a subduer, a forcer, and so on, psychologically prepares men to assume violently aggressive roles with others. Male sex-role socialization also teaches men that women are passive acceptors. This is why many men insist that women actually enjoy being raped, being dominated, being subdued. Interestingly, this is the same faulty logic used by some men in male–male sexual violence. While sex and violence are often linked in male-total institutions, they are also often linked in the outside world. There is no way of knowing how much male–male sexual violence occurs yearly in the United States. However, there is reason to suspect that it is much more common than many people realize. This type of violence, too, is related to male sex-role socialization. Many males fall victim to the same pattern of male dominance and aggression in the same manner as women. In addition, some gay males are victims of a masculine backlash where a "heterosexual" male seeks out a gay male for "fun and games" after which he heaps violence on the unsuspecting victim. In such instances, the gay male is victimized for one of two reasons. Either the "heterosexual" male feels that he is preserving masculinity in society by ridding society of "queers" or he is ridding that aspect of himself that is queer by heaping violence on his sexual partner, who, with him, has violated society's expectations for men. Whatever the reason, we can be sure that it is an inextricable facet of perceived definitions of masculinity in America. To say that recent changes in the male sex-role are welcomed is an understatement; to say further changes in the male sex-role are needed is a foregone conclusion.

CHAPTER 8

Male Sex Roles in the Future: Will "Prince Charming" Survive?

An Excursion into Fairyland

A decade ago many people felt that "Prince Charming" would be unable to survive the onslaught of several simultaneous social movements. The Women's Movement, the (male-led) Black Power movement, the men's movement, the Gay Movement, the youth movement, the sexual revolution, and numerous other "little acts of rebellion" all combined seemed on the verge of dismantling Prince Charming's masculinist castle in the early 1970s. Even "Prince Charming" himself was threatened with destruction during this period. However, as we look around today, there is substantial evidence that Prince Charming's castle remains intact; and Prince Charming, though battered, survives in the 1980s.

"Prince Charming," the hypothetical homophobic male who is controlling, aggressive, domineering, protective, condescending, and sometimes even hostile toward women and other men, resides uncomfortably inside his masculinist castle. He is surrounded by his strategies of nonempathy, inexpressiveness, self-nondisclosure, and dominance. Nevertheless, "Prince Charming" survives, and that is the pity of it all, because he is a pathetic figure. Actually, Prince Charming has grown "weak." Sometimes he makes feeble attempts to show expressiveness; he occasionally pretends passivity when interacting with others; and he even "helps" Cinderella around the castle, since she insists on working for pay in the village alongside male and female villagers. The "Prince" bemoans the fact that Cinderella is not with the royal children more, despite the fact that he still is unable to do anything about his "royal" schedule which has always limited contact with his "royal" children.

Prince Charming in his village activities still, as always, often misuses the village maidens, and seems leery of the male villagers. . . but he is growing weary. He keeps a stiff upper lip, though, because he wants his castle to remain strong. Can Prince Charming's castle remain intact? In fact, can Prince Charming himself survive? The prognosis for both is not good, despite the fact that a strong battle is being fought by the prince. It seems that his survival will depend on Cinderella and the minority male and female villagers. Cinderella has recently been accused by the minority villagers of helping Prince Charming to try to save his castle by supporting many of the prince's strategies listed earlier, and even adopting some of them in her social relationships. However, minority male and female villagers also lend support to the prince's struggle by waging ferocious battles among themselves. Many of them, much to the delight of the prince, have adopted some of the prince's strategies in dealing with each other, thereby supporting the prince in his efforts to remain in power. Cinderella and the villagers continue to claim that they want the castle dismantled; they want Prince Charming out; and they want to construct a new humanist castle. Presently, Prince Charming seems too shrewd to allow this to happen. But Cinderella and the villagers keep trying to dismantle the castle, although it is difficult for them to construct the foundation for the new humanist castle. Prince Charming's present "weak" state does attest to the fact that, before long, he may not be able to prevent the new foundation from being built.

Any discussion of American male sex-roles in the future is necessarily speculative. Even in a society as "advanced" as ours, there is no way of knowing all of the twists and turns a society will take during a decade. For example, during the heights of each of the movements mentioned in the beginning of the chapter, no one could predict that a major deterrent to these movements would be our society's economic difficulties, which came to the attention of the public in the late 1970s and persists into the 1980s. Few persons realized that society's economic problems would divert attention from the various movements' objectives and cause most people to focus, instead, on surviving and meeting basic human needs. Yet, this is precisely what has happened. Economic changes, however, will not have a lasting deterrent effect on sex-role changes in America. In this section, some of the possible sources of sex-role changes will be discussed, as well as the patterns some of these changes will take. We will begin our exploration into the future of male sex-roles by examining the implications of present-day male–female interaction (intrarace and interrace) for changes in the male sex-role. Following this discussion, we will consider male responses. The chapter concludes with a brief discussion of men's career paths toward sex-role equality.

The Implications of Male-Female Interaction for Changes in the Male Sex Role

White Males and White Females

Any discussion of White male–female social interaction patterns must acknowledge a discrepancy that exists between what women perceive as "ideal" social interaction patterns and the social interaction patterns most experience. It is safe to say that White women today, increasingly express a preference for egalitarian social interaction between themselves and White men. They realize, however, that what they are likely to experience is a White male-dominant pattern of social interaction. White women also understand that since their interaction with males is more than likely to be with White males, their strategies for social interaction must be constructed with the thought in mind that they will be dealing with the most "powerful" group in our society. Realization by White women that White men are powerful generally is accompanied by an understanding (as many do) that White men are not going to relinquish their power without an intense struggle. This kind of understanding has resulted in several types of responses from White women which have implications for future changes in the male sex-role.

One type of response is made by White women who refuse to accept their subordinate "lots." These are *"liberated" women*, who because of their desires for autonomy, social privilege, and mobility, reject "their places" in American society. Instead, these women behave independently of men and are not afraid to exhibit "competence," "intelligence," "authority," and even "power." Such traits are exhibited by some women despite the fact that men (and some other women) perceive them as violating societal expectations of women and norms of femininity. Nevertheless, behaviors such as these have implications for alteration in the male sex-role. The male sex-role is not biological; it is social. This means that the male sex-role is derived from social interaction. For men to understand that their social behaviors are not exclusive to an aggregate called "men" is a first step toward alteration of the male sex-role. This step is important, since it is difficult to imagine sex-role equality becoming a reality in our society without alterations in the male sex-role. *"Liberated" women* facilitate men's movement toward this first step.

The vast majority of White women, however, do not "refuse to accept" their subordinate lots. While many express resentment about their status, probably too few reject it in the manner discussed above. A great number of others take "paths of least resistance" and engage in male-dominant social interaction with men. Such interaction takes two forms. One form is characterized by male dominance although the female demands equity in social interaction. In the second form, the female simply assumes a submissive role, making demands neither for equality nor equity. Women interacting with men in the first form (let us call these women *"equity-oriented women"*) exhibit sex-typed behavior but demand that their outcomes are proportionate to their "feminine" investments. *"Equity-oriented women"* generally do not "rock the boat" and often are the recipients of the meager rewards that women receive during male-dominated interaction. These are the kinds of women who Harlan and Weiss say "receive the highest ratings in corporations from supervisors, who like the fact that they are older and less aggressive." Interestingly, more aggressive women are blocked in their efforts to move upward, despite the fact that they possess the necessary characteristics for high-level jobs. Regarding these older, less aggressive women who receive high ratings, Judith Thurman (1982) observes that "these were precisely *not* the kinds of executives whom senior management wanted for high level jobs" (p. 42).

Obviously when women enter into male-dominant social interaction and relationships assuming sex-typed roles, and, perceiving that they are receiving fair return on their investments, male dominance is supported. In fact, there is little likelihood that men will make changes in their behavior since they do not receive information suggesting that change is necessary. In effect, equity-oriented women suffer from the same destructive and debilitating sexism in America that millions of women before them have suffered. However, unlike more militant women today, their behaviors do not even serve to "inform" men of a possible need for change in the male sex-role since men may discern from their apparent acceptance that the token "rewards" received by them are satisfactory.

On the surface there may appear to be little difference between the behaviors of women who acquiesce to men but demand equity and those who simply assume submissive roles in the traditional mode. However, upon closer analysis, one finds that the two patterns of interaction have different implications for change in the male sex-role. Equity-oriented women help to perpetuate what Pleck (1976) has termed the "modern male sex-role" which is also characterized by male dominance but is somewhat less denigrating of women. *"Traditionally submissive women"* make no demands for equity. They "accept" their lower status as the "law of nature." These women come to believe that they have "unique capacities for sacrifice, caring, and mothering" (Chodorow, 1978). In other words, they assume the role they inherit from their mothers, who inherited the role from their mothers, and so on. As Thurman has suggested, this serves to reinforce the traditional sex-based division of labor and the inequality that goes with it. Just as important is the fact that when women simply assume submissive roles with men in social interaction with no demands for equity, they also encourage an alteration of the male sex-role which is *not in their best interests.*

Many persons writing about and/or discussing men who exhibit no appreciable changes in their sexist attitudes and behaviors toward women seemingly assume that it is due to "ignorance." Men are not aware, they imply, that changes for women will mean changes for them—that men, too, will become free (e.g., Nichols, 1978; Goldberg, 1979). To the contrary, today most men are very much aware of the male benefits that are derived from women's liberation, ranging from greater opportunities for sexual intercourse to sharing the breadwinner role. This is why women who participate in male-dominant social interaction with no demands for equity can be said to facilitate male sex-role change in ways contrary to their best interests. When such women make no demands for equity, they are in essence giving men more power by allowing them to reap all of the benefits from traditional masculinity while bearing none of the costs associated with the role. To put it simply, when men are given free reign, they can enjoy traditional male sex-role rewards, liberated male sex-role rewards, and none of the "hazards" of being "male." For these men, the male sex-role is altered in the sense that they become freer while the women with whom they interact from this perspective become even more oppressed.

Another White male–female interaction pattern that is occasionally seen in our society can be labeled *female-dominant.* This pattern is extremely rare for three reasons: females and femininity are devalued in society; females are associated with femininity; and males who allow females to be dominant are devalued. As stated often in this volume, most males learn to value their masculinity highly and to guard against threats to their masculinity from *"matriarchal women."* For a female to be dominant in social interaction with a male threatens most men's masculinity—even many so-called liberated men (who usually stress *egalitarianism* in male—female interaction regardless of the specific demands of a situation—We must keep "masculinity" in there!). Still, some men are becoming capable of passivity on occasions. These are men who realize that they do not have to dominate all social interactions with women. They also do not fear women assuming a dominant role in social interaction from any perspective—feminine, masculine, or androgynous. It is such a capacity that some men are developing, I believe, which will have the greatest impact on the male sex role. After all, men have always been dominant in our society. To allow women instances of dominance in social interaction will give men the opportunity to "see" dominance for what it is really worth, and/or to see it as "worthless." Perhaps when more White men have these experiences, male dominance in America will give over to White male–female relationships characterized by high-quality sharing—equal power and equal dependence.

Black Males and Black Females

All the Women Are White, All the Blacks Are Men, But Some of Us Are Brave (1982) is the title of a popular prize-winning book edited by Gloria Hull, Patricia Bell Scott, and Barbara Smith. A major theme running throughout this work, as the title implies, is that Black women continue to be the most oppressed aggregate in the United States despite the numerous contributions made by Black women to our society. Contrary to popular opinion, then, it seems that some Black women feel that they have gained little from two of the most important social movements in this century: the Black Movement and the Women's Movement. Proponents of this thesis certainly have economic and other social statistics confirming their claim that Black women remain the most oppressed group in America.

The reasons for Black women's continued underclass status are varied, however, some feel that part of the explanation lies in the nature of the abovementioned social movements themselves. For example, it has been pointed out that the Black Movement of the Sixties and early Seventies was a Black male-led movement. More than this, though, it also was a movement that exhorted the Black female to assume "a role more subordinate relative to the Black male than she had at any previous point in American history" (Franklin, 1980, p. 47). When she assumed this role, implies Wallace (1979), Black males betrayed Black females by not becoming the "Prince Charmings" they had promised to become. Coupled with this blow to Black women, many others (e.g. LaRue, 1970; Duberman, 1975; Wilcox, 1979) contend, the Women's Movement may not be in the best interests of Black women. There are arguments that the Women's Movement creates unnecessary competition between Black men and Black women for economic resources; and as a result, exacerbates tension between Black men and Black women. In addition, it is felt that White women are the ones who benefit from the Women's Movement, at the expense of Black women, since "they hoard the benefits of the struggle from Black Women" (Braithwaite, 1981, p. 90).

One response by a few Black women to both of these movements has been to develop an ideology that questions the idea that Black men are the main targets of White oppression. Instead, these Black women feel that Black men are to blame for their own victimization (Braithwaite, 1981). Feminist Black women contend that Black men are also oppressive and that the main target of their oppression is Black women, since they have limited contact with White women. On this controversial issue Braithwaite writes:

> Racism and sexism are inextricably linked to each other. Both manifest deleterious effects (economic, psychological, and social) on Black people. Building a separatist Black women's movement, wherein Black females collaborate with White females against the needs of their own people, is antithetical to the interests of the Black race (p. 90).

It is tempting to end this section with Braithwaite's quote. However, in all fairness to those Black feminists, I am not sure that their efforts operate against the interests of Black people. On October 20, 1982, in Columbus, Ohio at the Ohio State University, I asked Barbara Smith, the self-labeled Black feminist, just such a question, and her answer in no way implied that Braithwaite's inferences were accurate. Nevertheless, many Blacks, especially Black men, share Braithwaite's contention. This contention, I believe, is one of the sources of growing sexism among Black males who, ironically, are identifying with their "captors"—the White male. Growing sexism among Black men, and the decimation of the Black male population, are the two major factors affecting Black men and Black women's social interaction today.

Several authors (e.g., Jackson, 1978; Staples, 1978; Braithwaite, 1981) have explored the issue of increasing scarcity of Black men. The fact that the Black male infant mortality rate is higher than the Black female infant mortality rate, despite the fact that more male infants than female infants are born, begins the Black male decimation process. This alone, however, does not account for the alarming scarcity of Black men. The Black male sex-role contributes immensely to the problems as mentioned elsewhere in this volume. There is a shorter life expectancy for Black males than for any other aggregate; high accident and homicide rates prevail, as does drug addiction, and increasing numbers of Black men are in prisons; these, among other factors, contribute to the growing scarcity of Black men. If, as Staples (1978) suggests, there is only one acceptable Black man for every five Black women, regardless of the reason, this scarcity of Black men affects Black male–Black female relationships. Let us examine Black male–Black female social-interaction patterns, given Black male sexism and the scarcity of Black men; and, in addition, the implications of these patterns for changes in the Black male sex-role.

Black men and Black women, like their White counterparts, engage in a variety of patterns of social interaction, and Black women's responses are as varied as the responses of White women. Despite the fact that Black women are caught in the "double bind" of sex and color, and despite the scarcity of Black men, many Black women—just as increasing numbers of White women do in their relationships with White men—refuse to accept a subordinate position relative to Black men. In fact, it is commonly thought that slavery "sustained the Black men in a subservient and dependent role while fostering the dominations of Black women" (Braithwaite, p. 83). Many believe that this pattern has persisted and may be the cause of much conflict between Black men and Black women. Regardless of the source of Black women's rejection of male dominance, many do not (perhaps more than among White women) subscribe to the traditional female sex-role definition. As stated in Chapter 5, the independence, aggressiveness, and generally androgynous orientations of many Black women have significantly influenced the Black male sex-role. The influence has been in the direction of sex-role equality, although our society has frequently considered Black women's and Black men's social interaction patterns as deviant. Even today, some consider Black women's rejection of stereotyped notions of femininity and Black men's rejection of the stereotyped male sex-role as deviant. Braithwaite, for example, implies this when he says that Black male sex-roles and Black female sex-roles today are vestiges of the basic "slave" social order which inhibited more natural patterns of role definitions. If by "natural patterns of role definitions," Braithwaite is suggesting male dominance, he is correct; however, if he is suggesting that *failing* to accept traditional sex-role differences is deviant, I am sure that many progressive-minded Black men and Black women would disagree with his label. Unfortunately, this seems to be precisely what Braithwaite is saying when he notes that this slave experience inhibits the prospect for unification between Black men and Black women. To the contrary, I submit that, at this point in time, in light of the movement toward sex-role equality, the vestiges of the slave experience may better prepare Black men and Black women for social interaction.

Some Black women, especially since the late 1960s, do accept traditional female sex-roles and have become Black Cinderellas who suffer from all of the dysfunctions that White Cinderellas experience and more. Many of the Black Cinderellas who enter into Black male-dominant relationships but demand equity in the relationships discover that, unlike

White Cinderellas and White Prince Charmings, their Black Prince Charming does not have the resources to provide outcomes for them commensurate with their "feminine" investments. Needless to say, upon discovering this, many Black women who demand equity elect to withdraw from the interaction and continue their search for a "resourceful" Black Prince Charming. As implied throughout this section, however, for many the search is futile because of the scarcity of Black men—not to mention the fact that numerous Black men are unwilling to enact the Prince Charming role. One outcome for a portion of these women is that they begin to develop strategies for an independent and autonomous existence. In other words, while a search is continued, it is done so from a perspective that is much less supportive of male dominance and much more supportive of sex-role equality. In a sense, these equity-oriented women move closer to total rejection of a male-dominance ideology in male–female social interaction.

Within the Black female aggregate there also are a relatively small number of women who assume submissive roles with men and who do not demand equity. *"Traditionally submissive Black women"* are rare, due to the socialization process most Black women experience. Black mothers usually teach their daughters self-reliance, independence, assertiveness, and so on, while simultaneously giving them a more traditional message "find a husband to take care of you." The latter message, though, generally is given from a "physical" perspective where "take care of you" means "meet your sexual needs" and provide "physical" protection. There are some Black women, nevertheless, who do develop and internalize traditional definitions of what it means to be "female." Black male dominance is supported by these women and they assume the familiar "caring" and "dependent" roles with Black men. Many times such women soon become disillusioned when they discover that numerous Black men have not internalized nor are they prepared to enact the complementary "dominant" role in vital areas of social life. Like their White counterparts, "submissive" Black women in dealing with Black men (many of whom are androgynous to begin with) often have even more subjugated experiences. Black men interacting with "submissive" Black women enjoy similar double benefits and few costs to White men interacting with "submissive" White women. The effect on the Black male sex-role may be even more deleterious from a sex-role equality perspective. While many Black men, because of their sex and race experiences, may be "anomic" to begin with, unqualified support for male dominance by a woman may push them into the more sexist categories "routine masculinists" and/or "classical men," without the obligations that accompany the roles. The disadvantages of such occurrences for Black women should be obvious.

A common belief in American society is that too many Black male–Black female relationships and interactions are characterized by female dominance. This belief has persisted in the United States at least since the Moynihan Report (1965) received widespread publicity nearly two decades ago. Persons taking this position point to the high number of male children who are reared by Black mothers and the numerous Black women who assume primary-breadwinner and authority roles within the Black family. This means that Black males, unlike White males, know firsthand what it means to be in female-dominant relationships. From what was implied in our discussion of White female-dominant relationships, one probably can reason that many males, having experienced this kind of dominance, reject it and tend to endorse sex-role equality. Many Black males probably would endorse sex-role equality, I contend, if it were not for the fact that society still endorses male-dominant relationships. This results in many Black men rejecting female dominance *and* egalitarian relationships in interaction with women. Instead, in an effort to conform to society's definitions of masculinity, some Black men with female-dominant interaction experiences adopt the same male dominance strategies as White men. In essence, further experiences of female dominance do not seem to be necessary for Black men. While White men may benefit in the short run, from female dominance, further matriarchal experiences for Black men may be inimical to the goal of sex-role equality.

Interracial Male-Female Relationships

Interracial relationships and social interaction between Blacks and Whites have increased in the last several decades and, though few in number, are not as rare as they once were. Increased social interaction between the races has occurred despite the fact that the vast majority of Blacks and Whites still live in two separate worlds in the United States. Increased social relationships and social interaction between the races also have implications for changes in the male sex-role, since some of these relationships and interactions are between males and females from the two racial aggregates. In 1972, Franklin and Walum proposed that the Black Movement and the Women's Movement would have a combined effect on interrace–intersex relationships and social interaction. They suggested that sex-role changes within each of the racial aggregates would have the effect of increasing relationships between Black males and White females as well as those between White males and Black females.

During slavery, interracial relationships and social interaction occurred basically between White men and Black women. These relationships generally are thought to have been genital focused, involving little else. Undoubtedly many were, but some are likely to have been White-male-dominance-initiated ones which developed into more expressive, more emotional, and richer relationships. We can hardly expect such relationships between White men and Black women to be documented in history books since often they were clandestine affairs "ignored" and "accepted" by white women. Moreover, since such relationships were not "legitimate," in all likelihood society would have refused to accept their existence—except that the products (mixed race children) of their relationships substantiated their existence, even if little could be inferred about the quality of the relationships. Following the Emancipation Proclamation, there was a gradual decline in White male–Black female relationships as Black women became less subject to the personal whims of White men. To be sure, some Black women did experience coercive relationships with White men following slavery and some "voluntarily" engaged in relationships with White men. But, for the most part, relationships between Black women and White men have been largely nonexistent for decades. Despite the fact that White male–Black female marriages are not the only indicators of White male–Black female relationships, it is interesting to point out that according to the U.S. Census Bureau only 46,000 of these marriages existed at the beginning of this decade. Somewhat revealing, however, is that a trend may be beginning, since there was an increase of 22,000 such marriages between 1970 and 1980.

Many Black women have been reluctant to become involved in relationships with White men for historical reasons and due to Black subcultural norms prohibiting interracial relationships, especially those between Black females and White males. Though more tolerant of interracial associations than the White subculture, the Black subculture is most hostile toward Black female–White male relationships. The greater tolerance of Black male–White female relationships obviously is related to emerging male dominance within the Black subculture since the Black Movement.

Alvin Poussaint (1982) has pointed out that despite all the discussions about Black male–White female relationships, only about 120,000 Black men are interracially married. While there are greater numbers of these kinds of relationships today, the pattern is a relatively recent one. Certainly, scattered Black male–White female relationships have always existed but it was not until the past two decades that these relationships flourished. Moreover, unlike White male–Black female relationships, the rate of growth of Black male–White female relationships may very well be attenuated by the Women's Movement. A major source of Black men's attraction to White women, in addition to the "forbidden fruit" phenomenon, has been the perception that White women assumed "submissive" roles with men. Given increased aggressiveness, independence, and autonomy among White women, this source of attraction may soon no longer exist since Black men's perceptions of White women as "submissive" will most certainly change. Summarily, as White men become increasingly attracted to Black women who may be willing to allow them to assume a dominant role in social relationships, Black men and White women may be on a collision course. Many Black men seem to have developed sexist attitudes toward women (or at least Black women perceive them to be sexist). In the *Essence* "Quality of Life Survey" in 1980, 82% of the Black women responding (5049) "agreed that Black women encounter sexist attitudes and behavior as much from Black men as they do from White men" (Braithwaite, p. 92). It is unlikely that Black men can carry such attitudes into relationships with "liberated White women" who are just the ones with whom they are most likely to establish interracial relationships.

In addition to the above barrier to increased Black male–White female relationships, perceived increased competition from White females may also mitigate further increases in Black male–White female relationships. As White women have increased their visibility in societal institutions, many Black males have begun to perceive White females as competitors, and increased participation on the part of White females will more than likely enhance Black men's perceptions in this direction. The irony of all of this is that many Black men who are attracted to White women will eventually discover that they are attracted to White women who no longer exist. These men, then, will be ready to return to Black females and when they do, they may find that the Black woman is no longer available—she will have cast her lot with a male she perceives as more socially potent—the White male. What is important to remember about this entire discussion, however, is that we have been dealing with a relatively small number of males and females within both races. Little change has occurred in race relations in our society in recent years and little change is expected in the near future. Also in the near future, most relationships between men and women will be intrarace ones. Thus, the major factor that will affect male–female relationships for some time to come will be the extent to which sex-role equality is a reality in our society.

The Implications of Men's Interaction with Men for Changes in the Male Sex Role

Men's relationships with other men are dysfunctional to men, as we have seen, but these relationships today do show signs that they are being influenced by several factors and may be undergoing change. Some of the factors that seem to be changing the quality of men's relationships with men include (1) the Women's Movement, (2) the current economic crisis, (3) the proliferation of information concerning the negative aspects of the male sex-role and (4) the decreasing significance of race in social interaction between men. These four factors combined undermine and affect the rigid definition of masculinity which men have been expected to internalize and enact in social encounters.

The Women's Movement

The Women's Movement has affected the male sex-role in all of the ways discussed in Chapter 1. In addition, this movement has had the effect of drawing men together. While the "togetherness" has been awkward for many men who were reared to avoid intimacy and expressiveness with men, presently some of the awkwardness seems to be dissipating. Men are discovering that society is relaxing its rules against male social interaction. Part of society's response undoubtedly is due to a Women's Movement "backlash" which has both negative and positive consequences. The negative implications of this backlash are obvious and are directed toward women. The positive consequences are not so obvious and men have been the primary beneficiaries, although ultimately women may benefit.

The ideology of the Women's Movement has directed most of its attention to White men in power but its adherents have directed their activism toward all men. Some attempts have been made to exclude relatively powerless men from attack, but the attempts have not been recognized by these men. Powerless White men, Black men, Chicano men, Puerto Rican men, Native American men, gay men, ambisexual men, and others have felt the "effects" of the women's Movement. These men, too, have been accused of espousing male-dominance traits and exhibiting male-dominance behaviors—and rightly so. Such accusations have had the effect of giving men from diverse backgrounds a common characteristic which has created a kind of aggregate-consciousness among men just as large numbers of women with diverse backgrounds now recognize some commonalities between them. If nothing more, by obscuring distinctions between men, the Women's Movement has given men a label, which if you are a man, you must wear—in fact, feel compelled to wear. Even if a particular man cannot be a "provider," a "rational" individual, and an "inexpressive" person, he can "wear" the label many women assign to him, because the only characteristic he needs to possess is a "male" anatomical structure. "Wearing" the label places a particular man in the male category and once the label is accepted, attitudes and behaviors commensurate with it emerge. I suggest that this has occurred for numerous powerless White men and men from minority groups. Moreover, interaction between these men also is increasing. As interaction increases, we may also expect to see an assimilation of attitudes and behaviors occurring. If this happens, those men's behaviors that have usually been sex-typed certainly will be affected by those men who have been more androgynous, and vice-versa.

The Economic Crisis in the United States

In the early 1980s thousands of men have suddenly found themselves incapable of fulfilling the requirements of the male sex-role because of the society's economic crisis. Recognition of this fact has resulted in many alterations in the male sex-role. There are "classical men" and "routine masculinists" who no longer have the means for enacting the roles they internalized during the male early socialization process. This has meant that many of these men have had to begin a resocialization process. Resocialization often has involved an "acceptance" of dependence, a modification of men's "breadwinner" role, and a recognition of powerlessness, among other things. Undoubtedly many men have also had to alter their definitions of masculinity, recognizing that they no longer fulfilled their own requirements for being "men." Such a reorganization of male cognitions about masculinity is sure to affect masculinity in the years to come.

Proliferation of Information about the Male Sex Role

Newspapers, magazines, television, radio, public forums, men's groups, and the like frequently devote attention to the topic of male sex-roles. Practically no man can escape these sources which inform him about the "hazards of being male." That men have received the information is reflected in an increasing number of men establishing more expressive and more intimate relationships with other men. It is not the case that suddenly men's friendships and associates are as "personal" as women's, but men's relationships do appear to be becoming more "human." Such changes may be exactly what is needed to further efforts for equal rights for men and women.

The Decreasing Significance of Race in Men's Social Interaction

Historically, when men of different races have interacted in our society, race has played a significant role. Race has affected the quality and amount of interaction between men of different races—especially inter- action between Black men and White men. The major reasons race has been a significant factor are obvious. Another reason, though, is that men of different races generally perceive the world differently. These diverse *perceptions* often have inhibited and/or affected men's internal social interaction. For example, White males have generally perceived men to be dominant and decisive, and that those persons who were submissive and indecisive were not men. White males also have been taught that men are nonexpressive and nonemotional. Summarily, White males are taught traits of masculinity that are often opposite to the traits many Black males exhibit. Given increased interaction between Black males and White males, their perceptions of each other in all likelihood will be affected. White males and Black males will alter their perceptions of each other. Because many of the traits Black males exhibit are more androgy- nous than those exhibited by White males, and because the traits Black males exhibit are more compatible with sex-role equality, as race becomes *less* significant in men's social interactions, sex-role equality will become more of a reality in our society.

Men's Responses to Sex-Role Changes

Much of this volume has been devoted to an examination of those beliefs, values, and attitudes existing among males which justify the inequality governing the way men and women are treated in American society. The fact that men and women often exhibit different kinds of behavior has not been questioned but what has been questioned is soci- ety's differential valuation of those behaviors, resulting in sex stratifica- tion. As Perry and Perry (1983) have noted, "undoubtedly men are supe- rior to women in some activities and women are superior to men in others" (p. 284). This fact, however, does not justify the construction of an ideology which attributes superiority to men and inferiority to women in all things valued by our society. As we have seen, not only is there no justification for such a pernicious ideology, there also is no empirical basis for such a claim.

By now most American men have heard the rhetoric of the Women's Movement in one form or another. Even those men who have clung tenaciously to their rather rigid ways of behaving toward women have heard the voices calling for sex-role changes, and the responses of these men and others have been diverse. Some have honestly tried to change; others have staunchly resisted change; and still others frequently express confusion about the entire matter. Nevertheless, patterns of male–female interaction, as we have seen, occur which give us a glimpse of things to come on the sex-role frontier. An increasingly smaller number of men now fall into the *classical man category*. Classical men *conform to traditional definitions of masculinity* with all of its male advantages as well as the dysfunctions associated with the outmoded role. Another category of males today is comprised of men who routinely engage in the same behaviors as classical males while verbally professing to espouse "modern" views of sex-role equality. Let us call these men *"routine masculinists."* Still another group of men (which is growing in number) consists of those who have accepted the idea of sex-role changes but who feel "confused" about what their role should be relative to women. These men are labeled *"anomic men."* An interesting characteristic of such men is that they frequently lapse into "old ways" of behaving because they do not perceive alternative ways of behaving. Lastly, there is a rapidly growing male minority that can be categorized as *humanist men*. These men are at various stages of rejecting our society's sexist ideology, which keeps both men and women "in place." In addition, *humanist men* are in the process of constructing personal ideologies that have as an objective, sex-role equality. Humanist men certainly flounder in their attempts to exhibit behaviors congruent with sex-role equality but they also usually become aware of their failures and attempt to rectify them. Such men, it can be said, not only are constructing sex-role equality goals for themselves but also are confidently exploring alternative mechanisms for realizing these goals.

The Classical Man

The *classical man* is archaic in American society. To be sure, from time to time, one can hear supporters of traditional masculinist values calling for a return to "the good ole' days," when "men were men" and "women were women." Lamenting changes in sex roles, these voices often decry the fact that male rewards and prerogatives of power are threatened with sex-role-equality-based allocation procedures. While it is tempting to say that most *classical men* are in positions of obvious power, they are not. Many of these men do hold power in our society, but many more do not. Classical men can be found throughout the social strata, perceive that their position is "correct," and believe in it fervently.

Most men falling into the *classical male* category exhibit retreatist behaviors on issues related to sex-roles. Because they are likely to be challenged on their controversial stance, they rarely verbalize their beliefs in traditional masculinist values. However, these men's behaviors reflect masculinist attitudes and values. Ironically, while such men may take a protective posture toward specific females with whom they have a close relationship (e.g., their mothers, daughters, and sisters), hostile behaviors may be exhibited toward women they feel are "not in place." They tend to follow the logical "individual" implications of McConahay and McConahay's findings on sex-role rigidity and violence. That is, cultures in which sex-roles are rigid tend to have high rates of sexual violence directed toward women. I submit that men who are characterized by rigidly steryotyped sex-role behavior react in hostile ways toward women whom they perceive challenge their ideas about the "proper" roles for men and women.

Hostile responses from the *classical male* may not be all dysfunctional, since such responses are often met with equally hostile opposing ones. Certainly, such hostile confrontations have been disruptive for individual relationships but they have also been sources of "new" cognitions for those males who have somehow been bypassed by sex-role changes. The angry daughter who responds to a hostile, masculinist father, who, in turn, after reflecting on both responses, softens his traditional masculinist stance is an example of the above. It is not implied necessarily that the father comes to "accept" his daughter's viewpoint, but it is suggested that she gives him "food for thought" which may at least move him into the routine masculinist category.

Some classical men, when confronted with opposing viewpoints, can be dangerous, as we have seen in the case of the Lady Killer. Others, though, are relatively harmless in terms of physical violence although they may be deadly to others, especially women, psychologically. Fortunately, these men seem to be part of a disappearing breed of American males. Their eventual extinction is certain to be appreciated by many more progressive-minded men and women in our society. Just as important is the *reason* why classical men are a disappearing breed in America. Many seem to be entering another category due to increased awareness of sex-role issues. This category, as labeled and defined earlier, is the routine masculinist category.

Routine Masculinist Men

Routine masculinist men verbally acknowledge sex-role changes in America and claim to recognize the legitimacy of such changes in the presence of women. Many of these men appear on the surface to even accept the goal of sex-role equality. Their acceptance of the goal, however, does not prevent them from behaving in subtly masculinist ways toward women. Routine masculinist men, when in the company of men, will frequently give themselves away on the issue of sex-role equality. They often tell "little jokes" about feminists and imply that they are simply going along with this madness to "please" some woman—either their wives or someone they happen to be with at the moment.

Routine masculinists are expedient, and, having developed mechanisms for interacting with women, generally display those role behaviors they perceive a women to deem appropriate at the time. Such men do feel that traditional masculinity is outdated and, in fact, even appreciate that fact. However, their appreciation is steeped in male-dominance. These are the men who have recognized that women's liberation also liberated them and they take full advantage of both liberations. "Yes, I agree that women should work for pay"; "Of course, women should be sexually free"; "Certainly women should be able to realize their potential." These statements are likely to flow freely from the lips of routine masculinists. Yet, such men do very little to facilitate these activities for women. In fact, when such men are married, their wives soon discover that women's freedom to participate in the above activities is contingent upon being able to assume fully both those roles external to the home and those traditionally domestic.

Routine masculinist men are especially difficult for women because usually they are "experts" at playing a vicious psychological sex-role game—"give them enough rope and they will hang themselves." Now this does not mean that the routine masculinist is aware of his behavior. Instead, he simply continues to behave as always, which is diametrically opposed to the interests of women. For example, numerous women who began careers in the middle 1970s, only to find after one or two years that things were not working out, returned to "their places." These women usually are unable to explain "their failures" beyond "role conflict." Perhaps the most unfortunate aspect of such an explanation is that these women feel that the entire "awful mess" was their doing. The routine masculinist sits silently by, simply saying to himself, "I told you so." It is too early to say, but it is likely that such women will discover at some point in the near future that their original goals were possible to accomplish, given half a chance. Moreover, it would not be surprising to find that many discover this much sooner than their men anticipate. Actually, such discoveries may be the catalysts that routine masculinists need to "push" them into the next male category.

Anomic Men

Anomic men are "confused" about the goals of sex-role equality and what they should do about sex-role equality. Their behaviors with women and strategies for interacting with women usually reflect the confusion. These are the men who frequently indicate that they do not know what is expected of them or how they should behave with women. Anomic men, in interacting with progressive women, have experiences which range from extremely positive to extremely negative. The reason, of course, is due to the fact that anomic men's behaviors fluctuate from conservative to liberal on sex-role issues. These are the kind of men referred to in Chapter Six who exhaust women in the process of learning about and accepting sex-role equality. Far from not empathizing with women, anomic men do empathize with women but they do so inaccurately. In taking the role of others, one actually constructs the role on the basis of a perception of that role from one's own perspective. If one's perception of that role is faulty, even well-intentioned role-taking will be inaccurate. This is precisely what happens with anomic men when they empathize with women.

Many anomic men have been, at one time or another, classical men and routine masculinists. Their knowledge of women, from these perspectives, undergoes tremendous change as they become anomic. In fact, most of the original cognitions about women are discarded as these men attempt to develop new cognitions about women. These new cognitions are derived from interacting with "progressive" women, focusing on such women in the mass media, discussing "liberated" women with other men, reading about liberated women, and so on. Often, however, the resocialization process is devoid of self-change content. This means that anomic men, in trying to change their attitudes toward women, often focus only on the external and do not focus closely enough on their own needs for change. As a result, the barrage of information coming from numerous sources is haphazard and disorganized, resulting in confusion for anomic men. For example, a woman carrying a briefcase and an armload of books may decline an invitation from a male to carry her books into a building. Upon reaching the building, the same woman may be highly appreciative if the male would open the door for her. Perceiving himself as "rejected" earlier, an anomic male would not know what to do upon reaching the door. If the woman asked him to open and hold the door for her, he would probably shake his head, implying, "I never know what they want." Actually, it is all rather simple. It is not necessarily difficult for an adult who is not handicapped to carry both an armload of books and a briefcase for some distance. It *is* rather unwieldy for an adult to open a door when laden with such artifacts. Courtesy toward another human adult (male or female) would dictate opening and holding the door if the adult desired.

The anomic man's dilemma upon reaching the door is due to inaccurate role-taking rather than nonempathy. Not being able to empathize appropriately with women is a learning experience for men because the feedback received by men can inform them of "appropriate" role-taking strategies. Beyond "proper" role-taking strategies, however, such information also teaches men about the "status" of women. This kind of socialization, in turn, can be used (and often is used) by men to improve their role-taking abilities with women. The state of *anomie* concerning sex-role equality, which is said to characterize a great number of American men today, probably is necessary for men's growth. Out of such states of "confusion" men will develop stable sets of cognitions, feelings, and behaviors which are oriented toward sex-role equality. Such men will develop a humanist perspective. Humanist men are discussed below.

Humanist Men

A humanist man is one who has constructed for himself the goal of sex-role equality. Having rejected the outdated masculinist goal of male dominance, humanist men also reject the strategies and techniques used by some men to maintain and support sex-role inequality. Instead, these men seem more likely to endorse an androgynous sex-role orientation, where both "masculine" and "feminine" traits are valued and exhibited in social interaction. Humanist men are not locked into social roles, and are usually quite capable of responding to a specific situation in terms of the demands of the situation—that is, whether the situation calls for an "assertive" response or a passive response, an independent response or a dependent one. These men are in the process of constructing sets of cognitions, feelings, and behaviors which recognize the legitimacy and value of sex-role equality. Such attitudinal components are "stable" only in the sense that they are oriented toward creating and participating in a society where men and women are equally valued and where each participates equally according to individual predilections.

Career Paths Men Take Toward Sex-Role Equality

Men in American society today are likely to receive conflicting information about what it means to be a "man." Though somewhat less encouraging than a decade ago, societal institutions still support male dominance, male aggression, male violence, and male superiority over females, among other things. On the other hand, the impact of women's efforts toward sex-role equality has been felt by many men (although some have chosen to ignore the demands for women's freedom). While many men seem to be locked in or between "classical men's" roles and/or "routine masculinist" roles, some are beginning to move back and forth between the routine masculinist category and the "anomic men" category. A few men have even moved into the humanist men category. At the present time, no clear-cut path seems to apply to men who eventually pass successfully through the "anomic men" category and into the "humanist men" category. For one thing, contemporary men confronted with sex-role equality begin their movements at different stages. Men under twenty-five are more likely than their older counterparts to have experienced a "liberal" sex-role socialization. As a result, such men are more likely to have been "routine masculinist" than "classical men" as they began their adult men's careers. Later adult socialization experiences may have the effect of pulling or pushing these men into either the "classical men" category or the "anomic men" category. Young men who become deeply religious and/or politically conservative may be pushed from the "routine masculinist" category to the "classical men" category because the latter category is consistent with the religious and political socialization experiences such men undergo. On the other hand, young men who form social relationships with others who fervently believe in equal rights for women usually are pulled into the "anomic men" category. Still, others may remain in the "routine masculinist" category for an indefinite period of time. Generally, it seems to be the case that *men's social relationships with others* (both males and females) determine the direction taken with respect to sex-role equality. This is to be expected, since individuals react to objects on the basis of the meanings that objects have for them; and, the meanings of objects grow out of social interaction (Blumer, 1969).

Prince Charming's Emerging Form

With women continuing their struggle for human rights, with men broadening their latitudes of masculinity, and with more men as well as women constructing strategies designed to eliminate sex-role inequality in America, the male sex-role, while resistant to change, will undoubtedly undergo further changes toward sex-role equality. Will Prince Charming survive? It is unlikely that he will survive in his present outdated form. Hopefully, his emergent altered form will be more beneficial to men and women, and to American society in general. But what will be Prince Charming's *emergent altered form?* It is extremely difficult to answer this question, given recent social and political trends in our society that challenge whether most men and women in America can (or want to) achieve an integration of masculine and feminine traits. For example, some evidence suggests that while sex-role attitudes changed in the 1970s, stereotypes about differences in the personal attributes of men and women remained stable (e.g., Ruble, 1983). It is important to remember also Alperson and Friedman's (1983) conclusions that women attempting to adopt certain aspects of the male sex-role are unlikely to be accepted and validated in their choices. In addition, Lee and Scheurer (1983) infer from their study that psychological androgyny may be a feminist view of the ideal. They found that a predominance of masculine traits rather than a combination of masculinity and femininity accounted for higher adaptive scores for both men and women. Lee and Scheurer conclude that it may be more advantageous for men and women to possess those qualities we typically term "masculine."

In debating Prince Charming's likelihood of survival, it must be remembered, however, that presently we *remain* in Prince Charming's deteriorating castle. All of the research studies, findings, conclusions, and inferences are part-and-parcel of the prince's deteriorating masculinist structure. The foundation beneath this structure historically has not been based on sex-role equality. This is precisely why the structure is so resistant to total destruction. Optimistically, it is assumed that the new foundation being built will be based on sex-role equality, and that this will facilitate the emergence of Prince Charming in an altered form. I believe that this will occur if we can remember the words of Judith Arcana:

> It will serve us well to realize and remind ourselves, whenever we try to understand who we are, and what "human nature" might be, that the definition of the roles we play are not definitions of us. These definitions generally have more to do with the ideas of the people who create them, and the expectations of our friends and relatives, than they have to do with who we actually are, as individuals—woman or man (1983, p. 98)

References

Allen, B. The Price for Giving It Up. *Essence*, 1983, *February*, 60–42.

Alperson, B. L., and Friedman, W. J. Some Aspects of the Interpersonal Phenomenology of Heterosexual Dyads with Respect to Sex-Role Stereotypes. *Sex Roles*, 1983, *9*, 453–474.

Arcana, J. *Every mother's son*. Garden City: Anchor Press, 1983.

Bahr, S. J., and Day, R. O. Sex Roles, Attitudes, Female Employment and Marital Satisfaction. *Journal of Comparative Family Studies*, 1978, *9*, 53–67.

Balswick, J. Types of Inexpressive Male Roles. In R. A. Lewis, *Men in difficult times*. Englewood Cliffs: Prentice-Hall, 1969.

Balswick J. O., and Peek, C. W. The Inexpressive Male: A Tragedy of American Society. *The Family Coordinator*, 1971, October, 363–368.

Bandura, A. *Social learning theory*. Englewood Cliffs: Prentice-Hall, 1977.

Bannon, J. A., and Southern, M. L. Father-Absent Women: Self-Concept and Modes of Relating to Men. *Sex Roles*, 1980, *6*, 75–84.

Bartolome, F. Executives as Human Beings. *Harvard Business Review*, 1972, November–December, 62–68.

Baruch, G. K., and Barnett, R. C. Fathers' Participation in the Care of Their Preschool Children. *Sex Roles*, 1981, *7*, 1043–1055.

Bearison, D. J. Sex-Linked Patterns of Socialization. *Sex Roles*, 1979, *5*, 11–18.

Bell, A. P. Comment on Homosexuals in Heterosexual Marriage. *Sex Behavior*, 1972, *2*, 46.

Bell, A. P., and Weinberg, M. S. *Homosexualities*. New York: Simon & Schuster, 1978.

Bem, S. L. The Measurement of Psychological Androgyny. *Journal of Consulting and Clinical Psychology*, 1974, *42*, 155–162.

Berger, P. L., and Berger, B. Becoming a Member of Society. In P. I. Rose, *Socialization and the life cycle*. New York: St. Martin's Press, 1979.

Berscheid, E. and Walster, E. *Interpersonal attraction*. Reading, Massachusetts: Addison-Wesley, 1969.

Berscheid, E., and Walster, E. Physical attractiveness. In L. Berkowitz (Ed.), *Advances in experimental social psychology*. New York: Academic Press, 1974.

Berscheid, E., and Walster, E. *Interpersonal attraction*. Reading, Massachusetts: Addison-Wesley, 1978.

215

Best, D. L., Williams, J. E., and Briggs, S. R. A Further Analysis of the Affective Meanings Associated with Male and Female Sex-Trait Stereotypes. *Sex Roles*, 1980, *6*, 735–746.

Bieber, I., Dain, H., Dince, P., Drellich, M., Grand, H., Gundlach, R., Kremer, M., Rifkin, A., Wilber, C., and Bieber, T. *Homosexuality: A psychoanalytic study*. New York: Basic Books, 1962.

Biller, H. B. *Paternal deprivation*. Lexington, Massachusetts: D. C. Heath, 1974.

Birns, B. The Emergence and Socialization of Sex Differences in the Earliest Years. *Merrill-Palmer Quarterly*, 1976, *22*, 229–254.

Blakeley, M. K. He's A feminist, But. . . . *Ms.*, 1982, *October*, 44.

Blau, P. M. *Exchange and power in social life*. New York: Wiley, 1964.

Block, J. H. Assessing Sex Differences: Issues, Problems and Pitfalls. *Merrill-Palmer Quarterly*, 1977, *23*, 140–147.

Blood, R. D. The Husband–Wife Relationship. In F. I. Nye, and I. W. Hoffman (Eds.), *The employed mother in America*. Chicago: Rand McNally, 1963.

Blumer, H. *Symbolic interactionism: Perspectives and methods*. Englewood Cliffs: Prentice-Hall, 1969.

Blumstein, P. W., and Schwartz, P. Bisexuality in Men. *Urban Life*, 1976, *5*, 339–358.

Blumstein, P. W., and Schwartz, P. Bisexuality: Some Social Psychological Issues. *Journal of Social Issues*, 1977, *33*, 30–45.

Booth, A., and Edwards, J. N. Fathers: The Invisible Parent. *Sex Roles*, 1980, *6*, 445–456.

Brabant, S. Sex Role Stereotyping in the Sunday Comics. *Sex Roles*, 1976, *2*, 331–337.

Braithwaite, R. L. Interpersonal Relations Between Black Males and Black Families. In Gary, L. E., *Black men*. Beverly Hills: Sage Publications, 1981.

Braito, R., Dean, D., Powers, E., and Bruton, B. The Inferiority Game: Perceptions and Behaviors. *Sex Roles*, 1981, *7*, 65–72.

Brannon, R. Inside the Men's Movement. *Ms.*, 1982, *October*, 40–44.

Brown, R. *Social psychology*. New York: Macmillan, 1965.

Bryson, R., Bryson, J. B., and Johnson, M. Family Size, Satisfaction and Productivity in Dual-Career Couples. *Psychology of Women Quarterly*, 1978, *3*, 67–77.

Burke, R. J., and Weir, T. Relationship of Wives' Employment Status to Husband, Wife and Pair Satisfaction. *Journal of Marriage and the Family*, 1976, *38*, 279–287.

Caldwell, M. A., and Peplau, L. A. Sex Differences in Same-Sex Friendships. *Sex Roles*, 1982, *8*, 721–732.

Campbell, A., Converse, P. E., and Rodgers, W. L. *The quality of American life: Perception, evaluation, and satisfaction*. New York: Russell Sage, 1976.

Chafetz, J. S. *Masculine, feminine or human?* Itasca, Minnesota: F. E. Peacock, 1978.

Chessler, P. *About men*. New York: Simon & Schuster, 1978.

Chodorow, N. *The reproduction of mothering*. Berkely: University of California Press, 1978.

Cicone, M., and Ruble, D. Beliefs About Males. *Journal of Social Issues*, 1978, *34*, 5–16.

Cloward, R., and Ohlin, L. E. *Delinquency and opportunity*. New York: Free Press, 1960.

Connor, M., and Serbin, L. A. Children's Responses to Stories with Male and Female Characters. *Sex Roles*, 1978, *4*, 637–645.

Constantinople, A. Sex-Role Acquisition: In Search of the Elephant. *Sex Roles*, 1979, *5*, 121–133.

Cooley, C. H. *Human Nature and the Social. Order*. New York: Scribner, 1902.

Cosby, B. The Regular Way. In J. W. Petras (Ed.), *Sex: male/gender: masculine*. Port Washington, New York: Alfred Publishing Company, 1975.

Costrich, N., Feinstein, J., Kidder, L., Maracedk, J., and Pascable, L. When Stereotypes Hurt: Three Studies of Penalties for Sex-Role Reversals. *Journal of Experimental Social Psychology*, 1975, *11*, 520–530.

Curtis, L. Rape, Race, and Culture: Some Speculations in Search of a Theory. In M. J. Walker, and S. L. Brodsky (Eds.), *Sexual assault*, Lexington, Massachusetts: Lexington Books, 1976.

Dank, B. The Homosexual. In E. Goode and R. Troiden (Eds.), *Sexual deviance and sexual deviants*. New York: Morrow, 1974.

David, D. S., and Brannon, R. (Eds.). *The forty-nine percent majority: The male sex role*. Reading, Mass.: Addison-Wesley, 1976.

Derlega, V. J., Durham, B., Gockel, B., and Scholis, D. Sex Differences in Self-Disclosure: Effects of Topic Content, Friendship, and Partner's Sex. *Sex Roles*, 1981, *7*, 433–447.

Deutsch, C., and Gilbert, L. Norms Affecting Self-Disclosure in Men and Women. *Journal of Consulting and Clinical Psychology*, 1976, *44*, 376–380.

Donelson, E., and Gullahorn, J. E. *Women: A psychological perspective*. New York: Wiley, 1977.

Dowling, C. *The Cinderella complex*. New York: Harper and Row, 1981.

Drabman, R. S., Robertson, S. J., Patterson, J. N., Jarvie, G. J., Hammer, D., and Gordua, G. Children's Perceptions of Media Portrayal of Sex Roles. *Sex Roles*, 1979, *7*, 379–389.

Duberman, L. *Gender and sex in society*. New York: Praeger, 1975.

Ehrenreich, B., and Stallard, K. The Noveau Poor. *Ms.*, 1982, *August*, 217–224.

Emerson, R. M. Power-Dependence Relations. *American Sociological Review*, 1962, *27*, 31–41.

Epstein, C. F., *Woman's place*. Los Angeles: University of California Press, 1971.

Farrell, W. *The liberated man*. New York: Bantam Books, 1974.

Fagot, B. I. Play Styles in Early Childhood. Eric number Ed 175562, 1979.

Fagot, B. I. Continuity and Change in Play Styles as a Function of Sex of Child. *International Journal of Behavioral Development*, 1981, *4*, 37–43.

Fagot, B. I. Male and Female Teachers: Do They Treat Boys and Girls Differently? *Sex Roles*, 1981, *7*, 263–271.

Farley, L. *Sexual shakedown: The sexual harassment of women on the job*. New York: McGraw-Hill, 1978.

Farwell, W. *The liberated man*. New York: Random House, 1974.

Fasteau, M. *The male machine*. New York: McGraw-Hill, 1974.

Fein, R. A. Research in Fathering: Social Policy and An Emergent Perspective. *Journal of Social Issues*, 1978, *34*, 122–135.

Feinman, S. Approvals of Cross Sex-Role Behavior. *Psychological Reports*, 1974, *35*, 643–648.

Fitzpatrick, M. A., and Bochner, P. A. Perspectives on Self and Other: Male–Female Differences in Perceptions of Communication Behaviors. *Sex Roles*, 1981, *7*, 523–535.

Fling, S., and Monosevitz, M. Sex-Typing in Nursery School Children's play Interests. *Developmental Psychology*, 1972, *7*, 146–152.

Foreit, K. G., Agor, T., Byers, J., Larve, J., Lokey, H., Palazzini, M., Patterson, M., and Smith, L. Sex-Bias in the Newspaper Treatment of Male-Centered and Female-Centered News Stories. *Sex Roles*, 1980, *6*, 475–480.

Francher, J. S., and Henkin, J. The Menopausal Queen: Adjustment on Aging and the Male Homosexual. *American Journal of Orthopsychiatry*, 1973, *43*, 670–674.

Frank, E. *Ladies Home Journal*, January 18, 1983.

Franklin, C. W., II. White Racism as a Cause of Black Male–Black Female Conflict. *The Western Journal of Black Studies*, 1980, *4*, 42–48.

Franklin, C. W., II, and Walum, L. R. Toward a Paradigm of Subcultural Relations: An Application to Sex and Race in the United States. *Phylon*, 1972, *3*, 242–253.

Franklin, C. W. II. *Theoretical perspectives in social psychology*. Boston: Little, Brown, 1982.

Franklin, C. W., II. Black Male–White Male Perceptual Conflict. *The Western Journal of Black Studies*, 1982, *6*, 2–9.

Freeman, J. (Ed.). *Women: A feminist perspective*. Palo Alto: Mayfield Publishing Company, 1979.

Freimuth, M. J., and Hornstein, G. A. A Critical Examination of the Concept of Gender. *Sex Roles*, 1982, *8*, 515–532.

Freud, S. Three Essays on the Theory of Sexuality. In *The Complete Psychological Works of Sigmund Freud*, Vol. 7. London: Hogarth, 1953.

Freud, S. Mourning and Melancholia. In *The complete works of Sigmund Freud*, Vol. *14*. London: Hogarth, 1957.

Freud, S. Three Contributions to the Theory of Sex. In A. A. Brill, (Ed.), *The basic writings of Sigmund Freud*. New York: Random House, 1938.

Freudinger, P., and Almquist, E. M. Male and Female Roles in the Lyrics of Three Genres of Contemporary Music. *Sex Roles*, 1978, *4*, 51–64.

Fromm, E. *The anatomy of human destructiveness*. New York: Random House, 1973.

Fu, V. R., and Leach, D. J. Sex Role Preferences Among Elementary School Children in Rural America. *Psychological Reports*, 1980, *46*, 555–560.

Gerdes, E. P., Gehling, J. D., and Rapp, J. N. The Effects of Sex and Sex-Role Concept on Self-Disclosure. *Sex Roles*, 1981, *7*, 989–998.

Giarusso, R., Jounson, P., Goodchilds, J., and Zellman, G. Adolescents' Cues and Signals: Sex and Assault. Paper presented at the Western Psychological Association Meetings, San Diego, California, April, 1979.

Giels, J. Z. *Women and the future: Changing sex roles in modern America*. New York: Free Press, 1978.

Goffman, E. On Cooling the Mark/Out: Some Aspects of Adaptation to Failure. *Psychiatry*, 1952, *15*, 451–463.

Goldberg, H. *The hazards of being male*. New York: New American Library, 1976.

Goldberg, H. *The new male: From macho to sensitive, but still all male*. New York: New American Library, 1979.

Goldberg, H. *The new male: From self-destructive to self-care*. New York: Morrow, 1979.

Gordon, J. *The myth of the monstrous male*. New York: Playboy Press, 1982.

Green, R. Diary of a Native American Feminist. *Ms.*, 1982, *August*, 172–174.

Grier, W. H., and Cobbs, P. M. *Black rage*. New York: Basic Books, 1968.

Gross, A. E. The Male Role and Heterosexual Behavior. *Journal of Social Issues*, 1978, *34*, 87–107.

Gross, R. H., and Avery, R. D. Marital Satisfaction, Role Satisfaction and Task Distribution in the Homemaker's Job. *Journal of Vocational Behavior*, 1977, *11*, 1–13.

Haas, L. Determinants of Role-Sharing Behaviors: A Study of Egalitarian Couples *Sex Roles*, 1982, *8*, 747–760.

Hall, J. A. *Sex-role-related correlates of sensitivity to nonverbal cues*. Unpublished Doctoral Dissertation, Harvard University, 1976.

Hall, J. A. Gender Effects in Decoding Nonverbal Cues. *Psychological Bulletin*, 1978, *85*, 845–857.

Hall, J. A. Gender, Gender Roles, and Nonverbal Sensitivity. Paper presented to the 86th meeting of the American Psychological Association, Toronto, Canada, 1978.

Hall, J. A., and Halberstadt, A. G. Sex Roles and Nonverbal Communication Skills. *Sex Roles*, 1981, *7*, 273–287.

Hare, N. The Frustrated Masculinity of the Negro Male. In R. Staples (Ed.), *The Black family*. Belmont, California: Wadsworth Publishing Company, 1971.

Heim, M., Malamuth, N., and Feshbach, S. The Effects of Violent Aggression in Erotica on Sexual Arousal. Paper presented at the Western Psychological Association Meetings, Seattle, Washington, 1977.

Hemmer, J. D., and Kleiber, D. Tomboys and Sissies: Androgynous Children? *Sex Roles*, 1981, *7*, 1205–1212.

Herzog, E., and Saudia, C. Children in Fatherless Families. In E. M. Hetherington, and P. Riccicuti (Eds.), *Review of child development research*, Vol. 3. Chicago: University of Chicago Press, 1974.

Hess, B. B., Markson, E., and Stein, P. J. *Sociology*. New York: Macmillan, 1982.

Hetherington, E. M., Cox, M., and Cox. R. Divorced Fathers. *The Family Coordinator*, 1976, *25*, 417–428.

Hildebrandt, K. A., and Fitzgerald, E. Adults' Perception of Infant Sex and Cuteness. *Sex Roles*, 1979, *5*, 471–481.

Hill, C. T. Rubin, Z., and Peplau, L. A. Breakups Before Marriage: The End of 103 Affairs. *Journal of Social Issues*, 1976, *32*, 147–168.

Hill, C. T., Rubin, Z., Peplau, L. A., and Willard, S. G. The Volunteer Couple: Sex Differences, Couple Commitment and Participation in Research on Interpersonal Relationships. *Social Psychology Quarterly*, 1979, *42*, 415–420.

Hoffman, M. Sex Differences in Empathy and Related Behavior. *Psychological Bulletin*, 1977, *84*, 712–722.

Holcomb, B. Confessions of Domestic Men. *Ms.*, 1982, *October*, 39–49.

Hooberman, R. E. Psychological Androgny, Feminine Gender Identity and Self-Esteem in Homosexual and Heterosexual Males. *The Journal of Sex Research*, 1979, *15*, 306–315.

Hooker, E. Male Homosexuals and Their Worlds. In J. Marmax (Ed.), *Sexual inversion: The roots of homosexuality*, New York: Basic Books, 1969.

Hull, G. T., Scott, P. B., and Smith, B. *All the Blacks are men, all the women are White, but some of us are brave*. Old Westbury, N.J.: Feminist Press, 1982.

Humphreys, L. *Tearoom trade: impersonal sex in public places*. Chicago: Aldine, 1970.

Hunt, J. G., and Hunt, L. L. Dilemmas and Contradictions in Status: The Case of the Dual-Career Family. *Social Problems*, 1978, *24*, 407–416.

Ihinger-Tallman, M. Family Interaction, Gender, Status Attainment Value. *Sex Roles*, 1982, *8*, 543–556.

Jackson, J. But Where are the Black Men? In R. Staples, *The Black family: Essays and studies*. Belmont, California: Wadsworth Publishing Company, 1978.

Jacobson, M. B. Effects of Victim's and Defendant's Physical Attractiveness in Subject's Judgments in a Rape Case. *Sex Roles*, 1981, *7*, 247–255.

Janda, L. H., O'Grady, K. E., and Barnhart, S. A. Effects of Sexual Attitudes and Physical Attractiveness on Person Perception of Men and Women. *Sex Roles*, 1981, *7*, 189–199.

Jourard, S. M. *Self-Disclosure: An experimental analysis of the transparent self*. New York: Wiley, 1971.

Kanin, E. Sex Aggression by College Men. *Medical Aspects of Human Sexuality*, 1970, September, 28.

Kanter, R. M. The Impact of Hierarchical Structures on the Work Behavior of Women and Men. *Social Problems*, 1976, 23, 415–430.

Karr, R. Homosexual Labeling and the Male Role. *Journal of Social Issues*, 1978, 34, 73–83.

Kimmel, D. C. Adult Development and Aging: A Gay Perspective. *Journal of Social Issues*, 1978, 34, 113–130.

Kinsey, A. C., Pomeroy, W. B., and Martin, C. E. *Sexual behavior in the human male.* Philadelphia: W. B. Saunders, 1948.

Kinsey, A. C., Pomeroy, W. B., Martin, C. E., and Gebhard, P. H. *Sexual behavior in the human female.* Philadelphia: W. B. Saunders, 1953.

Kirkham, G. L. Homosexuality in Prison. In J. M. Henslin (Ed.), *Studies in the sociology of sex.* New York: Appleton-Century-Crofts, 1971.

Kitson, G. C., and Raschke, H. J. Divorce Research: What We Know; What We Need to Know. *Journal of Divorce*, 1981, 4, 1–37.

Kohlberg, K. A Cognitive-Developmental Analysis of Children's Sex-Role Concepts and Attitudes. In E. E. Maccoby (Ed.), *The development of sex differences*, Stanford, California: Stanford University Press, 1966.

Komarovsky, M. Cultural Contradiction and Sex Roles. *American Journal of Sociology*, 1946, 52, 182–189.

Komarovsky, M. Presidential Address: Some Problems in Role Analysis. *American Sociological Review*, 1973, 38, 649–662.

Kremer, E. G., Zimper, D. G., and Wiggers, T. T. Homosexuality, Counseling and the Adolescent Male. *Personnel and Guidance Journal*, 1975, 54, 94–101.

Kulik, J. A., and Harackiewicz, J. Opposite-Sex Interpersonal Attraction as a Function of the Sex Roles of the Perceiver and the Perceived. *Sex Roles*, 1979, 5, 443–452.

Kutner, N. G., and Brogan, D. R. Problems of Colleagueship for Women Entering the Medical Profession. *Sex Roles*, 1981, 7, 739–746.

Lamm, B. Learning From Women. In J. Snodgrass (Ed.), *For men against sexism.* New York: Times Change Press, 1977.

LaRue, L. Black Liberation and Women's Lib. *Transactions*, 1970, 8, 59–63.

Lee, A. G., and Scheurer, V. L. Psychological Androgyny and Aspects of Self-Image in Women and Men. *Sex Roles*, 1983, 9, 289–306.

Lehne, G. K. Homophobia Among Men. In D. David and R. Brannon (Eds.), *The forty-nine percent majority: The male sex roles.* New York: Addison-Wesley, 1976.

Lesserman, J. Sex Differences in the Professional Orientation of First-Year Medical Students. *Sex Roles*, 1980, 6, 645–660.

Lester, J. Being A Boy. *Ms.*, 1973, July, 112–113.

Lever, J. *Columbus Citizen Journal*, November 30, 1982.

Levinger, G., and Snoek, J. D. *Attraction in relationships: A new look at interpersonal attraction.* Morristown, New Jersey: General Learning Press, 1974.

Levinson, D. J., Darrow, C., Klein, E. B., Levinson, M. H., and McKee, B. *The seasons of a man's life.* New York: Ballantine, 1978.

Lewin, E., and Olesank, V. Lateralness in Women's Work: New Views on Success. *Sex Roles*, 1980, 6, 619–629.

Lewis, M., and Freedle, R. Mother–Infant Dyad: The Cradle of Meaning. In P. Pliner, L. Kramer, and T. Alloway (Eds.), *Communication and affect: Language and thought.* New York: Academic Press, 1973.

Lewis, M., and Weinraub, M. Origin of Early Sex-Role Development. *Sex Roles*, 1979, *5*, 135–153.

Lewis, R. A. Emotional Intimacy Among Men. *Journal of Social Issues*, 1978, *34*, 108–121.

Liebow, E. *Tally's corner*. Boston: Little, Brown, 1966.

Light, R., and Keller, S. *Sociology*. New York: Knopf, 1979.

Liss-Levinson, W. Men Without Playfulness. In R. A. Lewis (Ed.), *Men in difficult times*. Englewood Cliffs: Prentice-Hall, 1981.

Litewka, J. The Socialized Penis. In E. Shapiro, and Shapiro, B., *The women say, the men say*. Delta Special, 1979.

Lombardo, D. P., and Lavine, L. O. Sex-Role Sterotyping and Patterns of Self-Disclosure. *Sex Roles*, 1981, *7*, 403–411.

Maccoby, E. E., and Jacklin, C. H. *The psychology of sex differences*, Stanford, California: Stanford University Press, 1974.

MacKinnon, C. *Sexual harassment of working women: A case of sex discrimination*, New Haven: Yale University Press, 1979.

Malamuth, N. Rape Proclivity Among Males. *Journal of Social Issues*, 1981, *37*, 138–154.

Malamuth, N., and Check, J. V. P. Penile Tumescence and Perceptual Responses to Rape as a Function of Victim's Perceived Reactions. *Journal of Applied Social Psychology*, 1980, *10*, 528–547.

Malamuth, N. M., Feshback, S., and Jaffe, Y. Sexual Arousal and Aggression: Recent Experiments and Theoretical Issues. *Journal of Social Issues*, 1977, *33*, 110–133.

Malamuth, N., Haber, S., and Feshback, S. Testing Hypotheses Regarding Rape: Exposure to Sexual Violence, Sex Differences and the 'Normality' of Rapists. *Journal of Research in Personality*, 1980, *14*, 121–137.

Mallowe, M. The Lady Killers. *Savvy*, 1982, March, 38–42.

Mamay, P. D., and Simpson, R. L. Three Female Roles in Television Commercials. *Sex Roles*, 1981, *7*, 1223–1232.

McBroom, W. H. Parental Relationships and Socioeconomic Status and Sex-Role Expectations. *Sex Roles*, 1981, *7*, 1027–1034.

McConahay, S. A., and McConahay, J. B. Sexual Permissiveness, Sex-Role Rigidity, and Violence Across Cultures. *Journal of Social Issues*, 1977, *33*, 134–143.

McGhee, P., and Frueh, T. Television Viewing and the Learning of Sex-Role Sterotypes. *Sex Roles*, 1980, *6*, 179–187.

McIntosh, M. The Homosexual Role. *Social Problems*, 1968, *16*, 182–192.

McKee, J. B. *Sociology: The study of society*. New York: Holt, Rinehart & Winston, 1981.

McNeill, J. *The Church and the homosexual*. Kansas City, Kansas: Sheed, Andrews and McNeel, 1976.

Mercer, G. W., and Kohn, P. M. Gender Differences in the Integration of Conservatism, Sex Urge, and Sexual Behaviors Among College Students. *The Journal of Sex Research*, 1979, *15*, 129–142.

Miller, A. G. Role of Physical Attractiveness in Impression Formation. *Psychonomic Sciences*, 1970, *19*, 241–243.

Miller, B. Adult Sexual Resocialization: Adjustments Toward Stigmatized Identity. *Alternative Lifestyles*, 1978, *16*, 1–42.

Minton, C., Kagan, J., and Levine, J. A. Maternal Control and Obedience in the Two-Year-Old. *Child Development*, 1971, *42*, 1873–1894.

Mischel, W. Sex-Typing and Socialization. In P. Musen (Ed.), *Carmichael's manual of child psychology*, Vol. 2, New York: Wiley, 1969.

Michel, A. Comparative Data Concerning the Interaction in French and American Families. *Journal of Marriage and the Family*, 1967, 29, 337–344.

Moley, B. E., Skarin, K. and Weil, S. Sex Differences in Competition-Cooperative Behavior at Two Age Levels. *Sex Roles*, 1979, 5, 329–342.

Money, J., and Ehrhardt, L. A. *Man and woman/boy and girl*. Baltimore: Johns Hopkins University Press, 1972.

Moreland, J. Age and Change in the Adult Male Sex Role. *Sex Roles*, 1980, 6, 807–818.

Morgan, R. (Ed.), *Sisterhood is powerful*. New York: Vintage Books, 1970.

Morin, S. F., and Schultz, S. J. The Gay Movement and the Rights of Children. *Journal of Social Issues*, 1978, 3, 137–148.

Mosher, D. L. Three Dimensions of Depth of Involvement in Human Sexual Response. *The Journal of Sex Research*, 1980, 16, 1–42.

Moynihan, D. P. *The Negro family: The case for national action*. U.S. Department of Labor: Office of Planning and Research, 1965.

Neal, M. A. Women in Religious Symbolism and Organization. *Sociological Inquiry*, 1979, 49, 218–250.

Nelson, M. New Wave Feminists. *Ms.*, 1982, August, 92–93.

Neubeck, K. J. *Social problems: A critical approach*. Glenview, Illinois: Scott Foresman and Company, 1979.

Nichols, J. *Men's liberation*. New York: Penguin, 1978.

Noble, J. *Beautiful also are the souls of my black sisters*. Englewood Cliffs: Prentice-Hall, 1978.

Nordheimer, J. The Family in Transition: A Challenge From Within. *New York Times*, November 27, 1977: 1.

Nye, F. I., and Hoffman, I. W. (Eds.), *The employed mother in America*. Chicago: Rand McNally, 1963.

O'Brien, P. AIDS Causing Some Panic As Research Seeks Answers. *Columbus Dispatch*, Columbus, Ohio, June 28, 1983: Section B, p. 3.

The Ohio State Lantern, United Press International, Monday, November 15, 1982, p. 12.

O'Leary, V. E., and Donoghue, J. M. Latitudes of Masculinity: Reactions to Sex-Role Deviance in Men. *Journal of Social Issues*, 1978, 34, 17–28.

Orlofsky, J. L. Psychological Androgyny, Sex-Typing, and Sex-Role Ideology as Predictors of Male–Female Interpersonal Attraction. *Sex Roles*, 1982, 8, 1057–1073.

Parke, R. D., and O'Leary, S. E. Father–Mother–Infant Interaction in the Newborn Period: Some Findings, Some Observations and Some Unresolved Issues. In K. Reigel and J. Meacham (Eds.), *The developing individual in a changing world*, 2, The Hague: Mouton, 1976.

Pearce, D. The Feminization of Poverty: Women, Work and Welfare. *The Urban and Social Change Review*, 1978, 11, 1–2, 28–36.

Perlman, D., and Cozby, P. C. *Social Psychology*. New York: Holt, Rinehart & Winston, 1983.

Perry, J. A., and Perry, E. K. *The social web*. New York: Harper and Row, 1983.

Pettigrew, T. *A Profile of the Negro American*. Princeton: Van Nostrand, 1964.

Phillips, B. S. *Sex-role Socialization and Play Behavior on a Rural Playground*. Master's thesis, Department of Sociology, Ohio State University, Columbus, Ohio, 1982.

Pines, A., and Kafry, D. Tedium in Life and Work of Professional Women as Compared with Men. *Sex Roles*, 1981, 7, 963–977.

Pleck, J. Psychological Frontiers for Men. *Rough Times*, 1973, 6, 14–15.

Pleck, J. H. Man to Man: Is Brotherhood Possible? In N. G. Malbin, (Ed.), *Old family/new family: Interpersonal relationships*. New York: Van Nostrand Reinhold, 1975.

Pleck, J. The Male Sex Role: Definition, Problems and Sources of Change. *Journal of Social Issues*, 1976, 32, 155–164.

Pleck, J. H. The Work Family Role System. *Social Problems*, 1978, 24, 417–427.

Pleck, J. *The myth of Masculinity*. Cambridge: The M.I.T. Press, 1981.

Pleck, J. H., and Sawyer, J. (Eds.), *Men and masculinity*. Englewood Cliffs: Prentice-Hall, 1980.

Pleck, J. H., and Pleck, E. H. *The American man*. Englewood Cliffs: Prentice-Hall, 1980.

Polatnick, M. Why Men Don't Rear Children: A Power Analysis. *Berkeley Journal of Sociology*, 1973–1974, 18, 45–86.

Ponte, M. Life in a Parking Lot: An Ethnography of a Homosexual Drive-In. in Jacobs, J. (Ed.), *Deviance: Field studies and self-disclosures*. Palo Alto, California: National Books, 1974.

Poussaint, A. F. What Every Black Woman Should Know About Black Man. *Ebony*, 1982, August, 36–40.

Reiber, V. D. Is the Nurturing Role Natural to Father? *American Journal of Maternal Nursing*, 1976, 3, 443–458.

Reik, T. *Sex in men and women: Its emotional variations*. New York: Noonday Press, 1960.

Richardson, L. W. *The dynamics of sex and gender: A sociological perspective*. Boston: Houghton Mifflin, 1981.

Richardson, M. S. and Alpert, J. L. Role Perceptions: Variations by Sex and Roles. *Sex Roles*, 1980, 6, 783–793.

Riddle, D. I. Relating to Children: Gays as Role Models. *Journal of Social Issues*, 1978, 34, 38–58.

Robinson, J. P., Yerby, J., Fieweger, M., and Somerick, N. Sex Differences in Time Use. *Sex Roles*, 1980, 6, 783–793.

Roof, W. C. *Community and commitment: Religious plausibility in a liberal Protestant church.* New York: Elsevier-North Holland, 1978.

Rosenberg, M., and Kaplan, H. B. (Eds.), *Social psychology*. Arlington Heights, Illinois: Harlan Davidson, 1982.

Rosenkrantz, P., Vogel, S., Ber, H., and Braverman, D. Sex-Role Stereotypes and Self-Concepts in College Students. *Journal of Consulting and Clinical Psychology*, 1968, 32, 287–295.

Rosenthal, D., and Hansen, J. The Impact of Maternal Employment on Children's Perceptions of Parents and Personal Development. *Sex Roles*, 1981, 7, 593–598.

Ross, H. L. Modes of Adjustment of Married Homosexuals. *Social Problems*, 1971, 18, 385–393.

Ross, H. Poverty: Women and Children Last. In J. Chapman (Ed.), *Econom independence for women*. Beverly Hills: Sage Publications, 1972.

Ruble, T. L. Sex Stereotypes: Issues of Change in the 1970s. *Sex Roles*, 1983, 9, 397–402.

Rubin, Z. Disclosing Oneself to a Stranger: Reciprocity and Its Limits. *Journal of Experimental Social Psychology*, 1975, 11, 233–240.

Russell, D. Rape and the Masculine Mystique. Paper presented to the American Sociological Association, New York: August, 1973.

Saghir, M. T., and Robins, E. *Male and Female Homosexuality: A Comprehensive Investigation*. Baltimore: Williams and Wilkins, 1973.

Sampson, E. E., and M. Kardush. Age, Sex, Class and Race Differences in Response to a Two-Person, Non-Zero Sum Game. *Journal of Conflict Resolution*, 1965, 9, 212–220.

Santrock, J. W. Effects of Father Absence on Sex-Typed Behaviors in Male Children: Reason for the Absence and Age of Onset of the Absence. *Journal of Genetic Psychology*. 1977, 130, 3–10.

Sattel, J. W. The Inexpressive Male Re-Examined. *Social Problems*, 1976, 23, 469–477.

Schall, C. G., Kahn, 1., Diepold, J. H., and Cherry, F. The Relationship of Parental Expectations and Pre-School Children's Verbal Sex Typing to their Sex-Typed Toy Play Behavior. *Child Development*, 1980, 51, 266–270.

Segal, M. W. Varieties of Interpersonal Attraction and Their Interrelations in Natural Groups. *Social Psychology Quarterly*, 1979, 42, 253–261.

Serbin, L. A., Connor, J., Burchardt, C. J., and Citron, C. C. Effects of Peer Pressure on Sex Typing of Children's Play Behavior. *Journal of Experimental Child Psychology*, 1979, 27, 303–309.

Seyfried, B., and Hendrick, C. When Do Opposites Attract? When They Are Opposite in Sex-Role Attitudes. *Journal of Personality and Social Psychology*, 1973, 25, 15–20.

Slater, P. E. Sexual Adequacy in America. In C. Gordon, and G. Johnson (Eds.), *Readings in human sexuality: Contemporary perspectives.* New York: Harper and Row, 1976.

Slevin, K. T., and Balswick, J. Children's Perceptions of Parental Expressiveness. *Sex Roles*, 1980, 6, 293–299.

Spence, J. T., Helmreich, R., and Stapp, J. Ratings of Self and Peers on Sex-Role Attributes on their Relation to Self-Esteem and Conceptions of Masculinity and Femininity. *Journal of Personality and Social Psychology*, 1975, 32, 29–39.

Spence, J. T., and Helmreich, R. *Masculinity and feminity: Their psychological dimensions, correlates and antecedents.* Austin: University of Texas Press, 1978.

Spencer, M. *Foundations of Modern Sociology.* Englewood Cliffs: Prentice-Hall, 1983.

Staines, G. L., Pleck, J. H., Shepard, J. H., and O'Connor, P. Wives' Employment Status and Marital Adjustment: Yet Another Look. *Psychology of Women Quarterly*, 1978, 3, 90–120.

Staples, R. Masculinity and Race: The Dual Dilemma of Black Men. *Journal of Social Issues*, 1978, 34, 169—183.

Steiber, S. R. The Influence of the Religious Factor on Civil and Sacred Tolerance 1958–1971. *Social Forces*, 1980, 58, 811–832.

Stockard, J., and Johnson, M. M. The Social Origin of Dominance. *Sex Roles*, 1979, 5, 199–218.

Stockard, J., and Johnson, M. M. *Sex Roles: Sex Inequality and Sex Role Development.* Englewood Cliffs: Prentice-Hall, 1980.

Storms, M. D. Sexual Orientation and Self-Perception. In P. Kliner, Blanstein, K. R., Spiegel, I. M., Alloway, P., and Krames, L. (Eds.) *Advances in the study of communication and affect. Vol. 5 Perceptions of emotion in self and others.* New York: Plenum, 1978.

Stryker, S. *Symbolic Interactionism.* Menlo Park, California: The Benjamin/Cummings Publishing Company, 1980.

Taylor, V. M. How to Avoid Taking Sexual Harassment Seriously: A New Book that Perpetuates Old Myths (book review). *Capital University Law Review*, 1981, 10, 673–684.

Thruman, J. The Hangups, the Drives, the Price, the Joys. *Ms.*, 1982, December, 3946.

Tieger T. Self-Rated Likelihood of Raping and the Social Perception of Rape. *Journal of Research in Personality*, 1981, 15, 147–158.

Tiger, L. *Men in groups.* New York: Random House, 1974.

Tolson, A. *The limits of masculinity.* London: Tavistock, 1978.

Tyron, B. W. Beliefs About Male and Female Competence Held by Kindergarten and Second Graders. *Sex Roles*, 1980, *6*, 85–97.

United States Department of Commerce, Bureau of the Census. *Current Population Reports* (Series P-60, No. 127). Money, Income, and Poverty Status of Families and Persons in the United States: Washington: U.S. Government Printing Office, 1980.

VanderZanden, J. *Social psychology*. New York: Random House, 1977.

Varma, M. Sex Stereotyping in Black Play of Preschool Children. *Indian Educational Review*, 1980, 32–37.

Vittitow, D. Changing Men and Their Movement toward Intimacy. In I. A. Lewis, *Men in difficult times*. Englewood Cliffs: Prentice-Hall, 1981.

Wallace, M. *Black macho and the myth of the superwoman*. New York: Dial Press, 1979.

Walum, L. R. *The dynamics of sex and gender: A sociological perspective*. Chicago: Rand McNally, 1977.

Wapner, J. The Attitude, Feelings, and Behaviors of Expectant Fathers Attending Lamaze Classes. *Birth and the Family Journal*, 1976, *3*, 5–14.

Weinberg, G. *Society and the healthy homosexual*. New York: St. Martin's Press, 1972.

Weinberg, M. S., and Williams, C. J. *Male homosexuals: Their problems and adaptions*. New York: Penguin, 1974.

Weingarter, K. The Employment Pattern of Professional Couples and Their Distribution of Involvement in the Family. *Psychology of Women Quarterly*, 1978, *3*, 43–52.

Wells, L. *Essence's Quality of Life Survey Results*. College Park: University of Maryland Press, 1980.

Wheeler, L., and Nezlez, J. Sex Difference in Social Participation. *Journal of Personality and Social Psychology*, 1977, *35*, 742–754.

Wilcox, P. Is There Life for Black Leaders After ERA? *Black Male/Black Female Relationships*, 1979, *2*, 53–55.

Wilkins, R. Confessions of a Token Black. *Ebony*, 1982, *July*, 69–80.

Williamson, R. C., Swigle, P. G., and Sargent, S. S. *Social Psychology*. Itasca, Minnesota: F. E. Peacock, 1982.

Willis, F. N. Initial Speaking Distance as a Function of the Speaker's Relationship. *Psychonomic Science*, 1966, *6*, 221–22.

Wood, M. M. The Influence of Sex and Knowledge of Communication Effectiveness on Spontaneous Speech. *Word*, 1966, *22*, 112–137.

Yankelovich, D. The Meaning of Work. In J. M. Rosan, (Ed.), *The Worker and the Job*. Englewood Cliffs: Prentice-Hall, 1974.

Yates, G. *What women want: The ideas of the Movement*. Cambridge: Harvard University Press, 1975.

Index

LIBRARY
OF
MOUNT ST. MARY'S
COLLEGE
EMMITSBURG, MARYLAND